IN MY TIME

IN MY TIME
ROBERT STRAUSZ-HUPÉ

W · W · NORTON & COMPANY · INC ·

NEW YORK

Preface

When one no longer has anything to say about the world at large, one writes about one's own world, about oneself. Having squared accounts with the life of action, I survey the long columns of the entries and the blank spaces of the might-have-beens. The gaps of the record—the things that did not come to pass—are more vivid than the events, pegged and tagged. I have read through volumes that purport to be autobiographical, yet reveal little about the author except his determination to revise history and his own role in it. What is offered as a "life" is but a series of maneuvers for launching the barque, stranded on the beach of neglect and disfavor, back onto the tide of action. Not so surprisingly, this sort of autobiography absorbs the leisure of the unemployed politician whom neither dotage nor some irretrievable "public relations" error has stricken from the lists. Since I have found my beach livable and the view pleasing, since my barque will never float again, I need not concern myself unduly with voyages ahead and cock my ear anxiously to the distant rumble of the tide. Of course, I live with anxiety. But I have learned games to calm it. And, then, I have taught myself to believe that the rules are mine and that I am the umpire between my embattled self and the hopes and fears that trouble me.

I am sure that among the legions of men and women who

5

have sought to turn solitude to good account or to escape it the best and the strongest drew their portraits with firmer strokes than mine, their hands steadied by repose that comes from wisdom and does not falter before the last encounter with the unknown, and by unasking love. Of wisdom I have little, for I would still trade my book of maxims for the colors, sounds, and smells around me this very morning. Although I have traveled to the valley that disappears in the unscalable folds of the range, I still want to go I know not exactly where.

On second thought, to write about my life might be one way to find out about it, to discover what I thought I had always known, yet had never met face to face. Then, having found what I seek, I might stop searching for the random trophies that seem to be mounted for no other purpose than to be left moldering, boasts of unprovoked prowess. Then, my adventure no longer calls for a cast, for a hero and his victim, nor for an audience.

Avec la croix dans ma main . . . I do not think that I could have ever written (and proofread) this superb and somber phrase. But I would think my life to have been all I wanted it to be, awake and dreaming, could I say these words to myself (without troubling about the signs and symbols) during that unique transaction which necessarily extends beyond the scope of autobiography.

IN MY TIME

An unexamined life
is not worth living . . . .
Plato, THE APOLOGY

Chapter One

I was born in Vienna, the Vienna that history and stupidity have transformed from a metropolis into an overpopulated provincial town, its dullness being one of the most closely guarded secrets of the travel bureaus. Notwithstanding its antiquity and healthful climate, Vienna once had more in common with New York than any other European town. At that time it drew its airs and peoples from a score of races. Its tailors, bookmakers, and pastry cooks were Bohemians whose tongue had not lost the rasping twang of Czech; its nobles hailed from every corner of Catholic Europe, including the Hapsburgs' lost domains in the Lowlands, in Lombardy, Umbria, Silesia, and Spain, in the lands under the colonial rule of heretics and heathens, such as Wallachia, Greece, the Levant, Ireland, and Scotland; its most beautiful women and its most openhanded hosts had left their native Hungary and Poland to grace an uninterrupted succession of official and private festivities; and its most colorful soldiery was recruited from Bosnia, Hungary, and the Tyrol.

In Europe the monarchy, a frail repository of the residual ideas and splendors of the Holy Roman Empire of the German Nation, held the last rampart against nationalism. It stood in the way of virtually every *Idée force* of the late nineteenth century: English liberalism, French secularism, Pan-Germanism, Pan-Slavism, and the Socialist International. How these forces, so ill-assorted and so mutually antagonistic, managed to topple the Monarchy and, in the process, balkanize all of Eastern and part of Central Europe—this is the real inside story of World War I, the story that will be retold and garbled *ad nauseam,* long after the saga of Verdun, the White and Yellow Papers, Wilson's inspirational messages, Clemenceau's canny silences, and the chronicles of appalling military and political mismanagement—the first head-on collision of politics and strategy with modern technology—will have been forgotten.

My mother was a good woman. The wisdom of her folly gave me those few notions which nowadays are being called values. A most undramatic person, she did not tell me about Good and Evil, Right and Wrong. Rather, when I was a child, she taught me how to behave decently about little things, ignored steadfastly my tendency toward hypochondria, guarded my daydreams, encouraged my liking for adults, and made me display that deference and reserve without which any child can readily annoy and bore even the most tolerant adult.

Having left school when she reached thirteen, my mother turned to books in her fifties. Like every good German, she revered the poets and the thinkers whose busts graced the bookshelf. Beyond a few quotations, she knew hardly anything of their verse and thought. But she watched proudly my attempts to make sense, at the age of ten, of Goethe, Hegel, George, Rilke, and Schopenhauer. I understood hardly anything at all, but learned to leaf the encyclopedia, *Meyer's Encyklopadie,* which, because of its massiveness, I recall as the first durable birthday present of my memory.

This encyclopedia, incidentally, followed me for many years. Eventually, it came to rest in my Paris apartment. Then it disappeared with the retreating German major who, quartered in my flat, polished my Empire table and cared for the bindings of my first editions of Malraux, Gide, and Giraudoux. The most expen-

sive ones shared the major's homeward journey. After the war I
did not seek to find them, though I wish I could retrieve those
ungainly volumes of the encyclopedia, thumb to the item of
Johann Wolfgang von Goethe, and reread the summary of *Faust*,
in particular.

For this summary of *Faust*, under Johann Wolfgang von
Goethe, relieved me from the drudgery of plowing numbly
through the lengthy tragedy; thus freed for the afternoon, I
would spin my own more plausible yarns. As a marshal of Napoleon, for example, I sat my horse at Wagram and then, struck
by a musket shot, expired in the arms of a suitably distressed aide.
On foot, I rallied my infantry on the bridge of Arcole. With a
handful of men, musket in hand, I covered the retreat across the
Beresina. In fact, the first book I read because I wanted to read
and not because I felt I should, was Kircheisen's solid biography
of Napoleon. My mother, again, led me to Napoleon.

My mother abhorred violence and war. (At the end of her life
she turned to theosophy. She died, in the second year of World
War II, a firm pacifist.) She was a Saxonian, born and reared in
the village of Konnewitz, near Leipzig, where her father raised
roses and carnations for sale to the Leipzig florists.

Though a Lutheran—my grandmother's forebears lie in a small
churchyard in Wittenberg—my mother learned the little history
she knew from a Saxonian primer. The kings of Saxony professed
the Roman faith. Chastened by the profligacy of Augustus the
Strong, and defeated in war, the Royal Princes prided themselves
on their parsimony, dressed shabbily, and conversed with their
subjects, as well as among themselves, in the grotesque patois of
Saxonian people. They hated the Prussians who had despoiled
them in the Seven Years' War. A king of Saxony was Napoleon's
ally and stood by him, until his troops deserted, at the battle of
Leipzig. My grandparents had talked to men who said that they
were—and could have been—present at the battle.

After the defeat of Austria in 1866, the Saxonians again elected
defeat as well as surrender. The least warlike of the German
people, they chafed under the hegemony of Prussia. Their sly wit
contrived the best anti-Prussian jokes. Their remarkable business
acumen, untiring industry, and practical inventiveness made them

rich. But the legends of Saxony's brave struggle against Prussia and brief companionship-in-arms with Napoleon lingered into my mother's time. Indeed, my mother kept a lithograph likeness of Napoleon after David on her desk. Her heart went out to the great short man, distraught by the frivolity of Josephine. My mother sowed the seed; I still tend the grove of the hero.

Like Napoleon, I, too, was a studious child, fair at mathematics, scrupulously—perhaps compulsively—clean, and small of stature. I have read a good many biographies of Napolean and learned studies of the man, the ruler, the captain, and the mover of history, French, German, English, and Russian. I am content to avow today the belief I held long ago: among the greatest doers of history, all of whom wasted lives and treasure to make it, he stands least in need of apology or, what is worse in contemporary historiography, patronizing rehabilitation. The hero still stands on his own and well-shaped feet. The compelling eyes do not blink.

It is preposterous to judge Napoleon by the canons of post-Hiroshima quietism, by the survival mythology of Lord Russell. To say that Napoleon was a man of his times is both trite and true. Made of the stuff of the Colleonis and Pescaras, he stepped from his bastioned and clannish rock into the Age of Enlightenment.

The eighteenth century bridged its complexities by that serene cadence which ordered its music, architecture, and passions. A society in dissolution indulged its infatuation with every possible type of imposture and with geometry, with the Kabala and with science. The Middle Ages were still fermenting in miasmic decay beneath the polished floors of the Trianon; bats nested in the instrument-littered studies of the *philosophes*. A part of Napoleon belonged to the contrived symmetry of this age; another part of him, however, seems puzzlingly remote—out of the way, as are the island of his birth and the island of his death.

We know that Napoleon read those magnificent bores Corneille and Racine; Plutarch's *Lives;* the banalities of Voltaire, spiritual forebear of our more elevated columnists—and Goethe's *Werther.* Notwithstanding this intellectual fare, he mastered his trade, which was war, and cultivated his avocations, which were to make laws, to draw straight city streets and country roads, to write concisely, and to collect almost everything from obelisks to recipes.

Nowhere did his inspired dilettantism achieve more splendid results than in the field of public Relations: he wrote his press releases; invented, graded, and made easily accessible military and civilian decorations for mass distribution; devised the status symbols of democratic inequality; extended impartially the list of subscribers to Jacobins and ci-devants; and converted his memoirs into an action program. All this he did with obvious relish and, at times, with an engaging hilarity. In the crush of business, he neglected to bone up on technological developments and maritime navigation, oversights which accrued chiefly to the benefit of the English military establishment. A gunner, he did not improve the technical equipment of the French artillery; a trained geographer, he knew little about the high seas. He was a devoted son, a patient brother, and a doting father. Unlike most of his prominent contemporaries, he was free of avarice. He rewarded his captains generously and forgave them a long list of vices, including rank treachery. A part of him belongs to this century: he anticipated not only status society but also plebiscitary democracy, fetishist hygiene, and prestige scientism.

Appalled as I might be at the results, I do not choose now to defect from my adolescent hero worship. Napoleon prompted tendencies that issued from the womb of mass society. He reduced the obvious to order a generation before the ideologues scrambled it again. He provided the last great spectacle before state and art parted company. His pseudo-Roman was archaeologically no less authentic than Mr. Walpole's and the Romantics' Gothic and a great deal less neurotic. He made Europe, the good and the bad of it. Among the vanquished, he excited the nationalist spirit, for he, like all the great conquerors before him, was a cosmopolitan. His European dream, however, was deflowered by those "liberation" movements which, in our time, still rally around the tribal cooking pot; nevertheless, the European Common Market and the Atlantic Alliance owe him a monument in the good classic manner with appropriate *son et lumière*. And he fostered tourism. Ave Napoleon!

So I stand in the ranks of those innumerable European adolescents whom the Napoleonic cult marked for life. Like Napoleon, behind whom lurked the role-player, I wrote my scenario and lived it; for that matter, some of the roles I played so convincingly that I can no longer tell the difference between the actor and myself. I imagine, therefore I am.

This lack of sense-of-process is my father's gift. My father's charm suffused a variety of traits, such as his love of games and gaming and his restless passion for motor vehicles and small arms as well as novel designs for manufacturing both, and his ever-resurgent faith in a long succession of men with breakthrough ideas and insufficient capital. Possessed of a modest capital, he was little attached to his fortune, which he spent freely and, but for his ventures in technical innovation, well.

My father acquired an estate in eastern Hungary, not far from the town of Temesvár (now Timisoara) and, for a few years, engaged in farming. Though the monetary rewards were slight, this undertaking repaid him richly in kind; guests thronged the house and stayed for days, weeks, and months. Here my father, who played the violin mostly by ear, indulged his passion, which remained constant, for gypsy music. Here a retired artillery sergeant who had served with my father taught me how to ride, a skill which was to stand me in good stead in later years. And the seasons provided additional instruction and entertainment—sleighrides; the planting and harvesting of Indian corn (which was grown extensively in Hungary before its introduction to Central and Southern Europe), the pheasant shoots, the drying and curing of tobacco (I have been a consistent smoker since the age of twelve); suckling pig and goose liver (in its natural state) for breakfast; and the lazy oxen at the waterhole. Eventually, however, my father had to sell the farm. A short while later our family broke up.

Thereafter, my father divided his time between Vienna and Munich, where he devoted his leisure hours to the enjoyment of Wagner's operas and the company of musicians and singers. Of small stature and sallow complexion, he dressed immaculately; I am told that women thought him attractive. My father died in poverty in 1928, a few days after my return to Europe from a five years' sojourn in the United States. My mother, who had not seen him for many years, attended his painful illness and kept from him the cause of his death, which was cancer.

I grew up and reached manhood in the midst of disaster. I was eleven years old when World War I broke out. After my father was called back into service, my mother settled in Munich, where I spent my school holidays.

If anything had ever been settled in my unsettled family, it was that I should choose the military or the diplomatic career. Given the circumstances, these were not altogether unreasonable expectations, though fairly ambitious ones. In the old monarchy, considerable social prestige attached to both professions. The nobility enjoyed privileged access to the army, especially to the elite regiments. The great majority of the diplomats hailed from the great aristocratic houses of the empire. Yet the army was large, and there were not enough nobles to officer the line regiments. In the General Staff and the scientific branches of the army, especially artillery, officers of bourgeois antecedents, including not a few Jews, had gained advancement. The doors of the Foreign Ministry on the Ballhausplatz were opening, albeit not without some creaks and groans, to *bürgerliche* candidates. The idea of making a living did not occur to me. This matter had been taken care of by previous, more mercenary generations; moreover, it was unmentionable in that very reserved circle which I was destined, so I told myself, to enter. Since I could not help but overhear snatches of my elders' conversation, my mind was not entirely at rest. There were pitfalls along the road: to enter a cadet school and thus the regular army, not to speak of being admitted to the Theresianum (Diplomatic Academy) and thus to receive a pass key to the highest civil service, one had to have connections in high places. I took the measure of those of our "connections" in high places who consented to inspect me personally and did not always feel assured as to their devotion to my cause. Yet, were they to fail me, I still need not despair of the future; I could travel abroad, explore remote places, coast along tropical seas, sample exotic philosophies and return to Austria, a polished cosmopolite with an aura of adventurous exploits. This, too, was not altogether an unreasonable expectation, for the century was still young and my family fortune, depleted as it was by paternal extravagance, was still large enough to support a life of judicious leisure and studious travel.

The earth was still immense. Throughout most of it, men moved on ships at seven knots at best and mostly at lesser speeds, on horse- or muleback, on dog sleds and on foot. A great part of the polar regions had not yet been surveyed; large parts of Africa, most of Central Asia, the Amazon Basin, and all of Arabia's deserts were closed to all but the most venturesome and incurable explorer. Some of the living civilizations of the Far East, not to speak of their predecessors in antiquity, still kept most of their mysteries. The tremors of World War I had opened, here and there, cracks in the West's colonial edifice. Yet, a few miles beyond the coastal towns from Zanzibar to Aden and all the way to Shanghai and Hulatao, the lives of the peoples, together with their faith, their water wheels, their shaggy ponies, their women—painted, veiled, tatooed, secluded, and promiscuous—their potentates—bejeweled, incalculable, and tainted by Oxford or the Sorbonne just enough to make them all the more enigmatic—went on as it had long before the West had established its enclaves. That they should do so forever was the premise of Western rule. The Russo-Japanese War had made perfectly clear that the West could put up with anything— except the Westernization of non-Western peoples. Yet, in the early 1920's, this prospect, at once so flattering to Western culture and so ominous for its progenitors, still seemed remote— a matter not of years but of generations.

Thus the earth was still a Western preserve—a good deal of it still untrodden and in the alluring state of nature—which beckoned the select traveler in search of knowledge and adventure. Since the traveler had to start out with considerable reserves of money and even larger reserves of time, he was likely to be a man freed of the common concern for making a living. Indeed, with few exceptions, the kind of traveler of whom I speak—the amateur ethnographer-archaeologist-geographer-explorer, collector-journalist—belonged to that nearly extinct species, the cultivated man of leisure, of adequate means, and of no particular profession.

An eclectic, this man of leisure roamed many fields of interest and thus discerned affinities and relationships where the mere specialist could not; financially independent and not beholden for his livelihood to institutions, he could afford to embrace unpopular causes; back the perennial revolt of genius against academic rote; dabble in experiments without hope of financial gain and fear of academic censure; and, perhaps most importantly, act the middleman between the comers in the arts, sciences, and politics and the Establishment. His influence on the political and social development of England has been ever-present and deep; the "breakthrough" in the arts between 1900 and 1920 is as much the work of a handful of discriminating and well-heeled men and women of leisure as it is of the artists themselves; the foundations of modern archaeology, anthropology, ethnography, ichtheology, and ornithology were laid almost entirely by amateurs who footed the bills with their own money; the beginnings of aviation are inextricably linked to a galaxy of moneyed sportsmen who took to flying for no other reason than the thrill and the sheer beauty of it, and combined a flair for technical innovation with that indifference to danger which was the hallmark of the caste.

That, in my teens, I could contemplate such a "career" as an honorable and promising alternative to more stationary, though gentlemanly, employment, and could do so unruffled by even a *soupçon* of doubt about my claim upon permanent financial security—this quaint conceit belongs to the times, as do consols at four per cent, international travel without passports, the Sitwells-in-bloom, and *l'art nouveau*. Yet, the arts, the politics, the scholarship, and even the technical progress of the age are inconceivable without the contribution of the cultivated man of leisure.

In 1919 the Austro-Hungarian military establishment—or what defeat and desertion had left of it—followed the monarchy into limbo. The empire, despite its colorful extravaganzas, had been kept solvent by the great wealth of Bohemia and Hungary. Severe financial disturbances attended its dissolution. The Austrian crownlands and Vienna lost their hinterland, market for their products and source of their tax revenue. The purchasing power of money dropped precipitously. Every penny my parents owned had been invested in government bonds. Within a few months our once comfortable income shrank to a pittance. My personal prospects dimmed. The plans for my professional education needed drastic revision. The Peace Treaty of 1919 closed all military schools, a provision intended to ensure the pacific disposition of defeated Austria. Loss of Great Power status left Austria with a serious problem of technical unemployment: now, ten qualified diplomats were available for each meager foreign service job. Recruitment ceased; the service schools were closed. I awoke from my dream. At an early age I learned that it is safer to dream about the past than about the future. Whatever the future held for me, it would be neither an official career, aloof from all but the most portentous cares, nor gentlemanly leisure. My long search for a profession and a livelihood began. How well had milieu, family, and education endowed me for this quest?

My parents had not succeeded in rooting themselves firmly in any place or stratum of society. Upon their separation, my mother's home was mine. Moreover, the adults in my vision were either military or members of that Central European middle class that did not fit Professor Riesman's categories, and had only one common characteristic: the impenetrable partitions that separated it from peasantry and aristocracy, from the working class and the very rich. Within its ranks, the lines of separation between middle-rung government servants and merchants, between lawyers and physicians, schoolteachers and apothecaries, were tightly drawn. Since we lived on fixed income from government consols, we "rated" middle class; since my father had not found a niche in any of the professions, soon stopped trying to succeed in business, and then vanished in the eastern cantonments of the monarchy-at-war, we were left stranded on the margins of this not unkindly but fussy and anxious society. Intuitively, my mother understood that I would not fit. Narrow as were the passages through this labyrinthine edifice of bourgeois mores, bureaucratic hierarchies, and deferential snobbisms, one wide avenue led into the world and, for odd individuals of my kind, into freedom: arts and letters.

The middle class of Central Europe, somewhat embarrassed by

its own tolerance, was hospitable to the intellect, to the arts and to their irregular supporting troops such as actors, the makers of batiqued materials, the *Kunst* photographers—the jacks of all and any aesthetical trade who lived, wrote, drew, conversed, and cross-fertilized in the coffeehouses. Probably more than half of this fringe population was Jewish. The crucial role of the Jew in the Old Monarchy has only lately attracted the attention of Western scholars. Perhaps it has been the horrors and the humiliations of the Nazi period which have made its assessment impossible. How great was the contribution of the Jew to the life of Vienna and the German cities has become plain only now.

After World War II, the German-speaking peoples would have relapsed into the dull provinciality of the Germanies of two centuries ago had it not been for the cultural infusion administered by their conquerors. Even so, there is still a void that has not been filled, a heaviness of hand that weighs upon the present effort to rejoin the creative currents. So much of the German struggle for beauty-regained, for the lost horizons of the spirit, lacks authenticity, a dutiful matching of cultural refinement against complacent grossness, of abstract painting against Mercedes-Benz, of Karl Barth against the *Deutsche Bank*. These acts of penance will not revive the zest for playful innovation and the ruthlessness of creative thrust, the marriage of baroque imagination and surgical introspectiveness, which set off the arts and letters of Vienna and Munich and, later, Berlin, from those of the centers of Western Europe.

In 1920 I left school. (I did not return until twenty years later.) My mother and I had moved to Munich. Of the Communist rising of 1919 I remember only the stillness of the surburban streets, doors shut and windows curtained, the hush of fear, the menacing posters and the columns of Communist militia, bright red armbands against war-worn field gray, marching to intercept the approaching troops of General von Epp. And then the battle for the town. One day I bicycled along the Briennerstrasse on I know not what errand. A rifle barked, a machine gun sputtered, and then the frenetic clatter and stealthy silences of street-fighting opened to me the era of global civil war. I ducked with that self-effacing nimbleness which, under these and similar circumstances, makes up by spontaneity for the lack of systematic training.

Never have so many men ducked in so many places as in our century. By far the most infernal phenomenon of our age is the marriage of modern technology and civil war, particularly its consummation in modern cities. Its incongruous violence might be among the deepest roots of contemporary neurosis. To die, in the midst of metropolitan facilities, from a bullet fired from one knows not where, victim of the struggle between two concepts of civic order, mocks the one common aspiration of mankind in this century: security. And there is, of course, the mopping up.

The "Whites," who had defeated the "reds," were regulars. The Iron Brigade formed the core of the government troops. It had fought the Bolsheviki in the Baltic provinces and, after the Armistice, withdrawn slowly to Prussia. By spring of 1919 it comsisted almost exclusively of seasoned professionals, experts in guerrilla warfare—the dirtiest kind even before Asian ingenuity and Western technology refined this bastard branch of war—and in mass execution. Among the officers, not a few carried Rainer Maria Rilke next to the Mauser and, between massacres and muddy retreats, took refuge in Nietzsche, Houston Chamberlain, and drink. Others, the more extrovert type, contented themselves with plying their highly specialized trade, killing matter-of-factly and thus keeping alive that martial spirit which should have prevailed over democratic decadence—had it not been for the "dagger thrust" into Germany's back.

The "dagger" had been "thrust" by an assortment of villains— Socialists, pacifists, capitalists, aliens, Bolsheviks, literati, and Allied propagandists. The principal culprit was the civilian, domestic and foreign, and especially the civilian politician, domestic and foreign. If the men of the Iron Brigade were agreed upon anything beyond their collective contempt for all things civilian, including the government that employed them, it was upon the cause of Germany's defeat: when the soldiers were about to win the war, treason behind the lines robbed them of final victory. Indeed, the Allies had not exacted the surrender of the German forces in the field, and most units drew back from the front in fair order, carrying their weapons with them and receiving the accolade of the populace reserved for returning conquerors.

The Iron Brigade's reputation was based upon the fact that it had cut its way out of the depths of Russia, holding on to a part of the Baltic provinces against the Bolsheviks long after the conclusion of the Armistice in the West, and then complying reluctantly with the orders of the German republican government to march home. How much of this story of a great retreat— German historians and poets have always been fascinated with stiff-lipped retreats and Roncevallian last stands—is factual and how much of it shades into pure fiction, I do not know. The association of this body of modern *Landsknechte* with the infant democracy of Germany was no more incongruous than that of Frundsberg's mercenaries with the most Christian king who sacked Rome.

Having accomplished its mission, the brigade did not tarry long in Munich. In the shabby flat of a czarist exile, I met two young subalterns, one a taciturn and pimply Junker, the other a shy homosexual, quoting Stefan George and Rilke between digressions on varieties of automotive vehicles. The latter had commandeered the explosive motorbike of a dispatch rider, and allowed me to try it out. I drove up and down Munich's longest street, and this was one of the most blissful experiences of my adolescence. Finally, covered with grease, I drew up at the curb. My thoughts were on the bike, but not the lieutenant's. He invited me to join him in his quarters and look at Doré's illustrations of the *Divine Comedy*. I declined and we parted. On the way home, I relived my brief tryst with exhilarating motion.

Before I had gone halfway, however, lumps of embarrassment choked recollected pleasure. I had read about Alcibiades; contrary to widely held beliefs, at that time most boys of my age in Middle Europe, for all their familiarity with Krafft-Ebing and the Erotica of the Ancients, responded forthrightly to the other sex. Those who did not were average statistical exceptions. The glories of the Victorian Age had bypassed Middle Europe, especially its Catholic half; so had the tide of Victorian repressions and hypocrisies. On the whole, Middle European society accorded to sexual deviations a considerable latitude of tolerance. Had this not been so, the flowering of sex psychology in Vienna and Munich would have been an inexplicable phenomenon. Sigmund Freud could not have practiced in Victorian or Edwardian London. In brief, the notion of rampant homosexuality as the key to the collective psychosis of Middle Europe and, especially, its Nazi excrescence, is footless.

My first encounter with an erotic inclination I did not share left me uneasy and puzzled: exactly what shapes lie hidden beneath the lilies which float upon the pond? Fortunately, I had been taught by my humanist preceptors that tastes were not a matter of dispute and that a sense of measure was needed for dealing and living with what is askew and shocking to the senses. Implicit, too, in this pedagogy was the distinction between social mores and spiritual authority, the latter being, by a wide margin, the ultimate judge of the sins of the flesh. In practice, legal sanctions imposed upon offenders against the heterosexual standard have been more stringent, and certainly more publicized, in the Western Protestant or quasi-Protestant countries than in Catholic Middle and Southern Europe.

Simultaneously, I experienced the distinction between social mores and military authority, the military rule of Munich. The occupation of Munich was brief, but long enough to afford a full view of the military profession in the wake of defeat and the overthrow of the first Reich. It accommodated respectably, as could no other walk of life, the rejected, the misfit, the maimed knight, and the killer-by-avocation. From its studied monastic anonymity were to emerge not a few of the men who, some fifteen years later, administered the political and strategic affairs of the Third Reich, conceived in the union of romantic verse and the machine-gun stutter. In the intervening years, some of their ex-comrades had turned assassins, amateur or paid; others soldiered abroad, notably in the French Foreign Legion and the armies of the Chinese warlords. Meanwhile, the brotherhood spread over the earth; the beliefs, the deeds, the words spoken, and even the faces were virtually the same.

Forty years later I again met my friend the lieutenant. This time, however, he joined me on the terrace of Fouquet's, quoted Camus, expressed devotion to his pipe of dreams and his almond-eyed mistress. He had marched, during the five years since his

graduation from St.-Cyr, the whole length of the via dolorosa
from the jungles of Tonkin to the Kabylian Mountains. Again,
valor had prevailed—or could have prevailed, had it not been for
the lies of the politicians and the indifference of the masses. This
time, too, I felt that his country and his leaders had sent him on
impossible errands—and that with or without their leave he
would continue marching on the endless retreat from yesterday's
glory to today's usurious routine.

His glance swept the wide avenue, scabrous beneath the neon
signs and packed with cars and peoples. Not wishing to offend
me, he asked me whether this tawdry coating of the triumphal
way could not be put to the debit of "Americanization." Without waiting for my answer, he conceded his partiality, professional and private, for certain kinds of "American" gadgets, some
of them highly lethal. Then he took his leave, to pass a few hours
with his pipe and mistress before returning to his Algerian post
—for no purpose whatsoever that he could see. Our suspense at
the unfolding of the historical process is matched only by our
surprise at the repetitiousness of its outcome. Those who learn
from history are condemned to listen forever to its broken
record, the needle caught in the same groove.

Meanwhile, in Munich the street cleaner sanded and hosed the
patches of gore; the pockmarks on façades behind which another
last stand had crumbled beneath a heavier weight of lead were
plastered over; and new windowpanes were set. The Soviet
agents had melted away; the shops and factories reopened; and
the breweries resumed production. The surviving leaders of the
Communists insurrections—Eisner had been assassinated by Arco-
Valley, a fighter pilot home from the wars, and Gustav Landauer
had perished no one knows exactly how during the last days of
the fighting—were tried before the courts and sent to prison. By
contemporary standards of revolution, the sentences were light.

The Communist revolution in Munich, unlike the one in Budapest and the Spartacus rising in Berlin, had not been master-
minded by seasoned professionals.

In the course of that brief and inept experiment, the rift between the thinker and the doer, between Marxist philosophy and
Leninist practice, became visible to the naked eye. The leaders of

the Munich revolution—Eisner, Landauer, and Toller—were neither organization men nor practical "operators." On the contrary, they were Schwabing literati. Unlike Lenin's didactic briefs, their compulsive oratory flowed aimlessly above the heads of the perplexed militants.

There were many reasons for the purge of the intellectuals from Communist leadership and the monstrous retrogression in the Soviet Union of all the arts except the least intellectual of them, music. Had they survived, they would have joined the disenchanted chorus of the Koestlers, Orwells, and Djilases. In the West, their brief and awkward performance upon the stage of the world revolution was hardly noted (to the best of my knowledge, no Western study-in-depth of the Munich rising exists). Nevertheless, it is certain that those of the party hierarchy who had always doubted the Western intellectual's fitness for an executive position in revolution-making found their views confirmed by the Munich fiasco.

Bloody as was the transaction, however, it did not lack comic byplay: echelons of Bohemians, surfacing from their favorite taprooms and descending from their garrets, declaimed avant-garde poetry to captive audiences, the stunned rank and file of the Bavarian Red Army. For a few weeks they controlled the printing presses and the lecture halls, the Ministry of Education and whatever funds were left in the exchequer. The Munich revolution had been suffocated by reams of bad verse, obscure prose, and sectarian social projects; now it was drowned in the blood of its more primitive militants. The Soviet professionals undoubtedly miscalculated the exhilarating consequences of loosening Bohemia from the fetters of the bourgeoisie and the laws of aesthetical supply and demand.

Unlike this unorganized militancy in Munich, the Communist risings in Berlin and Budapest were fomented and led by seasoned professionals, civilian and military, bent single-mindedly upon the bloody liquidation of the opposition and thus upon committing their followers irrevocably to the cause of the revolution. Bela Kun, Lenin's emissary who was later executed by Stalin, and his associates were organization men (*apparatchiki*). Upon the fall of the Communist regime in Budapest, they made their way to Moscow and from there to wherever the apparatus assigned them, to China, to Spain, to the Americas, and back to Eastern Europe, hard upon the heels of the Red Army. Though letter-perfect in Marxist-Leninist dialectics, they were, far and foremost, efficiency experts in the making of revolution and the allied arts of conspiracy, guerrilla warfare, assassination, liquidation, and propaganda. If they were interested in philosophy, literature, and the arts, it was for the purpose of winning over minds to the cause of the revolution, infiltrating institutions of learning, exploiting the rift between the bourgeoisie and its alienated intellectuals, and identifying the Communist revolution with the "progressive forces" of the times. They were practical men and miles apart from the Schwabing literati, scanning the glory of proletarian revolution.

By the end of 1919, defeat, revolution, and counterrevolution had pushed what was already falling, the social order of Middle Europe. The war had been fought on credit; the bills were now coming in. No one in high places, either in the defeated countries or in the victorious ones, had figured out how industrial societies that once had lived by mutual trade and then had warred upon one another could absorb into their cost accounting such rubbery items as, for example, victory and defeat.

In the absence of clairvoyance, the matter was settled by accident and improvisation. The principal, though pained and unwilling, agent of the ensuing settlement was the middle class of Middle Europe. The spoliation by governments of the middle class through inflation and, specifically, through debasing the currency and thus in fact defaulting on the fixed-interest-bearing obligations of the state, constituted the single most important cause of the disintegration of Middle European society, of the radicalization of European politics, and thus of World War II. This amply authenticated fact has not been given the attention it deserves—perhaps because it holds up a retrospective mirror which does not flatter the neo-Keynesian countenance. I have burrowed my way through the vast literature in English on the decline of the Weimar Republic, the rise of Hitler, and the origins of World War II. Measured by its bulk, it gives scant space to the traumatic shock which inflation delivered to the Middle

European middle class—a class dispossessed in the literal sense of the word.

Germany's slow-motion descent into the economic abyss and prolonged political quarantine culminated in a psychological disaster. The remedial measures were applied piecemeal and late —too late. A great deal of the damage was beyond mending; the social order had fallen apart. And so had my own frail world.

Although inflation in Austria did not reach the dizzy proportion of the German orgy of paper money (housewives in Vienna, unlike those in Munich, did not lug baskets of paper money to the grocer), it effectively wiped out the rentier. The value of holdings that had yielded my mother an apartment complete with cook and maid, a three-months stay at Rapallo or Menton or Biarritz each year, and a fair dress allowance for distribution among Vienna's couturiers (she selected my suits and shirts from a London mail-order catalogue), shrank to exactly thirty-five dollars. We both were shocked but, since we had no idea as to what unpleasantness the future would bring, not worried.

My mother began selling her jewelry and, upon the advice of our increasingly uninterested banker, looked for work. She found it behind the counter of a Munich furrier who catered to the dependents of black marketeers and currency speculators. This new chivalry vied with a contingent of mysterious foreigners—White Russian generals, who had managed to salvage from defeat trunkloads of ikons and gold watches, and a vanguard of Dutchmen, Swedes, and Americans, who had discovered the German seller's craving for hard currencies—for the possessions of the middle class and the tables of the proliferating nightclubs.

My mother did well in her job, the first one she had ever held—well enough to ensure us a subsistence diet, that is, the occasional pound of butter and dozen of eggs which, after an hour's railroad journey and a five-mile hike, we extracted from the hoard of our pet farmer. This remarkable man, a limping veteran of Verdun, illiterate and possessed of two solitary incisors, stayed abreast of the daily and, sometimes, hourly fluctuations of the mark-dollar rate. How he managed to keep his finger upon the feverish pulse of the national economy—his remote hamlet did not boast a single telephone, and a horse-drawn mail coach provided communication with a distant railhead—has been one of the mysteries which I never fathomed.

These short trips into the country proved most refreshing. In this particular corner of Upper Bavaria, the cultivated valleys rise gently toward the Alpine foothills. Here crop and meadow lands are rimmed by serried pine woods, and small lakes are fed by cascading brooks, quick and clear. Puffy white clouds—obese seraphim—float grandly upon the translucent blue, the Bavarian sky celebrated in the banners of the Wittelsbachs, the blue and silver of the Amalienburg, and the billowing frescoes and ceiling paintings of the Asam baroque. In the Mediterranean and Caribbean I have seen deeper blue, and, in the Pacific, clouds as white and more resplendent, but only in the Bavarian highlands have I seen a blue as airy, a white as pristine.

If any one word describes the Bavarian landscape, it is freshness. Even in the warm summer air there is a hint of the coolness of brooks and lakes and the high mountains. Even the most venerable pines, slender and dark, are young. On my foraging marches along the macadam roads, in stretches lined with poplars and always casual, I came to know many villages, hamlets, and solitary farms perched on the high slopes, church steeples with bulbous domes—stranded envoys of Byzantium to the northern barbarians—and a few monasteries that still brewed their own, and notwithstanding a national shortage of hops and malt, strong beer. A stein of beer with white radishes and black bread—I cannot think of a more wholesome and tasty meal, especially after a long hike, burdened with a heavy rucksack and hardly any concerns about the future of man.

It was during these forays that I came to know the Bavarian peasant, sturdy and sly. The Bavarian highlands and Alpine valleys breed a durable and ugly race. If mountains nurture the spirit of liberty, plains and seacoasts favor the development of the human body. The sea peoples seem most abundantly endowed with physical beauty. A diet of fish and salty breezes narrows hips and whitens teeth. The Bavarian peasant is squat and bucktoothed; not infrequently, he is also goitered and cretinous, consequences of iodine deficiency and a great deal of joyless inbreeding. Notwithstanding these unfortunate eugenic conditions, the land is unspoiled to this day.

Perhaps my love of walking is but a conditioned reflex of the human condition. Throughout most of my youth I was poor and, not infrequently, penniless. Horses, sailboats, and shoots denote affluence and leisure. Since I was short of both, had been raised on the axiom *mens sana in corpore sano*—the battle cry of the Germanic Academy—and craved motion for its own sake, I took to walking on foot—and on skis.

Fortunately, the train fare from Munich to the ski slopes was cheap. Although I did not master the more elegant turns—the art was still young and my equipment rudimentary—I developed a fair skill at cross-country skiing. My companions and I planned our route so that an eight-hour run would bring us to a shelter (*Hütte*). We spent the night, tidied up, and were on our way at daybreak. Depending on snow conditions and the weather, as well as our professional scruples, we managed to keep going for three to four days and to cover a sizable terrain. Neither of us could pass as an expert skier or Alpinist, and our exploits were notable for misadventures—broken skis, wrenched ankles, and the hostility of the indigenous population—rather than for our sporting feats. We were exceedingly happy and perversely carefree.

Some of my older companions on such adventures had returned from the wars; the mud and the gore still stuck to their souls. Like soldiers before and after them, they found that those they had left behind had come to terms with their absence, that even those who cared could not enter their private cell in hell, and that protracted boredom, broken by flashes of fright and elation, had not prepared them for the even rhythm of making a living, going to bed with their wives, and watering the geraniums. Indeed, not a few of my older companions, older by only two or three telescoped war years, were hopelessly lost—more hopelessly than their comrades of the lost generation in France and Britain, who had at least the consolation prize of victory to show for their pains. They never got back onto the road. Some wrote haunting verse and made of their misdirection a sedentary profession; some followed even stranger and more asocial callings; some, the most dangerous ones, turned mystics or politicians or both, thus striking the very bottom of wickedness. The company of the lost and the irrecoverable roamed postwar Europe. In Middle Europe it was large enough to twist society into its own neurotic shapes and, in the end, to hold a whole civilization to ransom. Without them, the pied pipers could not have come to power.

I foresaw nothing. Healthy, lusting for life, and unworldly, I plunged recklessly and awkwardly into experience. Unsure about myself, I was content to travel with my friends and to assemble from their confidences—perplexed as most of us were, we talked a lot, and much that had been pent up now sought release in torrents of self-revelation—the proper image of myself, the image I would display to the world. My selections from vicarious experience must have struck others as extremely odd. My search for identity led me into ever more tangled underbrush and ever further away from being what nowadays is called an adjusted person—adjusted presumably to one's peers, one's place in society. I had no place in society and, as for my peers, they were the last to whom I could turn for pointers on adjustment.

Chapter Two

I HAD left school in 1920. For a few months I kept books for a grain dealer, doodling through evening courses in stenography and accounting. My employer suggested that my creative drive and aversion to office routine destined me for intellectual pursuits. I had no choice other than to take his advice.

About that time my mother returned to Vienna. I stayed behind and settled in one of the many *pensions*—a rooming house with board—which were to inspire Christopher Isherwood's masterpiece, *Goodbye to Berlin*. Mine accommodated chiefly actors and actresses, a stage director, a few men of letters loosely connected with small magazines and the experimental theater, and an art historian, von der Bercken, esteemed for his works on the paintings of the high Renaissance, his vicious attacks upon his fellow experts, and, notwithstanding his Prussian and aristocratic lineage, his contempt for all things German.

A friend of my parents, von der Bercken opened to me the doors and the credit of the *pension* and the world of painting.

Curator in one of the great galleries of the Bavarian state, he put me to work translating museum and auction catalogues as well as scholarly articles from the French. My compensation for these efforts sufficed to settle about half the weekly bill presented by my landlord, a pallid man torn between mercenary motivation and genuine reverence for the arts. Von der Bercken, a solitary and dyspeptic man, led me to the literature of cultural history— *Kulturgeschichte*.

In this field of study, German scholarship had reared a formidable edifice upon the foundation laid by Jakob Burckhardt. The impressment of sociology and archaeology into the service of a many-pronged approach to the comparative analysis of civilizations revealed constancies and unities where the traditional disciplines saw but the fenced-in patches of their specialization. In part, this development derived from the refinement of the tools of research and the ease of global communication; in part, its thrust toward synthesis—the idea of one pattern woven of many threads, the nobles and their portraits, the common peoples and their pots and shards, the warriors and their weapons, the builders and their tools, the princesses and their rouge pots, the seers and the signs and symbols devised in their name—received its impetus from one Olympian intelligence.

As far as I was concerned, if any one man stood at the point of origin of such Olympian intelligence, it was Goethe. Like many others educated in the German language, I read his works as school assignments, reread *Faust* in later years, and, well past middle age, sampled again the cadenced phrases which, so I thought, I had once known so well. Yet, each time I found new meaning and, as it were, each time I found the man's presence changed. Perhaps the explanation lies in the fact that Goethe lived long and that age did not impair his mind nor assuage his passions. Perhaps it lies in his Promethean busyness which led him into many important and many more frivolous pursuits. Whatever it might be, it has been said that Goethe's greatest work of art is his own life, and that his literary and scientific output consists of a mass of fragments. For example, his masterpieces are unfinished—as is Michelangelo's last and most moving *Pietà*. But nothing that is alive is ever finished, and perhaps no man was more intensely alive than Goethe.

For quickness of perception and sureness of expression, Goethe cannot compare with Shakespeare—whose great plays Goethe knew long before they appeared on Continental stages. Yet, whereas Shakespeare takes the measure of man—and takes it with unsurpassed astuteness—Goethe challenges the bounds of man's fate. Shakespeare-the-man, immolated in his creations, remains to this day a shadowy figure; the figure of Goethe dwarfs his work. Shakespeare's characters *are*. They are what they are —complex, magnificent, contrary, pitiful, and always fully fledged. Goethe's heroes transform themselves under our eyes, transcend themselves—they *become*, and the suspense lies exactly in the forever unanswered question as to what they might be. Shakespeare at his worst—and his worst is atrocious and disgusting—never flattens into banality, whereas Goethe, on occasion, returns from his sublime musings with one of those thumping platitudes which have been regurgitated by generations of German schoolmasters. Yet, such lapses from good sense and taste are but the contingent flaws of an ever-questing and speculative mind: Not the play, but the experiment is the thing.

There remains always the artistic problem of rendering, after a century and a half, a life from contemporary reminiscences. Yet, there can be no doubt about Goethe's personal magnetism. The most extraordinary and the least likely people succumbed to his seduction. Napoleon and Byron, perhaps the two greatest egocentrics of the age, paid homage to his greatness. Napoleon's acclamation at Erfurt—*Voilà un homme*—honors the man so addressed as well as the speaker. Always in love, yet always capable of extricating melodious stanzas and, incidentally, himself from the most soul-shattering involvement, Goethe was greatly loved; the same power of passion that overwhelmed the pastor's daughter of Sesenheim swept, sixty years later, Ulrike von Lewetzow off her feet.

Goethe is wholly and intensely German, and we should not let the classicist folderol and philosophical internationalism deceive us. Perhaps no other man has had as great an influence upon the education of his people as has Goethe (Confucius was not a man but an anthropomorphic composite of traditions). Rightly, Germany has hailed Goethe not only as her greatest poet but also as her *Erzieher* (educator). No doubt, the Shakespearean turn of phrase has shaped the English language, and the fables of Fontaine have impregnated generations of French schoolchildren with that pungent cynicism which is the Frenchman's impartial response to virtue and vice. But Goethe's pedagogical contribution is far more explicit: a part of the German mind is his. And this, perhaps, is the trouble: the other part has always denied him. This circumstance, too, stands to the credit of Goethe's clairvoyance. Long before the word was coined, Goethe defined the nature of schizophrenia: *Zwei Seelen wohnen in meiner Brust*.

Goethe's striving—his intent as artist as well as his intimate yearnings and quest for a personal style—is directed toward serenity and poise. Quietude, detachment, the exhaustion of the senses in unselfish labors, the noble renunciation of earthly passion and the individual's voluntary surrender to the service of mankind—these are the ideals extolled in Goethe's plays, poems, and novels. Yet, in fact, Goethe's creative genius finds its true expression in the evocation of man's insoluble dilemma, the daemonic forces within and around him—and the joys and sufferings of the creative genius, Goethe himself. The fact is that Goethe was a master of self-analysis and a colossal egocentric.

I do not know whether my first communion with Goethe—I was then still in my teens—helped or harmed me. Since then I have accumulated a great deal of intellectual baggage—and discarded much of it. In my attic molders the luggage of German philosophy, including the valise marked Schopenhauer and Hegel. There were all kinds of writers of no particular consequence and distinction which, at a certain turn in my life, moved me deeply or opened a new path of intellectual discovery. I hardly remember the names of the authors and still less the titles of their works. Yet I owe more to their mediation than to many a classic masterpiece. The idea of a Hundred Masterpieces of World Literature has always struck me as very, very funny. The only result their consumption guarantees is an acute case of constipation. For a healthy intellectual digestion I recommend a lot of roughage. The one exception from the massive turnover in suppliers of my intellectual guidance has been Goethe. I presume that this is due, in part, to my heritage and, in part, to *Wahlver-wandschaft*. The visceral affinity remains.

The principal furnishings of my room in the *pension* were books, piles of foolscap paper, and a window with a view on the tops of old chestnut trees. Most of the day I stuck doggedly to my translations, as tedious and exacting a job as any I have known. For relaxation I composed verse in the lugubrious Stefan George manner which then was still in fashion. In the evening I joined my friends in one or the other of the taverns which drew their regular clientele from the *Schwabing bohême* and its floating patronage from the ordinary noncreative public seeking personal contact with the arts and their purveyors.

For a few years Munich offered sanctuary to the arts, scholarship, and pleasure—especially the last. The great mass of Germans could not indulge their *Wanderlust* for want of foreign currency. Moreover, they were not welcome in the countries of the Allies; passports and visas were difficult to obtain. Munich, a beautiful town in a beautiful land, had always attracted tourists and expatriates.

An oasis of peace and quiet, furnished with many studios, *pensions*, hotels and comfortable villas, and a few tolerable restaurants and nightclubs, Munich now drew the rich, the eccentric, the frustrated cosmopolite and the displaced person from all parts of Central Europe. Munich's golden age began shortly after the restoration of public order. It ended in the mid-twenties. By then, the Weimar Republic seemed firmly established; foreign loans had helped to rebuild German industry; Berlin had resumed its role as the uncontested center of politics, finance, culture, and vice. By then, the quick and the gifted who had written, painted, talked, and made love in the Munich attic responded to the call of Berlin's well-heeled impresarios, art dealers, producers, and sundry gatekeepers of the Muses. Some, as for example, Dieterle, the stage director of the Schauspielhaus, and Elisabeth Bergner, the leading and precious actress of the same theater, pushed onward to New York and Hollywood—emissaries of the bizarre, mannered style of stage "expressionism" to which the "experimental" theater not only in this country but also in Paris and

London owes, to this day, a large and largely unavowed debt of gratitude. The fare was the rich and varied one of a tireless and resourceful repertory theater: the somber plays of Strindberg, the shockers of Wedekind, the hilarious one-acters of Courteline, Shakespearean comedy. Calderón's cape-and-sword, and the shouts and groans of Büchner.

Georg Büchner hurled the existential dilemma into the teeth of the universe. His muse was the French Revolution. He gave the German stage what it so conspicuously lacked: tragedy in the grand manner. There is oaken strength in Büchner, that irreconcilable protest of the German Gothic against Roman civility. There is also that fatality that is the essence of great tragedy. His hero does what he must do. To strip him down to what he is at heart, poltroon, coward, and lecher—no one performs this horrible operation with more skill than Büchner. Yet, then the loathsome wreck rises, ascends, steadfastly, and open-eyed, to the summit of his destiny which is the scaffold, and, with his last breath, exhales the sigh of all humanity.

I do not know whether Bertold Brecht's kinship to Büchner has been noted by any literary critic. Both belong to the same German tradition of immoderate revolt. The West's acclaim of Brecht, a humorless, didactic, ideological zealot, would be incomprehensible but for Brecht's overpowering, remorseless sense of tragedy. His art lies in his consummate stagecraft and the melodic cadence of his lines. Betwixt their monstrous doings, Brecht's lustful, hungry, thirsty, and desperate men and women manage to speak lines as lyrical, as sensitive, as terse as any written in the German language or, for that matter, in any language. That Brecht should have come to rest in the camp of a tyranny far more blatant and hypocritical than any his heroes seek to break, this is a German literary tragedy—a loss far more grievous than the easy, "safe," and royalty-wise, highly profitable defections of some notorious literary figures in other Western lands.

I found employment in the theater to supplement my meager earnings as a scholar. A young actress who wore her dark long hair in a coiled bun, spoke her lines in that husky alto voice which, in future years, was to become familiar on the world's stages as the tonal manifestation of troubled sex, and, between interminable rehearsals, cooked magnificent sinuous spaghetti, introduced me to Otto Distler, reader and script man (*Dramaturg*) of one of the leading repertory theaters. Otto lived austerely, shaved uncertainly, though incisively, wrote jerky and obscure verse, read quickly and voraciously, did not stand in awe before his own untested creative powers, and thus had the makings of an excellent dramatic critic. The stage directors valued his discrimination—from beneath mountains of unpublished and mercifully unpublishable manuscripts he recovered several "new" plays that were to establish the considerable reputation of their respective authors—and his flair for timing, for pace, which is the one indispensable attribute of stagecraft. Otto deposited a pile of French and English plays in my cluttered quarters, paid me a small retainer fee, and told me to furnish forthwith a brief critical summary of each. Otto, I believe, never really quite trusted my judgment. He read French and English tolerably well, and in not a few cases could have procured fair translations in print. A born pedagogue, Otto set out to train me, so to speak, on the job.

It seems I did not disappoint his expectations altogether. After a while he asked me to check the German translation of a play by Paul Claudel with the French original. Upon Otto's advice, the management acquired the rights, the play was produced and had a long run. I sat through the rehearsals; Otto adopted a few of the minute changes in wording which I had suggested. For the first time in my life I felt the pride of publication—a few lines of verse spoken as I had set them down. I thought my rendering quite superior to the French original. I was probably right at that, for Claudel can be tediously allusive, prone to a hyperbolic symbolism which leaves one waiting for a clue that never comes. Many years later I read his correspondence with Gide. Gide, a far less happy man than Claudel and not possessed of the latter's almost musical facility, stands up much better. A spoiled Calvinist wrestling with vice is just plausible, even if he slugs it out with the devil in the most meticulous and elegant prose; a suave diplomat in mystical communion with Catholic dogma is not.

My heavy chores were redeemed by irregular hours. In my later years I was to work and watch the clock. I have always found

timed labor intolerable. Then, with the consuming introspectiveness of youth, I noted neither the time of day nor the weather nor
the seasons. I was blissfully unaware of the existential condition.
The indifference of nature reveals itself only to the stricken and
the prematurely aged. I was too curious and hard-pressed to ask
for precise directions. Between bouts of despair filtered into dark
verse, I pursued zestfully my quest for great ideas and passionate
communion. Thus I lacked the solitary leisure to meditate upon
the nature of happiness. I meant to brood over my predicament. I
was easily diverted.

I had several occupations, a free library, a pass to the theater, a
call on spaghetti and, now and then, a bottle of Chianti, a window
on life, and hardly ever a sou in my pocket. After more than forty
years, I probe the treacherous depths of memory. The records I
kept, the letters I received are lost. Those I then loved are dead or
strangers who would tell me nothing—even if they cared to seek
with me the overgrown path. I wonder as to whether I do not see
myself across these forty years as I now want myself to have been
—not necessarily stronger and more poised, but happier and more
lucky. So much I strove for came to pass and, as is the caprice of
fortune, came to pass long after I had stopped striving.

What makes a revolution so unnerving is its penumbra of in-
definiteness. Conceivably, the men in charge know that they are
making a revolution or that they are crushing one. To have one's
head cut off in the full view of the *tricoteuses* must be a horrible
experience; it does clarify the issue. For the average men and
women things are not so simple. They do not know that they are
living through a revolution, that they are the generation of destiny. I was not dense enough to ignore the drastic change the
revolution had wrought around me. Yet I grasped but vaguely
the impact upon my own life of these horrendous political, economic, and social transactions. Like so many *émigrés* before me,
I thought that things would right themselves, that after a while
my rightful claims to privilege and possession would prevail.

The inertia of status defies the historical dialectic. I moved
from one fitful job to another, improvisations without issue;
dreamed my sumptuous dreams of canopied barges on the Nile

and throbbing Bentleys in Biarritz; woke with strangers in dank attics; nursed the one undarned, too tightly fitting suit—and plotted my escape. Try as I may, I cannot bring into focus the young man of twenty. If we were to meet today, we would have little to say to each other. His ruthless naïveté, his clammy embarrassments, his lyrical sensitivity in the throes of his own emotions, his stoic indifference toward the feelings of others, his flustered passions, his tortuous and transparent stratagems—I superimpose image upon image. Yet, no sooner done, the features melt and blur. How would he see me? The husk that he would be?

Fortunately, we are spared this melancholy confrontation. What sustained him so splendidly was his total lack of sense-of-process; what sustains me now is that I can order the past to suit my fancy of orderly progression. Were we to meet now, he would lose hope and I the knack of forgetting. The "I" I seek to recall stands out vividly against the backdrop of the without. I remember incidents and people, coordinates of my place in time. But the solitary man within is brittle bone and dust beneath the retrospective effigy.

Had I but known it, my predicament was not unique, and the world had been crumbling for a long time—at any rate, ever since the end of the nineteenth century. The chilling shadows of novel technologies and rising industrial powers had fallen, long before World War I, upon the glories of the Victorian age. Darwinism had seeped into moral speculation; for quite some time mass civilization had been creeping toward the secluded houses on the hill; the chosen few themselves were rattled by what they had read about the Satanic mills and natural selection; the many sensed how rattled were the few; sex was just about to shed its provocative concealments and encumbering ornaments and to strip for forthright, experimental action; the clinical thrust of Dr. Freud breached the walls, which heretofore had confined the senses and, in any case, closed the gap, but for a matter of inches, between sacred and profane love. Not that Darwin, the Fabians, and Dr. Freud meant to propound these absurdities: Darwin, a meticulous and cautious man, had neither inclination nor time for metaphysical speculation; Freud, though less resistant to the lure of platitude, did not conceive of his teachings as morally permissive; the Fabians were much too pleased with their own paradoxes and subtleties to let the vulgar in on their clever jokes. Be that as it may, the clichés of naturalism, Marxism (pure or Anglican), and moral relativism put a shade more succinctly what a new, matter-of-fact generation of the middle classes had meant to say anyway to its baffled elders. The war cut short what, then and there, might have turned into a great debate. The energies of the young were diverted into another kind of controversy.

After the war we resumed the discussion. The young had the better of it. Patently, the elders had made a mess of things. They had grown older and more flustered. The truth, the wisdom of the ages and the folly of its living guardians had exploded in the trenches. The young, redolent with the fragrance of latrine and dispensary, returned to tell their parents and teachers of love and death, joy and putrefaction. The over-all effect was stunning. The cord linking the generations, frayed by the attrition of forces on the loose long before the guns played catalyst, snapped with a deafening bang. The five years of the war might just as well have been fifty. This process of compression shaped and reshaped all things. It bore down upon the middle-aged, who sought to return to a past which the five years' nightmare had turned into an Arcadian legend; it bore down upon the survivors of the fighting, who now learned, to their surprise, that they had been accelerating history and in the rush had skipped their own youth. It stamped the postwar generation—mine. We were the genuine product of the great, the abrupt transformation. We did not even have to push what was falling; we were responsible for nothing; most certainly, it was not our task to put back the heads which stronger hands than ours had knocked off the statuary. We were, in a matter-of-fact and canny way, concerned with ourselves. At that time the solid citizenry began to bewail the *Verwilderung des Jugend*—literally, the growing wilder of the young.

My generation reached maturity in the twenties. I do not think that we were more ferocious and unruly than the same age group today or, let us say, twenty years before us. Rather, we were outsiders who, with no other guidance than their precocious wit, had to make their way across the wasteland. Quite obviously, the old rules did not fit. We had taken our place in the world before the appointed time. The war had taken a terrible toll of the male population. Boys, since they were taught the ways of men, quickly became men. Thus the natural balance righted itself. The authorities professed to be indignant—all the more deeply because the adjustment had come about quite casually. The distressing revelations of the revolution in sexual mores shocked everybody—except the parties most immediately concerned.

Had we but known it, we then crossed the threshold leading toward the democratization of sex. Up until then the guardianship of sexual mores had been pre-empted by the upper classes, and the lower orders honored the reigning taboos with the pretense of their compliance. This left to both a comfortable margin between theory and practice. Although the lower orders suspected that the well-tended privacy of their betters allowed for considerable latitude, neither photoreportage nor the motion picture had yet revealed to the masses the minutiae of upper-class life. On the other hand, the cycle of peasant life remained what it had been throughout the ages. Its reconciliation with public morality was left to the wisdom of the Church and its local disciplinarian, the village priest. After many centuries the result was a draw, a standoff between brutishness and civility.

The sons and daughters of the peasant, camping on the barren ground of the cities, were being taught new ways and new needs. Mass production and the daily press were the teachers. The workshop imposed its discipline; the press and, later, the cinema opened wider horizons: romance, sports, crime, high adventure, scandal in high places, politics, and the infinite variety of desirable things that could be bought for money.

Change of scene and pace was fraught with some disturbing consequences: on the land, men, women, and children worked in the open air; the rhythm of their lives and the cycle of the seasons were closely linked; the same roof sheltered cow barn, stable, loft, woodshed, kitchen, and bedchamber; the village clustered around its church. The enclosed monotony of the factory and the anonymity and dispersion of the city were as far removed from village life as village life was from the cave dwelling. Not all could make the adjustment. The tearing wrench left incurable cripples. It unchained monsters. In Hitler, the village took terrible revenge on the city. The story of Hitler's parentage and upbringing reads like any of the countless records of that community misfit who belonged to the village, as did the headman and the priest.

The masses became conscious of themselves, and out of this consciousness emerged new sets of values. These were assortments of all kinds of things, some new and some quite old. The ensemble was highly original. Its style—and style is everything —bore hardly any resemblance to that of upper-middle-class culture. For more than a hundred years the bourgeoisie had tried to fit its bursting affluence and prudish scruples into the code of the aristocracy. The new urban-industrial mores paid little heed to aristocratic decorum or its deferential adaptations by the bourgeoisie. To be sure, some of the most venerable taboos were incorporated in the new code of morals and manners—with a twist here and a foreshortening there. But the whole was everything but gentlemanly. The accent fell upon unblinking practicality, hard cynicism, coy sentimentality, sly wit, mock deference to fine manners, and mutual tolerance, the impersonal forbearance of the crowded tenement, the rush to work and to public gardens on a hot summer evening. The "lower" classes drew the logical conclusions, namely, that the mores of their urban-industrial milieu were authentically theirs and owed nothing to those of their "uppers" who could afford the luxurious anachronisms of their increasingly dubious station. The moral revolution from below seeped upward. The lower classes paid homage to their rulers by a smirking persiflage of elegant manners. The rulers took on by almost imperceptible osmosis the mores of the masses —a process described by Ortega y Gasset in this century's noblest statement of humanist culture, *The Revolt of the Masses*. Liza learned to speak as Dr. Higgins spoke; Dr. Higgins did as Liza did.

Chapter Three

My generation was the last whose childhood was cradled by the certainties of the Long Peace and the Gold Standard. We had been raised as little gentlemen; circumstance drove us into the street to measure ourselves with the sons of the great migration, uninhibited by, and hilariously contemptuous of, our code and, more often than not, more nimble than we. Some of us retreated in bewilderment; some of us took to the game and turned bullies. My generation, not the one that had fought the war, supplied the toughs, intellectual as well as brawny, that bludgeoned democracy into insensibility and carried Hitler to power. Some of us steadied, took bearings, and reached, relatively undamaged, the yonder shore of the twentieth century. We had a lot to learn. For example, we had to forget what we had been told about women. The knight had fallen off his charger. Worse, there was no longer anyone who needed his protection. The reticent maiden had leapt from her bower. Probably never, in all these hundreds of years, had women taken quite seriously their own cult, the cult of chivalry. Rid of this burden, they stepped into life. We discovered what all the powers of social convention had sought to hide, namely, that in not a few essentials women were not so different from men.

Before the great flood, society operated a complicated machinery for first taming and then titillating the mating instincts of the young—dancing classes, debuts, chaperoned balls, and rusticated trystings of the eligibles at Karlsbad or Wiesbaden or the Italian lakes under the watchful eyes of their elders. This machinery now broke down, for such elaborate preliminaries were far too costly for the inflation-stricken middle and upper classes. Now we met a great deal more informally, and, since no one among us had expectations of settled bliss, entered and dissolved partnerships more lightly. What our relations had lost in decorum was made up for by directness. Our watchword was the New Matter-of-Factness (*Neue Sachlichkeit*) which streamlined the formalities and speeded the proceedings. Of course, every so often we forgot to play by the new rules. But our transports and tragedies were those of youth of any time. If it is possible for the very young to feel nostalgic, we managed this sensation. The fleeting view of a well-cared-for garden, and then the gates are shut. We did not always take and break as ruthlessly as our hard-boiled script called for. Most of us, I suspect, suffered from an incurable hangover, for we had drunk, at a tender age, from the dregs of the Romantic.

Shortly after World War II, I saw a French motion picture entitled *Carnet de Bal*. The middle-aged widow of a successful businessman grows restive upon the terrace of her Italian villa. Still beautiful, she seeks happiness. To find it, she travels to the small French town where she grew up. In the chest of her mementos she has found a *carnet de bal*. This card, upon which her swains had inscribed their names to secure her as a partner, recalls her first dance. The *carnet* now serves as agenda. She seeks out, one by one, the charming young men who had danced with her to the tunes of haunting waltzes and stirred her girlish fancy. Although this should surprise no one, she is in for appalling discoveries: in the intervening twenty years some of her gallants have gone to pot; others have grown bald and paunchy, pillars of provincial mediocrity. Of course, they are no longer charming, and she is no longer sure that they ever were. Disenchanted, she visits that splendid ballroom in which the dance had been given. Of course, it is a bleak and musty hall, as bleak and musty as life in any small French town. By a clever trick of cinematographic montage, her reverie of the dance—the resplendent decor of the vast room and the rapturous faces of the dancers—is superimposed upon the shrunken, empty place in which she stands—illusion and reality, past and present fused together.

Throughout these years I managed to resist the temptation of such a sentimental journey into the past. I might have wavered had it not been for the encroachment of history upon the peoples and places of my youth and, perhaps more decisively, the one clear impression which those years engraved upon my memory: most of the time I was wretchedly unhappy.

The Central European Odyssey never reached Ithaca. Nearly everybody was drowned on the way or was devoured by the monsters or turned into a pig—and stayed a pig. From uncertain reports I gather that Otto Distler moved on to another town and theater. Otto was a Jew. After 1933 he seems to have been without a job, and then he disappeared. The mutual friend to whom I owed his acquaintance and Italianate fare vanished too. Her husky voice was stilled. Some time before the coming of the Nazis she threw in her lot with a stage director, undistinguished except for his vicious temper and Communist sympathies. She followed him to Russia. Both perished in the second of the great Stalinist purges.

Among my companions on the mountain, the one whom I called friend sought his luck in South America and returned to Germany with an Argentine wife. She was handsome, rich, and Jewish. He joined the Nazi party and by 1933 had brawled his way to a colonelship in the SS. I recall his open face, daring and patient in adversity. Somewhere along the ascent up the party ladder he rid himself of his wife, though not before having extorted from her a considerable amount of money. Some years after World War II, I managed to piece together the rest of the story: the colonel was promoted to general. In the campaigns against Poland and Yugoslavia the general acquired high honors and considerable personal property. Later he denounced his closest friend and faithful comrade-in-arms as an accessory to the attempt on Hitler's life in July, 1944. Fortune favored the informer to the end: he was killed instantly in a blackout accident. Not one other of those now dead whom I called friend was as lucky.

Had I kept any mementos they could guide me now in revisiting my youth. In Europe east of the Rhine and all the way to the Urals, the past forty years have been the epoch of liquidation— *tabula rasa*. First the dancers and then the ballroom vanished into the grinder. I wanted to try the experiment suggested by *Carnet de Bal*. Thus, a few months ago I halted in Munich and asked the taxi driver to take me to that great hall where, clad in my first and ill-fitting dinner jacket, I had sipped sweetish German champagne and made my debut as a vertiginous waltzer. I was braced for that shock of recognition and memories tarnished. In 1943 a bomb had flattened the place. In the roaring 1950's it had been rebuilt, no expense spared—an impressive cross between German modern and Conrad Hilton. I paid off the taxi and walked back to my hotel, trying disconsolately to recapture the mood of nostalgia.

During the immediate postwar period we danced whenever and wherever we could. The tango and the Boston, reputed to be sensual, were in fashion. And just about that time Europe negotiated awkwardly its transition from gliding motion to agitated shuffle. We tried to get the hang of Afro-American rhythm. We stood—or rather, jiggled—on the eve of the revolution culminating in the Charleston. Of all the things men have contrived to assuage desire and to forget, the dance is the most innocent and the healthiest—far healthier than drink and pills, far less insidious than gambling, and about as challenging as, and a great deal safer than, any sport that calls for skill. Every night we danced till sunrise, during the delirious weeks of the Munich Carnival. The Protestant countries, rejecting the rites of Rome, cut themselves loose from the web of mysteries. Of these, not the least cleansing was the Dionysian cult.

The Carnival is but the license of Christianity for the Dionysian rite of purification, the divine intoxication, and then the repentant sobriety of Ash Wednesday. To surrender oneself to the Bacchanalia one must be cloaked in anonymity, rid, so to speak, of one's identity—hence the mask that covers fame, fortune, beauty, ugliness, and infinite promise. The heartbeats of the Carnival were the great public *bals masqués,* preceded and followed by private parties in the houses of the rich, in the studios of artists, and in all kinds of likely and unlikely places that accommodated a crowd large enough to shelter anonymity. At the great public balls, the cavalier in the brocaded court dress, heavy with Mechlin laces, danced the polka with the Goddess of Reason scantily robed in a Chemise cut lovingly from a piece of sacking; the temple dancer of Angkor Vat, adorned with the treasures of one of the town's great collections of Asian art, waltzed with the Tyrolean peasant who, for all she knew, was indeed a Tyrolean peasant. Although the corks popped and glasses tinkled, hardly anyone got drunk. Nearly everyone was in motion, engaged in the bantering pursuit of willing game, all the more willing since evasion at any time was the mask's most sacred privilege. The white nights of the Carnival release the everyday self from its mean prison and give it unlimited license, license to be, until dawn, prince, libertine, hero, fool, and harlot. This release contains—and has perpetuated throughout all these Catholic centuries—the essential ingredients of psychosomatic therapy.

By 1923 the Munich Carnival had regained a great deal of its prewar gaiety and splendor. People from everywhere came to purge themselves of that grit called individuality. Without these cathartic few weeks I would have shriveled into that pathetic figure, the angry, nasty young man—too angry and nasty to enjoy life and to lift a finger to make it more enjoyable. Since then I have attended many a round table and conference that are supposed to further the exchange of many views and, by some sublime osmosis, the meeting of contentious minds. Much could be gained if all participants were masked and none could be sure about the hardened preconceptions of the other.

One late night, for example, my companion and I, teamed as Cleopatra and Marc Antony (thanks to the benevolence of the theater's chief costumer), drifted into a smallish party given by we knew not exactly whom. The setting was pleasing, the room of the watch above one of the city gates, the last survivals of the wall that ringed medieval Munich. Between dances we reclined on cushions and carpets and drank deeply from a deceptive peach punch. As was the custom, we toasted the venerable Mandarin who squatted, motionless and solitary, next to our encampment. We wondered how it was possible to be so impressively Mandarin—the magnificent silk robe, the headgear with the bird-of-paradise feather perched upon a globular bald skull, the disenchanted, drooping mustachio ends. Surprisingly, he spoke. Gravely he noted Cleopatra's blue eyes beneath black brows and paid homage to the true daughter of Macedonia. The files of the Celestial Empire, he conceded, contained intelligence on Cleopatra's nose: it was straight. Cleopatra did not concede. Her nose seemed straight only because it was in fact concave—just like the "straight" Doric column. By the time the music stopped we had examined the symbolic meaning of the assertive upthrusting mustachio ends of William the Second and the devious droop of Aristide Briand's whiskers, of the ferocious lion of the Assyrian fresco and the coy one rampant in English and Bavarian heraldry. We were pleased with our Spenglerian parody. The Mandarin invited us to follow him to Donisel's, an all-night taproom, and breakfast on white sausages and tawny beer. With immense dignity the Mandarin fell asleep. We forgot about him. After a while he wakened. We conveyed him to his quarters. He did not speak. We parted at his door. I glanced at the nameplate. This was my one and only meeting with Oswald Spengler.

Spengler is a war casualty. Since the Nazis tapped his *Decline of the West* and pressed some of his metaphors into the service of their propaganda, he has been denounced, particularly by American critics, as an intellectual accessory to the crimes of the Nazis. Spengler completed his book before the end of World War I. Prophetic though it was, it did not anticipate the revolt of the gutter or a Caesar with a diminutive mustache *en brosse*. In the *Decline of the West* there are a great many somber passages on the dark powers of blood and soil, but not the faintest hint at a racist philosophy of history, not to speak of anti-Semitism. Spengler's great book came to the attention of the Western public only in the late 1920's. It was only in the 1930's that Spengler's scholarship came under the heavy attack of Western critics.

Today it is easy to shoot holes into Spengler's academic armor. In the intervening years scholarly exploration, armed with wonderfully efficient tools, has turned up a vast mass of facts which were not available to Spengler, and proved erroneous not a few of his deductions. Yet Spengler did not conceive of himself as a specialist in ethnographic or philological research. He examined available materials, quoted his sources meticulously, and built upon the works of others his masterful synthesis of cultural history. What is surprising is not that he erred about so many things, but that, his errors notwithstanding, so much of his analysis and conclusion stands. Like Lyautey and Romain Rolland, he viewed World War I as a civil war, the internecine conflict among the members of Western culture. Unlike nearly all his contemporaries, politicians, soldiers, and scholars, he was right in his view. From his speculations he deduced that the epoch of the Caesars—*les horribles simplificateurs*—was about to open. For that conclusion, too, he was to be vindicated by events. Indeed, the present state of affairs still confirms the astuteness of his judgment; the future is likely to do so with a vengeance—and not necessarily only in countries of authoritarian traditions. The end is not yet.

Chapter Four

I HAD learned little that I could put to use and next to nothing that I could offer in exchange for money. Thus far my life had been as disorderly as the times. But the times were now about to settle down, I was old enough to know that I had come to a turning point.

I had not acquired one of those engraved and sealed certificates which entitle one to the practice of a remunerative and respected profession. I had neither melodious voice nor fine ear nor manual dexterity; I would never amount to anything as painter, musician, or actor. Fortunately, I had tried my hand long enough at writing to realize that I had much to learn and that, for the best amateur, the pickings were lean in the most competitive of all markets. For good measure, I was a foreigner in Germany, and the Germans, like everybody else in Europe, frowned upon foreigners of no particular qualifications who looked for jobs. I was haunted by the thought that my mother worked long hours for a pittance and that I did next to nothing to ease her lot. I cudgeled my brain. I wanted to leave Germany and Europe and look for work in one of the European colonies. I did not know how to go about it, for I did not always have enough money to pay even streetcar fare. I waited for the unexpected: it came in a most unexpected way. Fate selected H.M. as its improbable messenger.

At first glance, H.M.'s ancestry was as improbable as he was. The Ms were about as eccentric, corrupt, and crafty as any old family enured to wealth, power, and prestige. Even by the standards of European aristocracy, a population sample more polyglot than the inhabitants of New York and Singapore, the Ms' racial stock was unusually mixed. The graft of many strains, and a long succession of more or less notorious saints, heroes, statesmen, idiots, and scoundrels had flowered into fine-boned grace and a feline sensitivity to human foibles, wholly devoid of compassion. One of M's forebears had emigrated to Bavaria during the French Revolution. According to one version, he was a Picard nobleman of ancient lineage; according to another one, he had been a fashionable Paris wigmaker. Uncertain as may have been his pedigree, his physical appearance, according to contemporary portraits, was pleasing: he was darkly handsome and elegant. Moreover, within a few years after his arrival in Munich he obtained the patent of Bavarian nobility via marriage to a great, though somewhat plain, heiress, thus establishing a precedent to which his male progeny was to adhere faithfully for several generations. His great-grandson, H.M.'s father, who resembled strikingly El Greco's Conde Orgaz, served in the Bavarian legation at St. Petersburg. This man took back to Bavaria the swarthy daughter of a Polish magnate, high dignitary of the czarist court and owner of vast estates in Russian Poland. They loved each other passionately and abidingly. Countess M., moody, indolent, and addicted to strong cigars, bore her husband two sons. H.M., the older, inherited his father's haughty good looks and his mother's indolence.

Intelligent and lazy, H.M. had learned at a tender age to avoid any exertions except those rewarded with a variety of instant pleasures. His immense capacity for mischief was matched only by the ease with which he managed to extricate himself, at the expense of others, from the consequences of his exploits. The younger son, J.M., to whom the race apportioned a contemplative temperament and ecclesiastic mien, adored and abetted his older and more flamboyant brother.

H.M. made friends easily; his pursuit of experience was catholic as long as it was pleasurable. We met in the apartment of a professor in the University of Munich which H.M. briefly and inconclusively attended. Neither H.M. nor I kept our mind on the learned man's discourse on Germanic philology. When it came to a halt at some obscure line in a medieval epic, we saw our chance, gratefully bowed ourselves out and walked into a sunny afternoon. We bought a bag of cherries, found a bench in the English Garden and compared notes on the professor, learning, and life.

H.M. invited me to spend a few days in his parents' country house. I accepted gladly, notwithstanding H.M.'s hint at some troublesome, unfinished, and overdue essays on Germanic philology. At a village a few miles upstream from Salzburg we were met by a coachman in gray and green and silver-buttoned livery. After a half hour's drive we rolled into the courtyard of a moated building jutting into a small lake.

More than a hundred years earlier, a Bavarian Duke Elector, famed for his profligacy and exquisite taste, had, at the age of seventy, taken as his wife an Austrian Archduchess, aged seventeen. Widowed at nineteen, this enterprising Princess gave her hand to her Master of the Horse. The couple settled in England, rode to hounds, and discovered the Gothic revival. They returned to the Continent and, inspired by Strawberry Hill and Fonthill Abbey, set out to build their castle of romance and chivalry. The Princess selected from her considerable properties a long-disused keep perched upon a tiny island in a large pond. Within a few years, a Gothic fantasy rose above the still waters. Craftsmen from all over Europe, Italian stonemasons, Tyrolean wood carvers, Scandinavian and German painters of romantically gloomy landscapes and historic frescoes, Bohemian glaziers, and Flemish weavers had labored to concoct a fake medieval castle— more surrealistically medieval than any authentic product.

Piecrust battlements hovered over an inoperable drawbridge; richly carved furniture and profuse spiky paneling, studded with innumerable heraldic emblems, simulated the luxurious discomfort of a medieval interior—or, rather, what the designers of this disquieting decor believed a medieval interior to have been.

The materials had been carefully chosen and fashioned with superb craftsmanship, unmarred by the facility of industrial reproduction. Perhaps the secret of the castle was that its absurdity had been transfigured by a great love; perhaps what made it livable were the comforts which later generations had added somewhat surreptitiously to the original design.

In my bedroom, an electric bulb had replaced the wick; the drains were inoffensive, and in the hall stuffed *fauteuils* had crept between the oaken settees. After a while I felt at home in the castle.

H.M. handed me three pages, each blank except for the title of the essay pledged to the expectant professor. Humbly, H.M. asked me to jot down a few ideas to guide his endeavors, pleaded a slight indisposition and withdrew, with the trace of a grin, to his quarters, a light novel bulging in his pocket. I became absorbed in the work, just as H.M. thought I would. One essay completed, I dragged H.M. from his couch and novel.

Castle and lake were set in a large park laid out by an English landscape gardener. A short walk brought us to brook. There we fished for trout and then lay in the sun and slept until the tower bell called us to dinner. Meals were quickly served by two footmen in the gray, green, and silver-buttoned livery under the supervision of an impassive major-domo, spade-bearded as his master.

My astute friend had smoothed my path. Countess M. quickly moved from the fine weather to French literature and cinquecènto painting. I was safe; but I was not quite certain how deeply Countess M. had probed into Claudel's symbolism. Count M. looked at his plate and plucked his silvery whiskers. I had much to say and, so I thought, said it well. When I came to a halt, Countess M. melodiously quoted a verse by Mallarmé, and everyone got up. Count M. asked me to join him for a cigar in his study. He came to the point. H. needed steadying, and, among his friends, I seemed the steadiest. Would I help him, at a fee, with his studies, and, whenever I had an evening to spare, spend it with him? I told Count M. that I was younger than his son, worked for my living and despaired of obtaining an academic degree. Count M. brushed my reply aside with an impatient wave of his tapering hand. The matter was settled. We rejoined the others. Count M. proposed that we go for deer early in the morning. Countess M. finished her game of solitaire. Her sons kissed her hand, and we went to our rooms.

H.M. and I met nearly every day. His academic chores did not seem very demanding, and he assured me that the essays had satisfied the professor. He asked me to introduce him to my theatrical friends who could help him gain insight into the living drama.

One day I called at his quarters; the landlord told me that H.M. had departed to an unknown destination, leaving behind a sheaf of unpaid bills. After a few days had gone by without a sign of life, I called Count M. Within a few hours, Count M. arrived in Munich. I called at his apartment—without a word, he handed me a telegram posted from one of the gayer among the German spas—not only was H.M. in urgent need of money, but he also asked his father to bless his marriage, duly recorded, to a dancer renowned for her free technique and intimate association with avant-garde composers and poets. Count M. withheld comment on the union and called his banker. Then he asked me whether I still intended to seek my fortunes abroad. I said I did.

A few days later H.M. returned, alone and unmarked by the experience except for a slight mustache and a small scar on his forehead. The union had proved unstable and was about to be dissolved by mutual consent. Later the Count called his lawyer. Then he invited me to lunch at his apartment. A Dutch friend had informed him that a large rubber concern in the East Indies offered jobs to young men who would sign up for service as trainees and then as plantation mangers. H.M., the Count declared, was to go overseas with the least possible delay. Would I undertake to see him to Amsterdam and, upon his acceptance by the company, to the next boat? If I were interested in accompanying H.M. all the way, this could be arranged. The Count would ask his Dutch friend to recommend me for the position of planter apprentice. Count M. agreed to pay our travel expense, and another Dutch friend, a retired diplomat, would provide our lodging. I told the Count that I had to obtain my mother's consent, a passport, and luggage. The same day I left for Vienna.

Today I regret little, for my mistakes and misdeeds long ago fused into that hard layer of fatality which, with the years, seals off the most sensitive conscience. Life has atoned for me. Nothing could, nothing should have happened but what has happened. If it were otherwise, one could neither remember nor forget. This is all there is to the balance of the mind. Within the selective range of memory I believe in Free Will. The choices are few, and, in the end, there are none. Had I but stood for a moment and let the chase go by, I could have seen the opening in the thicket and the straight path beyond.

My mother's love was free of all possessiveness. An only child, I was taught to fend for myself and, in my woes and tantrums, not to seek maternal compassion. Yet she lived for and through me. Since my mother made no other demands upon me than that I grow strong and make my way in the world, I took it for granted that she expected no more. Of course, I loved her. But I did not love her enough to understand the terrible need beneath her stoic pretense. I told her about the Count's offer and that, if I passed muster, I would be sent overseas. Without hesitation she agreed, told me where to buy my luggage, and made out a list of the things I should pack. We went to an expensive restaurant on the Ring, and my mother ordered a bottle of wine. We clinked our glasses, and toasted the future. In the morning I left. I was not to see my mother again for five years.

By the time the train pulled into Munich I had made firm friends with a medical student who also wanted to go abroad. We found each other sympathetic listeners, for neither of us exceeded unduly the bearable quota of monologue. We were filled to the brim with our own expectations. We exchanged addresses and pledged ourselves to keep in touch. By the time I joined H.M. in our most favored café, I had lost the slip of paper and forgotten my new friend's name.

I did not think again of the parting in Vienna until I returned, at a late hour, to my quarters and tripped over my shiny new valises. My heart sank; had I not been drugged with fatigue, I would have written my mother that wherever I went her love would sustain me. I put the letter off until morning and fell instantly asleep. Next day much had to be done. There were other partings and other pledges. The young are able to bear the sufferings of others with great fortitude.

Two days later, H.M. and I traveled to Holland; the Rhine flowed beneath the coach window and, in the corner seats of the compartment, two black marketeers counted a variety of foreign money. We had warmed up to the alluring East and were in high spirits. We both had read a popular novel about the South Seas; we had learned from Kipling and Conrad about the White Man's burden and how deferential natives helped him to bear it; we envisioned ourselves, in tropical whites and topee, ranging the lush hills of Java and exploring the candid beauty of Bali.

In Amsterdam, Count M.'s diplomat friend bade us welcome. On the next day, a Sunday, our host, his two daughters, H.M., and I bicycled to a country inn, and feasted on hot chocolate and creamy cakes. The Dutch had come through the war unscathed. They had done fair business with both sides, and both sides had respected Dutch neutrality, an arrangement which seemed to profit all parties.

By temperament the Dutch, though deeply attached to their flat landscape and moist climate, are dealers in commodities rather than fighters for causes. Of all the Europeans they are the most stolid and, but for the Swedes who owe them decorative inspiration, the most bland. Unlike the Swedes and the Swiss, the Dutch did not suffer momentary qualms about the ethics of neutrality. They did not greatly care as to who would win, and most of them would not have been deeply disturbed had there been no winners at all. Their colonial produce fetched ever higher prices; their merchant ships carried plentiful cargo. They did not stint the calories; they tended meticulously their lush fields to the faint rumble from the west of Holland.

Partition atrophied the two halves of the Lowlands, a preview of things to come in the rest of Europe. Brussels, once one of the gayest and most graceful among European cities, is now a coarse counterfeit of Paris; Amsterdam huddles morosely by its stagnant canals. In our times, Belgium's contribution to the arts has been paltry; Holland's has been nil. The peoples of the Lowlands have always pursued gross fleshly pleasures; by all accounts, the contemporaries of Brueghel and Rubens did so lustily. Their latter-day heirs indulge themselves sullenly.

H.M. and I presented ourselves at the offices of the great concern. We were inspected and questioned. Our qualifications—good health and a willing disposition—seemed to satisfy the requirements. But some features of the job were depressing; we had to do clerkly chores in the home office while we learned to speak Dutch. Though this unlovely language does not present serious difficulties to German-speaking persons, we could not expect to master it before the lapse of a few months. Even more alarming were the contractual conditions: we had to pledge ourselves to five years' service overseas. But the most crushing blow to our hopes was dealt by the revelation of the place where we would have to spend so large a chunk of our young lives. The plantation of our destination was located in a remote corner of Sumatra, several days' journey from Batavia on Java and again twice that distance from Bali. Sumatra, we were given to understand, was neither beautiful nor healthful, and the natives were said to be churlish. We were deeply disappointed. We made what, under the circumstances, seemed the most prudent move: we said we would consider the proposition, and looked for a bar.

Our search brought us to a hotel. As we crossed the lobby, my eye was caught by a poster of the Holland-America Line. There was no need for further deliberation: I suggested to H.M. that, since we were launched upon distant adventure, we might as well seek it in North America, a country that, by common agreement, was new and fraught with unlimited opportunities. H.M., who was always attracted by new departures, agreed enthusiastically. In America we need not wrestle with the language problem that would have bogged us down in this dismal city, for we both considered ourselves fluent in English.

From two Americans, a retired army major and a young woman, I had some reliable information on America. The major, a native of Savannah, Georgia, had settled in Munich for an undisclosed reason, probably because his pension was small and life in Munich was cheap. His opinions on North and South anywhere in the world were settled: he pointed meaningfully to the affinities of rasping Prussian with Yankee English, of the Southern drawl with the soft accents of Vienna German. According to him, Northern peoples were pushy; Southerners were ladies and gentlemen. The American girl had come to visit her German grandparents and drifted into the Munich Bohemia. She confided to me her aspirations: to become an actress and never go back to Milwaukee. H.M. and I emptied our glasses. On the hotel's stationery, I informed the great concern that we gratefully declined its offer of a career in Sumatra.

The subsequent few weeks were crowded with events. A good deal of resistance had to be overcome. By then-prevailing German standards, the price of two steamship tickets to America represented a fortune. Count M. considered the bleak alternatives, raised the money, and entrusted me with making the travel arrangements. Then began the long watch in the consular anteroom. We joined the throng of pinch-faced people and waited for our visas. Thirty years later Menotti's *Consul* afforded me the gruesome opportunity of revisiting the purgatory of emigration. The dirge of the same questions and answers, prayers and protests rises to unbearable, impotent suspense. The fluttering applications are never quite properly completed; the grimy certificates of birth, health, and morals are never quite properly attested; and the door to the office of the consul, invisible guardian of fate, never opens. *Lasciate ogni speranza.*

It takes the mighty a much longer time than ordinary men to see a simple, though unpalatable truth. Conceivably, the free world market, the most glorious of the glories of the Victorian age, might have survived the World War, economic chaos in Middle Europe, and the amputation of Russia. The war, despite or perhaps because it had destroyed so much wealth, created new demands.

There was, however, one major basic condition which had to be met which the mighty, for more or less shabby reasons, were no longer prepared to meet. The pendant piece of the free movement of goods had been the free movement of persons. Right up to World War I the two reciprocating forces were roughly in balance. The war pulled the system awry. The immigration legislation, enacted by the United States after the war, tightened up in

1924, and quickly emulated by major countries of settlement, made certain that the system would be kept off balance. Industrialization and free trade had triggered the immense rise of world population. Economically—the exploitation of unused resources and specialization at least cost—the problem called for free circulation of goods, capital, and people; socially, for the adjustment of the masses to urbanization and, hence, for birth control; politically, for practical and decent policies governing migration. The indifference of rulers and, especially, the inertia of Roman Catholic dogma have brought mankind ever closer to the cozy intimacy of the rabbit warren; and the closed consular door has been the statesman's answer to the call of economic necessity and social justice.

Of course, the problems of "let my people go" and of how to square the procreative instinct with material progress are the most difficult ones confronting mankind. In all likelihood, modern civilization will "solve" them as it is wont to do: by a *reductio ad absurdum*, such as war; or by technological-administrative interventions, such as forced migration, compulsive sterilization, and stealthy pills, which invariably encroach on human dignity and freedom and destroy the few good and beautiful things that have not yet vanished in the rummage sale of ancient cultures. A good part of the human race is afflicted by claustrophobia. Nearly every state worth its sovereign salt tends institutions designed to cope with frustrated mobility, namely, refugee and concentration camps. Since both types of residence have one feature in common, namely, penning up people who would rather be elsewhere, it is not always easy, apart from similar structural features, to distinguish one from the other.

Since I belong to the vanguard of those who, after World War I, queued up for the stamp of delivery, I was spared much anxiety and inconvenience. Yet even a brief sojourn in the netherworld supplied Dante with enough material for evoking poignantly the ambience of the place. I, too, had given up hope. I no longer called every day to ask the same question and watch the same receptionist shuffle applications and polish her nails. Then, one morning, an inconspicuous notice summoned me to the Castle. I was free to go.

H.M. and I arrived in Bremen just in time to board the vessel in which I had reserved the cheapest outside cabin. A few hours later the liner cast off and stood out to the North Sea. The October weather was unusually fair. The load had been lifted. I stretched out on my bunk and fell asleep to the creak of woodwork and the beat of the waves against the hull.

Chapter Five

Toward the end of October, 1923, I arrived in New York. The voyage had been a pleasant one. The rates—cabin class—were low; the food was plentiful. For twelve days I had, every day, enough to eat and no worry as to how to pay for it—in fact, I thought the crossing much too short. At Southampton many Americans had come aboard, most of them tourists who had spent the summer traveling about England, France, and Italy. I made friends and exercised my English on a pair of New York music critics, a schoolteacher with a Grecian nose, and a physician's daughter of my own age who tried her best and failed to arouse me to the charms of a suburban idyl in the environs of Cleveland.

One fine, rough day, Samuel Barlow, composer and collector, settled in the chair next to mine and told me about the house he had bought, a pile of terraced, crumbling masonry hanging on the rock of Eze above Cap-Ferrat. On a clear day the peaks of Corsica rose above the horizon. Sam loved music and people, Debussy and dinners at well-appointed houses. Anecdotal and witty, he managed to contrive the image of an America of solid comfort, immense curiosity, and naïve snobbery, which was not at all the America I had come to seek, but which seemed closer to my scale than the enigmatic conventions of marginal Cleveland. Some ten years later Sam and I met again in New York. He had married Ernesta Drinker, composed an opera, and completed the restoration of what came to be known as the Chateau Barlow at Eze. He had launched his musical soirées on Gramercy Park, confluence of arts, letters, and fashion.

When I first arrived in New York I thought that I had found America. In this belief, I now realize, I was mistaken—all the more mistaken because I had sloughed off so many lesser preconceptions about America. For Americans, probably more than any other people, are made in their schools. In America, public school and nationality are synonyms.

To be sure, Waterloo was won on the playing fields of Eton. And the English child is taught, before it is taught anything else, to embrace discomfort, shun abstractions, and observe the rules of informal association. The fables of La Fontaine drill the French child in the strategy of civilized behavior, first lesson in the school of formal grace and practical cynicism. For in France, learning how to think and to behave is as deliberate and as canny an initiation into the tribe as it is in England. But the English and French educational systems are not designed for the foreigner. Englishmen and Frenchmen are presumed to be born. Education sees to it that they stay that way.

Compared with Europe, the American educational system is both more accommodating and more insidious. American education does not take it for granted that the family will initiate the child into the American way of life. On the contrary, the American public school is separated by a gulf of tacit assumptions, none exactly complimentary, from the private sectors of society, the family, the church, and the ethnic group. The product of the American school is an average of conformity. For good reasons, given the heterogeneity of cultural origins, the American school is as much concerned with effective social cooperation as with the learning of disciplines and the discipline of learning. Thus there are two kinds of Americans today, namely, those who have gone to the public school and those who have not. I belong to the second category. For after forty years in America I still stumble where conditioned responses guide my fellow Americans of category 1 along the American way.

Furthermore, before World War I, an educated Continental European was taught next to nothing about America. A course in world literature might have introduced the more curious student to Longfellow, Hawthorne, Mark Twain, Whitman, Thoreau, and perhaps Upton Sinclair, in the original or a fair translation; unfortunately, however, European universities did not offer programs in American studies. A few rare European scholars might have read de Tocqueville's unsurpassed masterpiece of empathy and Lord Bryce's more tedious, though painstaking, reappraisal of American democracy one generation after the Frenchman's visit to America's model prisons. But for that matter, even in the United States, de Tocqueville had to wait until the 1930's for a wider hearing.

Not having learned a trade, I was ill-equipped for the highly competitive business of making a living in America. For good measure, I was wholly unprepared intellectually for the American social and cultural scene. I carried a few letters of introduction. I was introduced to New York Good Society. I recall with pleasure its Victorian flavor, its good Anglicized manners, and its delightful mixture of cosmopolitanism and provincialism. But it was not at all what I had expected, since the America I had envisaged was the America of vast fortunes, spectacularly made and ostentatiously spent, of ruthless empire builders and the taciturn riders of the wider spaces. My New York acquaintances, in contrast, lived in comfortable houses, mostly snug, brownstone, and high stoop, and were concerned neither with building empires nor with roughing it on the frontier. They were not the least ostentatious. In fact, their social conventions were, to my amazement, a great deal tighter than those I had grown up with in Central Europe.

At that time the massive influx into America of educated young Europeans had not yet begun. A fair command of English, decent manners, and a touch of general cultivation sufficed as credentials to a society that opened its doors more readily to casual foreigners than to domestic interlopers. I came to the Great City to look for the unexpected. Like nearly every impressionable young man, I found it. Indeed, I would have liked to stay, for New York, so it seems to the European, turns her face to the east and levies tribute on the lands beyond the ramparts of the river so that, self-indulgent and self-willed, she can gratify her whims.

Had I but known it, back of the big cities there stretched the infinity of rural America with its small towns, its well-kept farms, its innumerable clusters of courthouses, churches, banks and factories, and its Republican politics. Most of the successful men had come from these small towns and the farms around them. The concourse of their great fortunes, prizes of rugged individualism, nourished New York. The city grew and raised its monuments to anonymity. In another few years its power and its mores were to unmake the entire country. Flushed by the success of her global debut, America stood at the threshold of universal urban culture.

Then, for a brief span of time, America tarried in the pre-automotive age of innocence; her thousand towns were still divided into the two sides of the railway track. On one side were well-to-do, most of whom belonged to the ethnic groups that had assimilated to Anglo-Saxon culture. On the other side were the poor and the South and East European immigrants and their sons and daughters. With luck, the latter could cross the track; in fact, nearly all of them believed they could, and it was this belief that mattered. The afterglow of this age warms Mr. Lippmann's well-publicized nostalgia. Its problems, even its gravest ones, were relatively simple.

I was fated to arrive in America shortly after rural America, Baptist, steel-rimmed, and Fundamentalist, had won its last major victory or, rather, its last major rearguard action against urban culture. I could not understand either the purpose or the observance of Prohibition. I was baffled, too, by the Americans' crusading zeal for Good Government and their delight in a rich folklore of transgression. Some of my new friends were lawyers, graduates of the law schools of Harvard, Yale, and Columbia. They were almost wholly uninterested in the philosophies of history and the social and economic theories which then preoccupied literate Europe. Their passionate concern was with legal theory and the ethical foundations of law. They viewed the process of social transformation as a cadence of legal and, so it seemed to my ignorance, often quite contradictory opinions. In America, the Constitution is the true Ark of the Covenant, and universal faith is alive in the veneration bestowed upon the Law and the Amendments. It is this faith, and this faith alone, which nourishes the national consensus. In every American community a secular priesthood ministers to it. The United States Supreme Court is America's St. Peter.

In Europe, the knowledge of constitutional provisions is the possession of a few specialized jurists. The average educated man or woman or, for that matter, the average politician or public servant does not trouble about his country's constitution. No one bothers about the document—except on those rare occasions when it is being torn up and replaced by another one. For a long time the English, for example, attached to tradition and well-worn clothing, have refrained from changing their uncoded constitution radically. Yet, although most Englishmen will agree not only that theirs is a constitutional government but also that it is the best in the world, only two Englishmen, one of them a former Cabinet member and the other a law lord, managed to explain to me the English Constitution. As they kept on explaining it, its lineaments grew more indistinct.

In America, on the other hand, nearly anybody who has gone to school has read the Constitution and memorized the Preamble, and nearly all educated and a good many not-so-educated people believe firmly that they know, if not the text, then at least the intent of these revered documents. Thus, Americans are remarkably conversant with what the law says. Yet Englishmen, and even Germans, Swedes, and Swiss, are not less law-abiding than Americans, the fact notwithstanding that in these countries the legal profession does not hold as large a quota of public offices as in America.

Forty years ago my ignorance of legal usage and law observance in America was matched only by my ignorance of the effects of hard liquor. My legal friends applied themselves to remedying both deficiencies. It does not reflect upon the earnestness of their endeavor that I failed to resolve the paradox of legal principle and Prohibition. Of course, I read up on pragmatism only much later. But as things turned out, the systematic violation by so many loyal citizens of the Prohibition act repealed the hateful law *de facto* long before the general will struck it, in 1933, from the statute book. This episode reveals a realistic bent which old Europe lacked. In France, for example, a sumptuary law, had it ever gotten into the statute book, would have been enforced rigorously. After a while the enraged populace would have taken to the barricades and re-established the monarchy. The distinctions between law and law-that-is-being-enforced is incomprehensible to most Continental Europeans. If, for example, a French government does not enforce a particular law it acknowledges itself as being too weak to enforce any law. Hence, it is no longer worthy to govern, and there is really no other way for dealing with the intolerable situation than to overthrow the government and replace it with another.

Our stay in New York was short. Our ultimate destination was Chicago, where we expected to enjoy the hospitality of the Ns, a German-American couple.

Twenty years before, Mr. N. had left his Bavarian village and traveled to St. Louis, where he quickly rose to the rank of brewmaster. He moved to Chicago and, with a few other Bavarians, started his own brewery. Prohibition overtook him. In 1922 he and his German-born wife visited Germany. At the eve of World War I both had acquired American citizenship. Times had not been easy for brewers and Americans of unmistakably Teutonic origin. N. would have liked to remain in Germany. Yet he soon discovered that the returning emigrant was expected to do more than kiss the soil of the land of his birth and tell tall stories about his exploits at the frontiers of Western civilization. His friends and relations, failing to persuade him to back a variety of local business ventures or simply to lend them money, lost interest. Within a few months, he came to feel himself as being completely, deeply, and truculently American.

The Ns returned to America. Before his departure, N. took leave of his brother, a priest in a mountain village. In the same parish happened to reside an acquaintance of my mother's. My mother had met the priest and told him that I intended to go to America. The priest remembered and told his brother. Mr. N., in the expansiveness a quart of beer engenders, suggested that my friend and I be his guests in Chicago, and promised that he would find us jobs. The priest conveyed the invitation, and H.M. and I duly consulted. We might as well go to the heart of the matter and seek our fortunes in the most venturesome part of America. We wrote Mr. N., whom we had never met face to face, that we accepted.

We entrained in Hoboken for Chicago. At that time railroads still stood first in the economy of the country. They moved men and things; upon them had been built the great American fortunes; and, ever since the Civil War, the same entrepreneurial zeal that, in the post-World War II era, was to spark the electronics industry, had found release in the development, improvement, and consolidation of railway systems and in the shuffling of their shares. American railways differed in many respects from those in Continental Europe. Their spur was wider; their tickets folded like accordions. They were privately owned. I concluded from railway schedules that, if I wished to go from one city to another, I had the choice of at least two railway lines, their respective tracks having been laid, in places, no more than a stone's throw apart.

Pondering this fresh insight into the meaning of competition, I ascended to the upper berth. In the morning I shaved in the lounge. I was joined by the conductor, a handsome and heavy man of middle age. Upon his silver-buttoned waistcoat rested a heavy gold chain. He asked me what country I came from. I told him. He informed me that a good many Czechs had settled in Chicago. I told him that I was not Czech. He countered that I looked like one. He asked me what my job was. I replied that I had none, and that I hoped to find work in Chicago. He told me that, though many people were out of work, I might make a living washing dishes or cleaning windows. A wintry sun rose over the marshaling yards of a factory town somewhere in Ohio. The conductor looked at his fine watch and left.

In Chicago the wind stood to the north. During most of the

journey H.M., who had kept late hours in New York, slept or read *La Madonne de Sleeping,* a popular novel said to have been inspired by the amorous adventures of an English actress born into a ducal house. Having settled himself in a taxi that took us to a four-digit street address in West Chicago, he asked the driver to take us past sights of historical interest. The driver jammed the brakes, looked appraisingly at both of us, changed course and pointed out the Wrigley Building. In German, H.M. informed me that Chicago was an Indian word meaning *Feld der Wilden Zwiebeln* (field of wild onions). He suggested that we return to New York forthwith and work our way to São Paulo in Brazil, where the climate was temperate and healthful. I pointed out that our joint reserves amounted to thirty-eight dollars.

The taxi drew up to a small stuccoed building between two empty lots. I paid off the taxi, aghast at the fare of seven dollars. I knocked at the door. After a while we were greeted by a middle-aged stocky woman, bleached hair fringing a Bavarian peasant face. She told us that she had kept us waiting because she wanted to be sure who we were. She had telephoned her husband who agreed that she could let us in. Only a few days before, gunmen had beaten and robbed her neighbor. She bade us welcome and served us coffee. After an hour or so, Mr. N. arrived.

Mr. N. did not manage to dissimulate his consternation at seeing us and our considerable luggage in his living room. After the briefest exchange of civilities, he told us that his brewery was shut and that he had lost a good part of his savings in "the market." We did not know what that "market" was in which one could lose one's savings. But we understood that our host proposed to shelter us for a few nights and urged us to find a job. That night H.M. and I slept in a single bed, a novel experience for each of us, who had never shared a bed, single or twin, with a male companion. In the morning our host supplied us with a list of employment agencies and directed us to the streetcar stop. We seated ourselves in the lobby of the Drake Hotel and surveyed the situation.

The job openings which we examined did not offer large incentives. H.M. recalled that one of his father's friends had married the daughter of a Chicago industrialist. We consulted the telephone directory. There we found Count M.'s address. We left our calling cards. Count M. telephoned and suggested that we should come to his apartment between six and seven p.m. H.M. told our story well. Count M. undertook to introduce us to the head of one of the city's largest department stores. Warmed by the Count's excellent Scotch and then helped into our coats by a deferential English butler, we returned to our anxious hosts.

By noon of the following day we had found employment in the stock room of the store's art department. Our wages were set at twenty-five dollars a week. We were put to work wiring paintings and retouching damaged frames. Business seemed to be brisk. The picture gallery displayed a variety of oils, mostly flowering mountain landscapes or jolly monks drinking beer. Less costly were the lithographs. Among these, if I remember rightly, one listed as "Indian Summer" was much in demand. Before closing time, the manager told us that, with some application, we might satisfy his requirements. That same evening, we collected our luggage and took leave from our hosts, who seemed greatly relieved and somewhat dismayed by our good fortune. Mr. N. would have wanted to see us start from the bottom. The second floor of Chicago's largest department store was not close enough to the bottom. We found lodgings in a rooming house a few blocks from the lake. The rental was high, but we were confident that better things would come our way.

Had I left America then and returned forty years later I would have noted many a change but none as striking as the evolution of taste. America has launched herself upon the quest for beauty as purposefully as she has gone about making herself rich and powerful. Modern techniques of reproduction—catalogues; illustrated monographs; reproductions on sheets of great paintings and casts from statuary; the international circuit of loan exhibitions; scores of art magazines and special sections on art in mass-circulation periodicals, such as *Life* and *Look;* the proliferation of both "art appreciation" courses and art historians; and sundry didactic exhibits in universities—have broadened and sharpened the public's awareness. Nowadays it is so easy to move about. It is possible now, within a matter of a few months, if not weeks, to tour every public museum of art and archaeology in the world and thus to visualize development of all the schools of painting and sculpture, of decorative arts and architecture, past and present, as a simultaneous process.

In America the aesthetic revolution shattered the philistine crust, razed architectural monstrosities, swept Whistler's Mother into the attic, and liberated tastes and talents. Since World War II the pace has quickened. The artist has taken his place next to the scientist as one of the symbolic figures of the age. Of course, this breakthrough has been attended by a good deal of corniness and slick promotion of the art "industry." Smart money is going into the arts. But the fakers and the money-grabbers are but the weeds in a rich harvest. The aesthetic revolution in America is a real and a wondrous thing. Having first come to America at the nadir of aesthetic awareness and having served my time in the chamber of horrors, I qualify as a witness of change.

As Christmas approached and sales quickened, H.M. and I were detailed, after store hours, to rush deliveries. We carried our precious burden of rustling brooks, Swiss mountain cottages, and jolly monks to their various destinations along Lake Shore Drive. Thus, I entered many a festive home, usually by the delivery entrance. From what I saw I concluded that our merchandise was not out of place. More often than not, butler or maid took delivery. Occasionally, however, master or mistress opened the door, requested me to unwrap the package and place the objet d'art in the appropriate spot. Nearly always I was shown an easy friendliness which the European bourgeoisie does not extend to delivery boys. Nearly always I was tipped a quarter. Yet our financial situation did not improve. Our joint income of fifty dollars a week, though supplemented by gratuities and occasional winnings at cards, did not cover our fixed expenditures, not to speak of fringe costs.

Count M. had introduced us to some of his many friends. We received invitations to dinners and dances, concerts and operas. We found that the expense of keeping ourselves in clean starched shirts and escorting our hosts' daughters to parties—carless in Chicago, we depended on taxis—exceeded our budget. We skipped lunch. We walked to work. We halved cigarettes. But even these measures failed to restore the balance. We were in debt. We worked six days a week. We were given to understand that our chances for advancement were slim.

When the holiday season ended, business perceptibly slackened. We were kept busy at inventories and the repair of damaged items. But the evenings for which we had not secured an invitation grew longer. Almost everywhere in Continental Europe we could have found refuge in the café or corner bistro. Not a few psychological and social disorders can be ascribed to the absence from the American scene of this institution, with its therapeutic effect upon loneliness, boredom, and introversion.

We made one friend in the neighborhood. One winter evening H.M. ejected a tin can through the window. It dropped onto an alley, but not before it had struck a member of the Chicago police force. He forthwith entered our apartment. H.M., who hardly ever extended himself for anybody except women, rose to the emergency. Persuasiveness and tact blunted the edge of the crisis. H.M. movingly addressed our visitor, named Patrick, one son of the Church entreating another to display forbearance. Patrick showed us the photograph of his brother, a seminarian in Rome. Patrick took to our last bottle of Scotch and commented poignantly on law enforcement in Chicago. As our minds met and the bottle grew lighter, the line of demarcation between law and lawbreaker, between crime and punishment, between the slayer and the slain faded. Patrick had charm and wit. His broad understanding of human frailty would have stood him in good stead had he been able to achieve his life's ambition, which was to take orders. I like to think that he did, and that he sat among the two thousand fathers of the Church Ecumenical Council convened in 1962 to keep dogma in step with historical change. His wisdom, distilled from the reconciliation of probity with the understandable wish to stay alive, could have made a signal contribution to the Council's deliberations. He came to see us at odd hours, and always on Sunday morning. He prevailed upon us to discharge our spiritual obligations.

Spring came to Chicago. H.M. and I decided to return to New York. A Hungarian industrialist whom I had met in Munich and whose collection of early Italian masters, brought to safety in

Switzerland, was to ensure him a comfortable retirement upon Hungary's conquest by the Communists, visited Chicago. I asked him to sample the works of art offered for sale by my employer. He came and saw. The effect was instantaneous. Spontaneously, he proffered his help in finding me another, any other, employment. He paid our debts and fare to New York. A few days later we left Chicago.

Despite the generosity of the Hungarian industrialist, we were still faced with the problem of maintaining minimum subsistence. For a while a Russian émigré family gave us food and lodging. Our host, a former Guards officer, had fought with Denikin's army and been evacuated on a British warship to Constantinople. There, he married the daughter of a Cossack colonel. They were a handsome pair, and they had many friends among their fellow refugees.

Next to Paris, New York had drawn the largest number of czarist exiles. With a few notable exceptions, the women adjusted themselves successfully to the change in fortunes and to the new milieu. They hired themselves out as domestics, opened dressmaking shops, and prepared the borsch and blinis served in the multiplying Russian restaurants. Against the heaviest odds, they kept their good looks and perfect manners. Their men, too, went to work, but very few learned a trade, entered the professions, or advanced in the world of business. Not a few started out as taxicab drivers and stayed taxicab drivers the rest of their working lives, acquiring, over the years, the manners and the philosophy of their trade. Their wives remained countesses and princesses, tended their samovars, read French novels, and did not acknowledge the privations of the past and the penury of the present by one flicker of their long lashes.

Even in New York factional strife divided the community of Russian exiles. Those who had escaped from Denikin's disaster blamed Kornilov and Kolchak for the defeat of the Whites. Those who had fought with the White armies denounced Kerensky and Milyukov as traitors who had delivered Russia to the Bolsheviks. The divergencies between nobility and bourgeoisie had been carried into exile. Most of the nobly born and the ex-officers of the czarist army and navy wanted to restore czarist autocracy; the bourgeois exiles, merchants, and members of the professional classes, wanted to settle for a constitutional monarchy and, if it had to be, for a republic. The "absolutists" accused the "constitutionalists" of connivance with the Bolsheviks; the latter denounced the former as reactionary numskulls. One faction suspected not only the motives but also the practices of the other. Futhermore, the Communists had infiltrated, for a certainty, several exile groups, and probably all of them. The abduction of a czarist general by Bolshevik agents and the disappearance under mysterious circumstances of other exile leaders exacerbated the mutual distrust of the émigré factions.

I owe my Russian friends a liberal education in the politics of exile and the dynamics of revolution. The more I learned about the ease with which the Communists defeated their opponents, superior in material resources and at least equal in courage, the more I became convinced that the most significant feature of communism is the linkage between theory and action. Marxist-Leninist doctrine is based upon a theory of social conflict and disintegration; Communist strategy and tactics are designed to hasten disintegration—to push what is falling—and exploit conflict. The ethnocentric preconceptions of their opponents have greatly assisted the Communists in executing their wrecking projects. For all practical purposes, though not on the strength of their scholarly achievements, the Communists have been better historians and sociologists than their opponents. They have understood how to exploit social as well as national cleavages and to foster factionalism—the kind of sociological jujitsu that manipulates the heavier opponent into throwing himself.

I tried to isolate common elements of the experience of my Russian friends and of my own and to discard the adventitious and the exotic. I am sure that no one, not even the most systematic maker of systems, can achieve so antiseptic a state of mind. But try one must, lest the obvious be never reduced to order. Perhaps the most dangerous trap—and no one knows how to set it more expertly than the Communists—is Marxist economic theory. Forty years ago I found the so-called theoretical writings of Marx and Lenin unspeakably boring; I do so even now. Yet the mechanics of Communist political and psychological warfare

are today of greater interest than they ever were, for they have been tested in the crucible of action.

My Russian friends kept late hours. We talked interminably. Among any ten Russians there is always a powerful voice to sob out songs of war and love. We talked on, drank tea or the bottle of cognac which a recent arrival had smuggled in from abroad. V.M., a former naval officer, whose famous father had gone down with his ship at Port Arthur, launched a caviar import business. V.M. hired one of my friends as a salesman, who on festive occasions contributed sample kits to our menu. There were many festive occasions. I do not know whether M.'s business prospered.

One of my acquaintances, a pianist in a Russian nightclub, introduced me to M.C. and his wife, who seemed enthralled by Russian cuisine and Rimsky-Korsakov. Mr. C., who conducted a real-estate agency on Fifth Avenue, offered me a job and a small advance on commissions. In the mornings I compiled listings of apartments for rent and buildings for sale. In the afternoons I telephoned likely prospects who wanted to rent an apartment or buy a building. I learned to distinguish between a choice neighborhood and a neighborhood not so choice. I obtained permission to inspect the premises and to show them to my clients. Though my start was slow, Mr. C. and his partner, Mr. L., whose casual good manners compensated for the minuteness of my drawing account, retained their faith in my potentialities. After two months or so I met an operatic producer of Italian ancestry. I searched for a plot of land suitable for the erection of a small opera house. Exploring Greenwich Village, I had come across a string of abandoned stables. The operatic producer bought them. My share of the commission was nearly six hundred dollars. I had won my spurs as a real-estate broker. Unfortunately, the combination of operatic promoter and vacant stables was a nonrecurring one.

Flushed by success, I quit the rooming house in the Forties and together with an Austrian friend leased a fair-sized apartment in the mid-Fifties. The building, formerly a private residence, had been converted into flats. The living room was sunny; the ceilings were high and so was the rent. My drawing account soon caught up with my earnings. My roommate had found employment on Wall Street. He suggested I try my luck in banking. I sought out my friend the Russian pianist and asked him whether he knew a banker. He said he did not, but that, if among the regular patrons one would turn up, he would let me know. A few days later I stood in the presence of one of New York's leading bankers, B.S.

Mercifully, B.S. did not ask me, as would today's other-directed top executives, to declare the motive that prompted me to choose a banking career. He inquired why I thought that I could be of any use to a banker. Of course, I could not think of anything of fair value to any banker, and said so. B.S. had traveled in Europe before and after World War I. He asked me as to whether I thought the Germans would pay up on their reparations. I replied that I had not met a German who wanted to pay up or thought that Germany could square her accounts even if she wanted to. The French thought that, because they themselves had paid to Germany a war indemnity of three and one-half billion francs after the war of 1870-1871, they could now expect the Germans to fork out easily ten times as much. Yet in 1871 France had suffered little physical damage, had fought for only a few months, and had not been blockaded by the Germans. B.S. said that the United States wished to collect on the debts of its allies and thus had a stake, though indirectly, in the reparations Germany had agreed to pay. It bespeaks my own ethnocentric rigidities that this idea had not occurred to me. B.S., as if he had read my mind, said that Germany had signed the peace treaty which included the war-guilt clause. Hence, the Allies had a legal and moral right to claim damages. By international law, the Germans had to pay up. B.S., although a power in the Republican party, as I was to find out later, said that he regretted America's failure to ratify the peace treaty of Versailles not only because the League of Nations thus lacked America's support but also because the Allies could not maintain a common front on the issue of German reparations.

I was so absorbed in these matters of high policy that I forgot why I had sought the interview. Somewhat brusquely, B.S. brought it to a close and suggested I call on M.F., partner in a brokerage firm and member of the New York Stock Exchange. Mr. F., pale, gray and lean, told me that I must learn the business "from the ground up." There was an opening for a runner and I could have the job. I took it and stayed at it for the better part of a year.

To work hard at a chosen task is no hardship; to succeed in it is, in a Protestant country, the most respectable form of self-indulgence. During my first years in the engine room of Wall Street I worked hard because I had to. I do not think that hard work at a low wage improves anybody's character. I was poor, as shabbily and furtively poor as all the poor in a big, rich Northern city.

I learned, and then I ran. I ran to and from the brokers, carrying notices of securities sold and purchased. From a leather bag slung across my shoulder, I dispensed bundles of precious certificates. My boss was the cashier. The cashier and his clerical helpers were kept in the "cage," an area separated from the rest of the office by a strong wire netting. The cage harbored some of the firm's assets. Here were examined and counted those polychrome certificates which documented their owners' claims to two kinds of possessions, a share in corporate business or corporate mortgages and debentures. The paper was expensive. Though pliable, it conveyed the impression of weightiness and dignified stiffness. Sometimes it was decorated with the engraved emblem which identified the nature of the issuer's business. In my day, the engraver's artistry reflected the taste of the Victorian age for classic mythology and chaste seminakedness, as, for example, a freight car and the god Mercury running interference at hip-level with a cloud or a harvesting machine guarded by cloud-wrapped goddess Ceres. More often than not, the sumptuousness of the decor stood in inverse relationship to the document's quoted value on the stock exchange.

In the outer office, the boardroom, men talked knowingly and often with great emotion about the fluctuations which swirled around these reassuring and reposeful lithographs. I wondered at the links joining my polychrome pieces of paper with a steel mill which I had never seen and which probably most of its certified shareholders would never see either.

Modern civilization makes tremendous demands upon man's power of abstraction. Almost everything, like military power, industrial productivity, and government, must be imagined in order to be believed. On a clear day Pericles, standing on the Acropolis, could view Athens' entire army in the plain of Attica and her entire fleet riding at anchor at Piraeus. The shops of the artisans—all of Athens' industry—were clustered at his feet. He could assemble his public servants by shouting at them and, by blowing the trumpet, he could summon the entire Athenian electorate, within about fifteen minutes.

Today, even the mightiest in the land, possessed of every gadget of communication and mobility, will never perceive with their senses more than a tiny fragment of physical reality. On Wall Street the knack of imagining unseen things and relationships is an essential part of the needed intellectual equipment. It is as indispensable to the financier as an innate sense of form is to the artist. It is as if the immense varieties of things were driven through a sieve and shredded into dollars and cents. In a matter-of-fact way this operation is being carried on by the men of finance, supported by technicians such as statisticians and, especially, lawyers. The psychological strain upon the operators is enormous. The tension breaks all but the strongest or most insensitive men. Wall Street awaits its Dante who will sing of its maimed soul writhing in the purgatory of schizophrenia.

Wall Street intensely scans the world around it; yet Wall Street, by reducing the world to a quotation, alienates itself from reality. Isolated from the rest of humanity, it looks inward. Like all introverts, Wall Street is terribly sensitive to itself.

Wall Street's principal contribution to the psychology of the American people has been this peculiar introversion. The "market" supposedly reflects the state of American business. Since American business and the public in general take their cue from the market, the state of business is what Wall Street says it is. Because the mirror of Wall Street is distorted, Wall Street is never "right" about the state of business—except after the event. Speculative paroxysms disturb the state of business. Who mirrors whom? Paper gains and losses enrich and impoverish the whole economy. Once the market has made up its mind, it is as if whole cities had risen or been razed overnight. The weird psychological game that Wall Street plays with itself creates giants and then destroys them, and gives people the psychological lift to buy, without cashing in on their winnings, fine things, and, conversely, casts them, though they have not taken their losses, into fear of penury.

Anyone who has lived for any length of time in New York has seen what the market can do to the city's business. I do not believe that this psychological instability of mood proves one thing or the other about the capitalist system. Highly intelligent men can will themselves into illness and out of it; but capitalism is not utopia—it is one of the several imperfect institutions which, together, support political freedom. And no man possessed of a sense of measures will waste his time on utopian pursuits. The ambitions of the tyrant are measureless, and tyranny is an absolute; none of the working institutions of political freedom can be operated without a sense of measure, and a sense of measure is little else but self-restraint. The capitalist system, more than any other, depends for its effective operation on self-restraint.

Fortunately, just as my last pair of serviceable shoes was about to give out, I was transferred into the "cage," and, shortly thereafter, into the outer office. Speculative fever, meanwhile, had been rising. Some of my Russian friends who had saved money, being the sons and daughters of the old Russia, wanted to gamble. They turned to me as the most proximate initiate into the mystery of the market. They opened accounts with my employers. They were joined by the landlord of my building and the corner druggist. My employers raised me from my clerical status to the rank of customers' man. Rank confers privilege. I was paid twice as much for getting to work half an hour later and signing off half an hour earlier than the clerical staff. I had sole use of a roll-top desk, swivel chair, and telephone. I bought a Brooks Brothers suit, dark blue. The villein had risen to yeoman.

But by now protracted physical exertion and leaden boredom had turned me into a skeptic; I had not grown wiser, but rather more distrustful of my star. I had lost some of the insouciance which had buoyed me thus far through the vicissitudes of fortune. My fellow runners had been a few years younger than I. I

realized that time had gone by and that I had not much to show
for it. At my age, Nelson commanded a squadron; Alexander had
defeated Darius; Napoleon had conquered Italy; Einstein had developed his theory; Mozart had completed more than half his
work; the younger Pitt had governed England; and Raphael had
painted his most highly prized Madonnas.

Accidentally, I had strayed into a business about the inner
workings of which I knew nothing. I was not sure that I belonged to the community. Relations with my fellow workers
had settled down to a standoff. At that time I must have seemed
to them an odd fish; my mannerism of speech and stance now
amused, now annoyed them. Moreover, most of the clerical
workers were Irish. In spite of Patrick's indoctrination, I did not
catch on to their wit. I was too sluggish to rise to the bait; they
soon turned to other, more responsive game. The secretaries, neat
and pretty, tended the welfare of the partners. These exacting
and sometimes extramural labors seemed to exhaust their interest
in males of marginal status. They made their homes in exotic
places such as Brooklyn and the Bronx. I had no small talk and
little money. Moreover, it would have been indelicate to trifle
with the welfare of one's employers.

A social system based on private property needs a capital market. The workings of any kind of machinery must be judged by
how efficiently it generates energy. Wall Street has generated
vast energies; yet its performance has been attended by a waste of
resources which should not be tolerated by a society which has
made efficiency its watchword. Wall Street, aware of its appalling inefficiency, has propagated a number of soothing myths.
One of these is that standards which govern trade in general
govern, too, the so-called capital market. Do they? Now, it is
possible to specify the nature of a pound of coffee or a bale of
cotton, a pound of copper or an ounce of gold or a ton of steel,
since for these commodities strict quality standards have been
developed. Changes in supply and demand may raise or lower the
market price of these goods. He who has bought dear might lose
money; he need not fear that the pound of coffee that he bought,
cheap or dear, turns out to have been a pound of molasses or two
pounds of gravel. In brief, it has been possible for a long time to

deal and speculate wildly in a good many commodities and still enjoy a high degree of protection against fraud. This condition did not obtain in Wall Street when I served my apprenticeship.

Without the daring of nervy gamblers, backed by their retinue of promoters, middlemen, moneylenders, and Jacks-of-all-trades, America could not have been built, and certainly not built as quickly. American folklore endowed the gambler with virtues which more settled societies condemn as downright antisocial vices. The puritanical element of the American tradition, ever suspicious of all human instincts, could not fail to anathematize the gambling instinct, just as it anathematized love on Sunday and alcohol on any day. The public, overawed by its moral censors, withheld approval from licensed gambling and lotteries. The rules of most games of chance are relatively simple. Even the most besotted client of a casino knows that he is taking considerable chances and does not harbor the illusion that he is "investing" in an ordinary business venture. Licensed casinos in almost any Western country refrain from cheating, this practice having been found by managements to be unprofitable in the long run. No licensed casino is permitted to tell its clients that it offers any other opportunities than those inherent in a game of chance. In America the prohibition upon licensed gambling has left to the vast mass of law-fearing citizens, bent on easy money, no other place to go than the market. In fact, though not in name, the world's largest casino occupies most of the floor space in our financial district and caters from there to millions of clients.

The rules of this particular game of chance are far from simple. There is a spate of regulations designed to keep it clean. Yet no more than one among a thousand players has even the vaguest notion of their finer points. Only lawyers can decipher the small print of stipulations contrived by the shrewdest lawyers in the land. The management of the Casino, backed by the highest legal and moral authorities, has persuaded its clients they are gambling on a sure thing and, for good measure, "doing the nation's work."

What has been licit, though disreputable, for a long time becomes respectable through usage. Shooting craps is not respectable, but taking a flyer on a ten per cent margin in Far Offshore

Oil Inc. is. Of course, I speak here of the Wall Street of forty years ago. Since then much has changed—the margin requirements have been stiffened; the legendary promoters of my mythical Far Offshore Oil Inc. have been suspended by the New York Stock Exchange and now ply their trade as investment consultants; management has had to bone up on many more regulations; and raids by public authority upon the premises have become more frequent. Yet the sufferings of the management inflicted by government and occasional outbreaks of public indignation have been compensated by a vast increase of eager "investors." The prospectuses have grown into paperbacks and their print is getting ever finer.

Wall Street serves many other purposes than share-pushing and taking bets on the market. The moneylender enters the history of civilization with the warrior, the priest, and the prostitute. Not all civilizations esteemed him highly—the Middle Ages assigned him to one of the lowest rungs of the social ladder. Within the past five hundred years of Western history, however, the mounting needs of war, commerce, and, later, industrialization, have transformed the despised moneylender into the respected banker. Despite the social ascendancy of scientists and intellectuals, the banker still retains the highest position in American society. Banking is not only a profession; it is also a club and a very exclusive one.

The great banks of Wall Street, under the watchful eyes of the Federal Treasury and the Federal Reserve System, regulate the flow of money, that is, they lend money at less than usurious rates of interest. The moneylender performs a socially necessary service. He places the savings entrusted to his care and his own capital at the use of those of his fellow men who need money for a variety of purposes, including buying the things which others refrain from buying in order to save and lend. For this service the banker exacts surety and interest. Interest is as high as the traffic will bear. In American society which has accumulated a vast and widely shared fund of savings, the interest charged by the moneylenders is generally considered to be fair, or close to it. No one, not even the Church at the height of its secular power, has been able to define satisfactorily the nature of usury. The American public does not believe that its bankers are usurers. Most bankers are convinced that they are not. Of course, a society as articulate and as ingenious as ours excels in devising new semantics for age-old practices. Rates charged on consumers' goods payable in installments would have been considered usurious by medieval society. But, since both sides seem to be happy with the bargain, this kind of moneylending does not have the air of usury.

The moneylenders on Wall Street have served American society well, perhaps not quite as well as their own public relations men will have it but much better than their ideological and demagogic critics are prepared to concede. I suppose bankers know their fellow men better than these know themselves, for had bankers not put this vital knowledge to the good use of society as a whole, not only they but also our affluent society as a whole would be a great deal less affluent. Moreover, most successful bankers I have known—I have known many under various circumstances and have observed them from various elevations—equaled in rectitude and intelligence the best men in any profession and in public life. Most of them looked askance at what I have called the Casino. Most of them deplored the frailties of its management. Most of them said that they would welcome stricter rules than those imposed in the past. Yet every well-entrenched trade union seems to develop, side by side with its equitable rules, an incurable propensity toward featherbedding and other kinds of institutionalized waste.

Chastened, Wall Street now spends vast amounts on improving its public "image." Yet the management is loath to revise the rules, and fortunes, big and small, still disappear in the sinkhole of speculation. Perhaps this seepage is organic; perhaps this is the way the capitalist body evacuates. It is surprising that Marx and Lenin, who thought of so many unpleasant things, did not discern this possibility. Fortunately I did not think of it either when I started to learn the language of Wall Street.

Although the intellectual endowment of my fellow customers' men varied, they had in common a suave aloofness which assured the customer that his cares received judicious attention. The firm I served had prospered for fifty years. The partners, grandsons of the two founders, had passed through Harvard and Yale, respectively, and belonged to the appropriate town and country clubs. Most of my fellow customers' men had been chosen for their affinity to the same or analogous institutions. I had not shared their formative experience, nor did I excel in sports such as tennis, squash, golf, fly-fishing, and fox hunting exalted by genteel Anglo-Saxon tradition. The companionability and humor of the locker room flavor male sociability in America. Not that the young men in the office wished to make me feel an outsider; but they talked readily about themselves in that uninhibited and unguarded fashion which Europeans of the same age and background find embarrassing as well as indiscreet. Had I been less self-conscious and could I have told my story as simply as they told theirs, we could have become friends. In later life this lack of rapport was to cost me dearly. I mourn the stillborn friendships more than those that died, worn away by separation, quarrel, or simply the attrition of time.

And, then, just when I had learnt to talk meaningfully about capital appreciation, many years of irregular hours, skipped meals, a diet of cigarettes, and haunted sleep took their toll. I fell ill. Today I am quite certain that a deep distress, a sense of frustration and emptiness, spawned the variety of my physical disorders. I longed to see my mother. I had been away for five years. Of Europe I knew little but its middle countries. I wanted to stroll along the fabled boulevards of Paris. And I wanted to stand again on high ground, above mountain lake and valley. The physician agreed that I needed a change of air and scene. I quit my job. I converted my savings into a letter of credit. I reserved a berth on a French liner, and bought a couple of expensive valises. I felt greatly improved in health.

Chapter Six

IN THE summer of 1928 I sailed
for Europe. Although I was eager to see my mother after a five
years' separation, I stopped off in Paris for a few days. At the
age of seven, I had eaten a delicious chestnut glacé with whipped
cream at Rumpelmayer's on the Rue de Rivoli and ridden a paddle
steamer up and down the Seine between the high quais lined with
trees. This is all I remembered. Now I went to the Louvre, found
Mona Lisa as enigmatic and disappointing as she appears in any
fair reproduction; I sat on the terraces of recommended cafés,
fashionable or literary; made the round of the *boîtes* of Mont-
martre and Montparnasse; and, with a young man's undemanding
zest for well-authenticated pleasures, clutched my collage of
Murger's *Bohème*, Toulouse-Lautrec's posters, and *Vogue* (Paris
edition).

When at last, one hazy morning, I drove past gluttonous market stalls to the station and took the train for Munich I could not
account for what I had seen of Paris. Had I sampled the essence
or had I been fobbed off with a cheap pastiche? I vowed that

when I returned to Paris I would spend my days in the Bibliothèque Nationale, sit meditatively on a bench in the Luxembourg, visit Napoleon in his tomb, and stand where St. Louis had knelt in the Sainte-Chapelle. Although I returned to Paris many times and even settled for a while, thirty years passed before I redeemed my pledge.

Paris has drawn millions of foreigners to her; she welcomes them with her easy grace and forgets them before they have gone. At heart, Paris is fastidious and xenophobe. Only her own people know her, for they take her for what she is, a big city with fine trees, abundant bakery shops and bistros, acrid subways, well-kept public gardens alive with children at play without raising their voices, not-so-well-kept monuments for the sight of which strangers have come from afar; and all kinds of accommodations and places of entertainment for which only foreigners uncomplainingly pay exorbitant prices. The Parisian loves his city in a matter-of-course way, and goes about his business.

At the station I was met by my mother. She told me that my father had come to Munich, taken lodgings in a boardinghouse, and fallen gravely ill. She had arranged his transfer to a small clinic in the care of our old family doctor, whose cool hands, long white beard, and gentle brown eyes had comforted me in a succession of childhood afflictions. A nurse admitted me to a darkened room. My father was heavily drugged, and for the first time in my life I was at close quarters with death.

The mustache, which I remembered stiffly upturned and carefully trimmed, drooped limp onto the unshaved chin. My father opened his eyes and said that he was glad I had come. My father always liked to talk about far-off places to which he had been or wanted to go. I said that, as soon as the physician would agree, we would travel together to Sicily and from there to the island of Corfu, where he had spent a few spring days as a young man. I talked on, and my father put his moist hand upon mine. He fell asleep. I returned to my mother's apartment. In the morning my mother woke me and told me that my father had died. A few days later the coffin was lowered into the grave. The pastor looked up from a slip of paper and said that a wanderer, far from his native land, now rested in peace.

I stayed on for a few days. A German town gains little by an approach via Paris. I asked my mother whether she would like to settle in Paris, a city which she had visited frequently before the war. She agreed, and we made plans for the gay adventure about to begin. The letter of a Budapest lawyer advised me that my father's properties were heavily encumbered and that my presence was needed for the settlement of the estate.

Budapest had changed little. Horse-drawn vehicles still outnumbered motorcars. The cafés and restaurants were crowded. Peasants carting their produce to the markets still wore high boots and embroidered coats, nonchalantly draped over the shoulder. Although defeat in World War I had entailed heavy territorial losses, Hungary still retained the best part of her agricultural lands, the richest in Europe, and her industries. While Vienna, once so resplendent, had turned shabby, Budapest had quickly regained its racy opulence.

I took a room in a hotel on the embankment of the Danube. From here I commanded a view of the river, the chain bridge, and on the crest of the hill, of the Royal Palace and Citadel, stage setting for a period piece in the manner of Elinor Glyn. Then I set about my serious errand.

I did not like the looks of my father's lawyer, who seemed to be on the most cordial terms with an assortment of moneylenders and professed himself deeply hurt when I caviled at the vertiginously steep rates of interest. I quickly realized I was in need of impartial counsel. I recalled that one of my father's friends, a pensioned army officer, lived in Budapest, and I set out to find him.

To the south of the Danube rise frowning hills. Beyond them curve easy valleys. Nearest to the city is the Cool Valley. At that time, villas of various sizes and styles were scattered about its slopes. Turning the corner of an unpaved road, I came upon a two-story structure in the midst of a weedy garden. It owed its architectural inspiration to that hybrid Monte Carlo Casino-Paris Metro style which, from the 1890's onward, swept Eastern Europe, notably the Balkans. Though derived from diverse influences and put to a variety of uses, this creative effort stamped whatever it wrought with a high degree of uniformity. In most

Eastern capitals, it is not always easy to distinguish between the principal railroad station, the Royal Palace, the National Bank, and the most highly reputed house of ill-repute. The same unitary spirit had materialized, though on a greatly reduced scale, in the house to which a manservant in striped waistcoat and long apron now opened the door.

My father's friend, a bachelor, seemed to prefer a small chamber at the back of the house, where a narrow window afforded a view on the desolate garden, to the stately, uncarpeted, and unfurnished rooms in the front. The walls were lined with prints depicting small groups of valiant Hungarians fighting off the Turkish hordes and photographs of stallions and relatives. Colonel B. sported the long sideburns and large curved mustache which were the common adornments of Hungarian country gentlemen, their coachmen, and yeoman peasants.

The colonel was deeply grieved at the news of my father's death. He said that my father's legal counsel was a scoundrel as were all lawyers and politicians with the exception of Count Tisza, Hungary's fierce premier who was murdered after the war, and his own nephew who, because of a visual defect, had gone into the law rather than the army. The manservant served sweetened Turkish coffee and plum brandy. My father's friend inquired about my life in America, a country which he regarded, so he assured me, as the innocent and abysmally ignorant tool of French and English politicos, mostly lawyers. He gave me the address of his nephew, admonished me to tell the Americans the truth about the unspeakable Romanians, Czechs, and Serbs and to polish up on the Hungarian language, and sent me on my way.

The nephew, a pleasant young man a few years older than I, expressed himself delighted to make my acquaintance, for I was the first client in many a day. Having examined briefly the technical aspects of my case, he concluded that the lawyer in charge of my father's estate was a notorious shyster, and that, since I did not stand a chance in a protracted court battle, we had to resort to shock tactics. These he proceeded to apply forthwith—he called the shyster and, from my limited knowledge of Hungarian, the most virile language on earth and rich in turns of endearment and invective, I surmised that the man on the other end of the wire now understood more clearly if not the intricacies of the law, then at least my counsel's opinion. This gambit completed, the latter suggested that, the time being noon, we take a walk on the quai along the Danube and then on to Gerbaud's, where we might join some friends over a glass of sherry.

At this hour of the day the sidewalk was crowded with people strolling in the bright sun. The Hungarians are a well-made race. Even Hungary's enemies, who are many, concede the beauty of Hungary's women, blue-eyed and lithe, the cheekbones slightly raised and the skin kissed by the sun and the wind of the great plain. The men, whether handsome or not, carry themselves well. Few run to fat or shift their eyes.

The Magyar is said to come from Ugro-Turkic stock and thus to belong to the family of the Mongol peoples. Certainly his speech has nothing in common with the languages of the Indo-European peoples, and many a face of strikingly Asian cast stares impassively at the traveler passing through the villages of the great plain. Yet the horsemen from the East who conquered, a thousand years ago, the land which the Romans called Pannonia, numbered only a few thousand men, and the native population must then have exceeded the invader by about fifty to one. Mongol blood is strong; a few drops seem to have had a catalytic effect on the Russian Slav. It is unlikely, however, that today's Magyar is the product of so remote an accident in eugenics.

In the thirteenth century Hungary again fell, albeit briefly, under Mongol domination. From the sixteenth century onward until the beginning of the eighteenth, Hungary suffered a series of Turkish invasions and occupations. The Turks, themselves a member of the Ugro-Turkic group to which, incidentally, the Finns also belong, ruled Hungary for a hundred twenty years, and Turkish pashas worshiped Allah in a graceful mosque planted upon the hill of Buda. Yet, had it not been for the natural environment, these reinoculations of the Mongol strain might not have kept alive this enclave of Asia in the midst of Europe. Of all the regions of Europe to the west of the Prut and Dniester rivers, the Hungarian plain resembles most the level lands of inner Asia. Steppe lands border areas of tillage; reed grass fringes the banks of muddy streams; and riders on small, close-coupled horses drive herds of cattle to waterholes or walled, circular wells visible from miles away. The smells, that pungent mixture of dung, charcoal fire, and the lather of horses, are, too, of Asia. The land undulates toward the horizon, smudged in the far distance with the smoke rising from a herdsman's fire or a cloud of dust that, like a banner, waves above horses and cattle on the move. It is not anthropologically certain how genuinely Asian the Hungarians really are. But they feel as if they were, and they proudly assert their kinship to the fierce riders of the steppe; the land around them confirms them in their preconceptions.

Throughout the past hundred years the Hungarians have managed to acquire the unenviable reputation of the most nationalistic people in Europe. They are intensely patriotic and, since 1848, the professional Hungarian patriot-in-exile has been a fixture of international conferences, lecture platforms and drawing rooms. Patriotism, so the saying goes, is the refuge of the scoundrel. Undoubtedly, in many instances, it is; so is internationalism, humanitarianism, or any other "ism" out of which, depending on the public climate, unscrupulous men and women can make an easy living under the pretense of unselfish and noble motives.

In the course of their history the Hungarian people as a whole have intensely avowed their love of country—and have made of it only a poor and very dangerous living. Their misfortune has been to live at the crossroads of imperial traffic, athwart the path of several great and expansionist powers. The Pannonia of old was first conquered by the Romans and then ravaged by Hun, Teuton, and Bulgar. The Magyars found themselves in the way of the Germans, the Turks, and the Russian Slavs. Only a people as possessed of a superlative ego and courage as were the Hungarians could have retained its identity—and a striking identity at that. For not the least wholesome exercise in historical recollection is the evocation of Hungary's not so distant past; the Turks were ejected from their last toehold in the Danube basin only at the beginning of the eighteenth century and driven back to the Balkans only some eighty-odd years ago. The Hungarian rising of 1848 under the banner of national and democratic freedom was suppressed by Russian arms.

IN MY TIME

Every virtue has its vice, every vice its virtue. The Hungarians' love of country has bred a fiery intransigence and contemptuous arrogance which have frequently affronted the great powers of Europe and always Hungary's immediate neighbors.

The Hungarians' record of valor is gashed by a cruelty which, too, is part of the Asian patrimony of the race. Professor Toynbee, whose explorations only casually touch upon Southeast European history, could have found in Hungary ample evidence sustaining his theory on challenge and response. Notwithstanding a series of national catastrophes, some quite recent, the Hungarians have produced probably a larger quota of gifted men than any other country of its size. From Petöfi, Lenau, Liszt, and Jókai to Szilard, Teleki, Molnár, Dohnányi, Teller, and Kármán and on to Koestler and Ormandy, to mention only a few, the list of Hungarian genius has grown at a fabulous rate, a hall of heroes in the arts and sciences that stands upon the summit of achievement. Only an exceedingly tough, versatile, restless, and passionate people could have kept on, against unusually heavy historical odds, raising its crops of perfections.

The crowd on the Danube quai thinned out for the midday meal. My counsel and I strolled to Gerbaud's, a fabled confiserie that served a special chocolate cake, ice cream, tarts, hot chocolate, sherry, port, and goose liver paté sandwiches. "Everybody," that is, the smart set and those who wanted to mingle with it, made it a habit to be seen at Gerbaud's before the midday meal. My counsel seemed to know "everybody." Whatever it was that his friends practiced it was not time-consuming professions. A few joined us.

We then headed for a popular restaurant, and, over a copious and spicy meal and to the strains of band music, we talked politics. Politics meant the Peace Treaty of Trianon, which had deprived Hungary of two thirds of her territory and population. As far as my companions were concerned, there were no political problems, national or international, worth talking about except the bereavement of Hungary and the likely ways and means for revising the iniquitous treaty which, having torn the finest jewels—Transylvania and the Banat—from the crown of St. Stephen, had driven hundreds of thousands of Magyar settlers

89

from their ancestral lands. So intense waxed the emotion of my companions, who were of both sexes, young and handsome, and who had seemed, over Gerbaud's sherry, so carefree and gay, that I felt as if I stood in the presence of an impersonal physical force.

The spirit of irredenta, like a screaming, taloned bird, had swept over the whole city. On billboards and walls, brightly colored posters showing the prewar map of Hungary and, in blood-red, the lines of partition, bore the legend: "Nem, nem, soha!" (No, no, never!) Hardly a day passed without some public meeting devoted to keeping alive the memory of the "lost communities."

Living in a large and powerful country like the United States, it is not easy to fathom the depth of a small and weak people's resentments and aspirations. On the face of it, the idea of national self-determination seems both plausible and simple of realization. Yet people, not being vegetable, move about.

In most parts of the world the peoples who most stridently demand self-government themselves contain in their midst one or several national minorities. These national minorities, too, can and usually do claim the right of self-determination—and so on *ad infinitum*. Thus, for example, the Czechs as soon as they had achieved national independence and ceased to be a national minority within the Austro-Hungarian Empire, became themselves the target of national minorities under their rule, namely, Slovaks, Sudeten Germans, Carpatho-Ukrainians, and Hungarians. And there is a surprising similarity between the charges leveled by these minorities against the Czech minority group and those hurled by leaders of the Czech independence movement such as Masaryk and Beneš against the monarchy. As a matter of fact, the strife between the dominant and the lesser national groups grew fiercer than it had ever been under the Hapsburgs.

Thus World War I, far from settling the nationality problems of Eastern Europe and the Near East, created at least three new ones for each problem purported to have been solved. On the reduced scale of European geography the conflicts of nationalism in Eastern Europe after World War I anticipated virtually every turn and twist of the drive toward national self-determination in

Asia and Africa after World War II. I am deeply convinced that there is no such thing as "just nationalist aspirations." The claim of people A against people B to national self-determination is as good or as bad as the prevailing distribution of power makes it. In brief, the claim of a people to national independence is rightful only if it can make that claim stick. The problem can never be settled by statistical compilations or plebiscites. In each country can be found a region where one or several national minorities exceed in numbers that ethnic or linguistic group that makes up the majority of the country as a whole.

In a world order under justice, a people should have the right to speak its own language, cook its favorite dishes, and enjoy the good things that its labor produces. And this is about all there is to the cussed business of national self-determination. If these conditions are met, then it should matter little whether a people flies a flag that is red, white, and green, or black and blue with a unicorn rampant, or no flag at all. If, upon its liberation from some foreign domination, it proceeds to look for national minorities in its midst in order—tit for tat—to oppress them or to despoil and eject them, then the principle of the right to national self-determination shrivels into a bad and nasty joke.

There is not a nationalist frustration anywhere in the world that does not, sooner or later, grow into an international cancer. Once upon a time nearly everybody who counted in the international equation was involved in the Polish Question. Now, in 1928, the European powers were up to their elbows in the politics of Hungary and her neighbors. The French backed their allies, Romania, Yugoslavia, and Czechoslovakia, who had divided among themselves the Hungarian loot in satisfaction of their just national aspirations. As a matter of course, the Italians, although they, too, had been rewarded for their inconclusive pains in the Allied cause with a slice of Hungary, discovered that, after all, there was considerable merit in Hungary's demand for the "revision" of the Treaty of Trianon to which they themselves had appended their signature. Times had changed, and Italy, dissatisfied with the 1919 distribution of the spoils, prepared to change sides.

The English, who had always liked the Hungarians as a sport-

ing people, looked upon growing French influence in Eastern
Europe with mixed emotions. In 1848, English public opinion,
always ready to back a brave little people—other than the Irish
—against foreign rulers, had acclaimed the Hungarian rising, led
by Kossuth and Deák, against the Hapsburgs. Old memories
stirred: Was France not growing too cocky for the good of the
European balance of power, and were those who opposed the
pretensions of France and her clients not worthy of encouragement? Then English diplomacy, so sensitive to any attempt at
consolidating the affairs of the Continent under a single management, might have, sedately and in its own good time, swung
around to the support of the Hungarian "revisionists." As it was,
accident took a hand and with unseemly precipitateness plunged
English public opinion into the turbulent waters of Danubian
politics.

As all great dramatists know, comic byplay heightens the sense
of tragic doom. My visit to Budapest coincided with the unfolding of a strange epic on which my elated Hungarian hosts did not
tire to elaborate. Years later I tried to reconstruct the plot, and,
though some of the finer points in this Ruritarian parody may
have escaped me, I believe that the facts were as follows: Some
time before World War I a Viennese girl of modest station and
striking appearance was married to a Hungarian noble of impressive pedigree and slender means. Shortly after the war the
young woman, unaccompanied by her princely husband, made
her way to Paris. Her well-serviced establishment lacked neither
ample comforts nor sumptuous decor. She had gained the confidence and esteem of Viscount Rothermere, one of the great English press lords and master of a daily paper read by millions.

The Great War, to whose victorious conclusion the peer's
fiery denunciations of German atrocities had contributed so
much, was fading into memory; the world was at peace and
business was fair. There was a slack in newsworthy happenings.
The peer scanned the horizon for topics which would arouse the
public from its deplorable complacency and, incidentally, increase the circuation of his daily. The Hungarian lady was the
highly photogenic bearer not only of an ancient and famous
name but also of a great national sorrow. It was as if the misfor-

tunes of her adopted land cast a shadow over her youthful and otherwise fair countenance. Rothermere, who had brought Hearst's reductive journalism to Fleet Street and entertained but the vaguest notions on East European geography, now eagerly examined the lay of the land and the complexities of the Hungarian Question. No longer baffled, as were most of his countrymen, by the phonetic similarities of Budapest and Bucharest, he embraced the cause of the former capital and denounced that of the latter. At last Hungarian revisionism had found a powerful friend.

The *Daily Mail* started a campaign that was to air—day in, day out—the territorial grievances of Hungary, the sufferings of Magyar minorities under Czech, Yugoslav, and espesially Romanian domination, and the moral and legal imperatives for revising, without further ado, the shameful dictate, the Treaty of Trianon. English public opinion awoke to the plight of the chivalrous and sporting Hungarians; Hungarian restaurants, staffed with excellent cooks and vivacious gypsy musicians in pink hussar jackets, were mobbed by London's fashionable set; and visiting Hungarian nobles who, unlike most Continentals, dressed as English gentlemen should, were feted by London's Best Society. Hungary responded enthusiastically.

Before the accession of the Hapsburgs, the crown of Hungary —like that of kindred Poland—had not devolved upon its bearer by heredity but by election. In fact, the Hungarian nobles had called in foreigners and crowned them king whenever they could not settle the question of who among them should ascend the throne after the demise of a king. Why not resume now this venerable practice?

Responding to discreet feelers, Rothermere, pleading the pressure of business and his ripe age, shyly abstained from pressing his candidacy. But he conceded that his adult son, who had gone —as he himself had not—to the right schools and recently married a daughter of good family, might wish to visit Budapest and feel the pulse of Hungarian sentiment. Thus what started out as the informal visit of a honeymooning couple became, by dint of the Hungarian public's rapt acclaim, a triumphal pageant—the Union Jack flew together with the Hungarian flag; the path of the visitors was strewn with flowers; and the great, including the dour and fleetless Admiral Horthy, extended the bewildered couple the splendid, and a shade savage, ceremonial welcome which Hungary still reserved for visitors of state. Had nature been permitted to take its course, Hungary might then well have taken unto herself an English king and lived happily ever after or, at least, for as long a time as is vouchsafed any small country of passage.

But of course nature was soon brought under control. Hungary's neighbors rose in their wrath at what they denounced as the Magyar's contempt for international legality. The Quai d'Orsay sternly warned the Hungarians to desist from their English romance and, though this is a matter of conjecture, remonstrated with Britain to keep a check on her roaming press lords. Thus the young man and woman who innocently had unleashed these diplomatic storms departed from Hungary and, soon thereafter, withdrew for good from the race for scepter and crown.

After a while Rothermere's attention strayed from the woes of the Maygars to the frustrated aspirations of more populous and potentially more powerful nations as, for example, the Germans. Although not always judicious in his choice of the causes to which he lent his support, he expanded the circulation of his daily. It is today larger than it has ever been, notwithstanding or, perhaps, because of the wide swings of its editorial policy. The patriotic lady who had rallied the peer to her country's defense bravely hid her distress at the failure of her mission and, for a while, played host to a remarkable assortment of Mid-European politicians—who later were to cause the Western democracies a good deal of inconvenience, but then seemed merely anxious to put their claims to other peoples' property before Western public opinion, preferably through the mediation of the peer's daily.

All things must come to an end. World War II broke out, and the ardor of British public opinion for righting the wrongs of the treaties concluded at the end of World War I cooled considerably; so did the peer's interest in Middle European affairs. The Princess, after considerable vicissitudes, found a safe haven on a distant shore. The passage of time erases the memory of many a noble failure.

Budapest, despite national adversity, was then the gayest city of Europe. I did not know or greatly care whence flowed the wealth that rewarded the exertions of Budapest's countless restaurateurs, gypsy orchestras, and sundry entertainers. I had not yet acquired that sense of social responsibility that should have urged me to investigate the hidden cracks in the class structure. Instead, unburdened by sociological preoccupations, I followed my exuberant friends on their diverting rounds.

Although, since the 1870's, the capital had grown apace with industrialization, Hungary was then still predominately an agricultural country. Most of my Hungarian friends, for example, came from the land and, on holidays and during vacations, returned to their homes or stayed with one of those country cousins of whom there seemed to be an inexhaustible supply. Then, too, Hungarian hospitality was still what it had always been— unlimited. Guests stayed as long as they liked, and to ration one's visit to a weekend would have been taken by one's host as a discourtesy or, in the case of a foreigner for whom allowances must be made, as unfamiliarity with Hungarian customs. In Hungary, although some of the magnates maintained vast and sumptuous establishments, the average country squire lived in a plain though comfortable manor and in close propinquity with stable and barn. Country life still happily reconciled simplicity with plenitude. I was lucky enough to taste its joys before the coming of the great flood.

As far as I have been able to ascertain, not a few of my Hungarian friends have shared a unique distinction: having been thrown in jail by the Nazis upon the occupation of the country by German troops in 1944, they were kept there—some for months and some for years—by the Communists when the latter took over so that Hungary could rejoice in the blessings of the United Nations Charter. Although one of my friends did not survive the experience, others managed to make their way abroad, where, being neither young nor skilled, they live in penury.

At long last the court handed me my father's estate, greatly diminished. I left Budapest after a moving celebration. We drove to the Citadel and saw the sun rise over the blue hills beyond the

Danube; and then I returned to Munich. Shortly thereafter my mother and I traveled to Paris, followed by a vanload of my family's remaining possessions. My last tie with Middle Europe had been cut.

Chapter Seven

Upon my return to New York, in the spring of 1930, a small banking firm asked me to take charge of its foreign business. My new employers controlled an investment trust, that is, a company that held a mixed bag of securities of all kinds, supposed to have been chosen judiciously by the managing company. My employers did the managing and compensated themselves for their pains by a cut in the profits. While the investor received a claim to the contents of the bag, the knowledgeable and ever-watchful management decided what to put in and take out. This type of business—a holding company on shares, trading in a variety of shares—was then a novelty in the United States, though it had flourished for a long time in Scotland and England. My employers, knowledgeable and ever watchful as they had been, had been caught like nearly everybody else in the stock market crash. The long list of securities which they had selected fared no better, and probably worse, than would have a bunch of stocks and bonds picked at random by a blind man from the closing-prices columns on the financial page.

In the mid-1920's, Wall Street had noted the spectacular recovery of Europe and launched itself vigorously upon the flotation of European securities in the American market. The firm I now served had eagerly entered the competition, particularly since it found that European borrowers were willing to pay unusually high commissions on the distribution of their IOUs to the American investing public. Not content to be merely middlemen, my employers, in their capacity as managers of the investment trust, had taken substantial positions in the bonds and stocks of European undertakings, public and private. Thus the holders of the mixed bag found themselves proud possessors of a sizable foreign portfolio. In it were not only German but also a colorful selection of Eastern European securities. I never plumbed the inwardness of their selection. All I knew was that they were on the ledger. In 1930 it looked as if they would be there forever.

The governments of Germany and most of her East European neighbors, prompted by sharp declines in foreign exports and the accelerating flight of capital, blocked payments in foreign exchange. Thus, for example, an American investor in German securities could sell them, provided he was lucky enough to find a buyer, in Germany and receive payment in German currency; but he could not convert the proceeds into American dollars. In the lingo of the trade, his account was "frozen." Thus most of the European assets of my investment trust were frozen and were, for all practical purposes, worthless. My employers now assigned me the task of ascertaining exactly how worthless they were and sent me to consult with certain European bankers on what could be done to melt frozen marks, pengös, zlotys, and leis into liquid American dollars.

In high finance there is always a way of detour. European experts, it was rumored, had devised various ingenious procedures for moving the immovable. I was to go to Europe forthwith.

My friends gave me a farewell party. We saw a bad play in a half-empty theater and went on to the city's best-guarded speakeasy, tucked away just off Fifth Avenue. I felt that at last I had a hand in great affairs. My friends rejoiced in my good fortune. Since I would not be gone for long, I felt as if I were going on a holiday. And so I sailed. As it turned out, I stayed for more than a year.

As soon as I arrived in Europe I consulted the experts on the Continent and in London. Finally, on a sparkling May morning, I arrived in Berlin. A German banker of our connection invited me to stay at his house, a commodious villa in the suburb of Dahlem. The northern spring had come to its well-kept garden. I walked along the graveled path and took out time to think; I tried to sort out my impressions and appraise the situation as I had observed it in London and Paris.

From my talks with some of the important bankers in London and Paris I concluded that one could attain financial eminence without ever having read a book on history. These were intelligent men; in the community their names stood for integrity and charity. Their decisions affected deeply the course of events, the fortunes of great undertakings, and countless lives at home and abroad. They commanded a large network of intelligence. They enjoyed the confidence of political leaders. Yet so specialized was their concern that they excluded from their deliberations all those varieties of life that did not enter into one decision, namely, when and what to buy and sell.

Nearly all of them had traveled widely. They had sampled the scenic beauties of the Rhine and the German Alps. They had stayed at the best hotels in Berlin and Munich; they counted among their friends and acquaintances the leaders of German finance and business. And they saw no reason to concern themselves with obscure and disorderly occurrences such as street forays in grimy workers' suburbs and demagogical rantings in vulgar beerhalls. After all, the Germans were an orderly people that kept to the sidewalk and did not step on lawns marked *Verboten*. Intellectuals could be swayed by the battles of ideologies, but the practical men of action would surely be able to cope with the rabble-rousers and their eccentric political movements which, so their German business friends assured them, were passing and trivial phenomena.

Furthermore, after World War I, Germany's economy had recovered quickly. German industry had done a magnificent job of modernization. Of course, the first few years had been troublesome, and for such average persons as wage earners and pensioners inflation had been a painful experience. Indeed, because of their excessive faith in the solemnly pledged stability of the German currency, many people had lost their fortunes. But now Dr. Schacht had done away with bundles of worthless banknotes and the bonded obligations, equally worthless, of the imperial government. The mark was again as hard as the dollar and the pound sterling.

Naturally each country in Europe had its share of political radicalism. It was infinitely preferable that radicals should not come to power. But if perchance they did, they were apt to settle down, sobered by real responsibilities. Neither Lloyd George nor Clemenceau, who each had championed radical causes, had laid hands on basic political and social institutions. Mussolini seemed to get along with the best people in Italy and even with the Vatican. Moreover, some kind of radicalism might have prophylactic value: the radical Right checked the radical Left, thus permitting the middle-of-the-road parties to tend the status quo.

A few men—politicians out of office and intellectuals withdrawn from the crush of affairs—discerned the forces at work and the shape of things to come. But the men of affairs of London and Paris did not. In fact, nearly all of them were surprised by Hitler's accession to power.

Not that the parties of the democratic Left in England, France, and other Western countries made a better showing than the representatives of high finance and big business. The Left-wing intelligentsia, since it contained a larger quotient of Jews than the intelligentsia on the Right, was more sensitive to, and denounced more vocally, Hitler's racist ideology; yet it seemed more reluctant than the circles of high finance and big business (which, too, counted many Jewish members) to draw the appropriate conclusions. If Hitler was as dangerous as the men of the Left quite rightly thought him to be and as much in cahoots with German high finance and big business as they quite wrongly asserted, then surely the Western democracies should have girded their loins and forced a showdown, the sooner the better. Nothing could have been further from the mind of the Left, especially its intelligentsia, than to prepare for all eventualities, that is, to get ready for military action. The Left's opposition to Fascist aggression *and* to any and all wars had been noted by Mussolini when the English Left condemned Italy's rape of Ethiopia—and subscribed to a peace resolution.

The Communists claimed they wanted to fight Mussolini and Hitler and their backers, the capitalistic exploiters, to restore, of all things, national unity, and to strengthen national defense. In Germany the Communists, though they fought the Nazis in many a street affray, did their best to hamstring the Weimar Republic. Their chosen enemies were the democratic parties, the Socialists and Catholic Centrists who had founded the republic and governed it. For the Communists' strategy has always been to destroy what they cannot control. In Germany the aim of their policy can be summed up in one word: chaos. They meant to destroy the republic which had so successfully resisted their attempts at control.

As the Communists saw it, the collapse of the Weimar Republic would give rise to a general disorder which they could exploit. Failing a revolution in Germany, Hitler, whom the Communists thought a mere stooge of German capitalism, would then turn Germany against France and England, thus restoring the European balance of power. The imperialists would confront one another, and the Soviet Union would thus be able to await developments and throw its weight, at the right moment and in the right place, into the balance. It is now quite clear from Stalin's dealings first with the Western democracies and then with Hitler that the embroilment of the "imperialists" ranked first among Stalin's objectives. The Western Communist parties were expendable. Their task was to keep the pot boiling until the great day when the imperialists would wage war upon, and destroy, one another and the Soviet Union could pick up the bits and pieces. Apparently the Communists, too, had not read *Mein Kampf*.

Why the Western democracies did not take the appropriate measures that could have altered the foreseeable course of events is now an interesting intellectual question. Their failure set in motion a long sequence of events that need not have happened— the coming of World War II and the successes, during that war's first phase, of the Nazis; and the making and unmaking of alliances; the partition of Germany; and the Communist conquest of Eastern Europe.

Perhaps the most important single cause of World War II was the persistent misreading by the West's statesmen and peoples of Germany's history and German national character. To begin with, Western public opinion failed to note the terrible odds which faced democracy in the Germany of the 1920's. Only a handful of Western observers realized how deep had been the wounds which inflation had inflicted upon the German populace's psyche. Subsequently, when Hitler had come to power, the Western democracies, since they could not find fault with themselves, transferred their guilt feelings to the German people as a whole. That they themselves were accessories to the fact was a horrid idea. Somebody had to be found upon whom to pin the blame for what had gone wrong. That somebody was not so much Hitler as the German people collectively.

Up until that time, ever since World War I, the Western democracies had exercised unchallenged political and economic mastery of the globe. The Soviets, though they had consolidated their control over Russia and, through the world party, reached into the affairs of many countries, did not dare to contest Western domination openly. Thus the world could have been what the Western democracies cared to make it—had they combined their resources and managed them wisely. Nor did they keep their respective houses in order. Had they taken timely action, the economic crisis beginning in 1929 could perhaps have been avoided or certainly kept within bounds. For in 1929 the economic resources of the Western democracies were more plentiful than they had ever been; the roots of democracy were deep. Yet even in America, Britain, and France the economic crisis touched off serious social and, in the case of France, political disturbances. Germany, only barely restored from war and inflation, had little surplus fat to lose; democracy was still a novel and delicate graft on tradition. Is it surprising that Germany succumbed to calamities which even the older, wiser, and richer democracies escaped only by the skin of their teeth? For three years the despair of mass unemployment ate at the vitals of Western society. At long last the Western democracies got the better of the disease. In

Germany, a weaker organism, the disease had by that time injured the heart.

Walking to and fro in a German garden, I tried to fit the pieces of the puzzle. I was twenty-eight years old. For a good many years I had not troubled about the great issues of the times; I had been wholly absorbed by the business of survival and the intermittent pleasures of living. Mine is not the stuff seers and prophets are made of. In Isaiah Berlin's metaphor, the hedgehog goes to ground clutching the one great truth; the fox chases many. I have run with the foxes, for I have never found one great truth.

In 1931 I did not foresee the Third Reich triumphant nor did I anticipate for one moment how wise or foolish Western statesmanship would turn out to be. I had not pondered views on the causes of the Great Depression and its likely remedies.

An Austrian diplomat in London had presented me with a copy of *Mein Kampf*. As the train pulled out of Dover for Paris I started on page 1 and, by the time I reached Berlin, had burrowed to the last. Long ago I had read Spengler's *The Decline of the West*. A few years later I had marked a copy of Ortega y Gasset's *Revolt of the Masses*. Spengler's cunning Caesars and Ortega y Gasset's barbarians from within, sprung from the womb of mass civilization, are none other than the "horrible simplifiers" of whom Jakob Burckhardt had warned his contemporaries bemused by the universal belief in progress. Allowing for his unique vulgarity, Adolf Hitler fitted the composite image. From what I knew, the definition of mass civilization applied to Germany. This, perhaps, was all one needed to know.

The sun was setting and a chill breeze stirred from the eastern plains. I went into the house. The son of my host suggested that we drive to the Kurfürstendamm and see what it had to offer. Berlin's night life had withstood politics and economics. The nightclubs were crowded and the drinks flowed freely. There were many foreigners about, who seemed to prefer Scotch to wine and French champagne to the saccharine national product. Not a few of the establishments were lavishly decorated, ornate gold-and-white paneling, rococo curlicues, and tall candelabra topped by pink lampshades. In other places, the trimmings were reassuringly unsubtle. A musician pounded away at jazz, a suggestively hoarse singer simulated Marlene Dietrich, and hardly anyone paid any attention. The hostesses—cheer-girls (*Animier-mädchen*), as they were called by the trade—were young and pretty, and made the champagne-drinking customers feel at home.

Some places catered to a highly specialized clientele. Nowhere, except perhaps in the reclaimed caves and hole-in-the-wall *boîtes* of the Left Bank, cavorted as weird an assortment of freaks as thronged those establishments which contributed most notably to the international renown of Berlin night-life. Though the industry sought to satisfy every possible and impossible demand of its customers, its combined effort at amusement yielded less gaiety than a zither and a few bottles of sour wine in the least of the inns along the fringe of the Vienna woods. Even in the best of times the Germans are not a gay people and, like Americans, work hard at having a good time as if it were a business chore or an athletic contest. These were not the best of times. Even deep in their cups the revelers could not shake off that clammy suspense which choked the city. Something was about to happen. In Christopher Isherwood's *pension*, stray nymphs, beat journalists, and petty imposters gulped their pleasures, one ear cocked to the thud of marching boots.

At the time the Kurfürstendamm was lined with terrace cafés. For the equivalent of fifty cents one could linger indefinitely over coffee or chocolate and a slab of pastry, and look at the passers-by. Most Continental Europeans love to promenade, perferably late in the evening, up and down broad avenues. Thus, along the Kurfürstendamm walked staid married couples, young girls and men in twos and threes, respectively, hard-faced women bearing enormous handbags, and old men and women singly carrying soiled parcels or net bags bulging with indeterminate objects. They had come to take the air, to look at one another, at the crowd in the cafés, and at the creamy pastry on the tables; to ply all kinds of nightly trades or for no purpose at all.

In Berlin, several hundred thousand people had been out of work for months or years. The dole paid for bread. The mass of unemployed kept to their quarters in the north and east of the city, the very sections that were walled up thirty years later. Yet a trickle of their emissaries seeped into the well-lit and well-policed reservations of the well-to-do Berlin along and to the west and south of the Kurfürstendamm. Clearly, they did not belong. They did not keep step with the strollers; they shambled as will all the hungry and poor.

Poverty is a relative concept and so is opulence. To my neighbors on the terrace opulence meant a chromium-hooded roadster and a flashy diamond on a pudgy finger; to the man hugging a soiled parcel, the badge of poverty in all big cities, opulence meant a piece of cake dabbed with whipped cream. All over the world the newly rich are likely to be conspicuous. To spend money discreetly is an art which is perfected only after many years of practice. But the German newly rich seemed unteachable. The destruction of most of Germany's old wealth and the eclipse of the old ruling classes deprived the newly rich of visible standards upon which they could have modeled their conduct. Thus, in the 1920's, the newly rich—those who had made their pile during the inflation and those who had skimmed the cream from the recovery boom—thronged to Berlin. Rapacious and gross, they put their stamp on the city's business and amusement.

In Berlin, the pace was fast, the baubles gaudy, and manners brash. Fortunes were being quickly made and quickly lost. These characteristics and a genuine zest for innovation suggested to Europeans the analogy of an American city. Even Americans held Berlin, of all European capitals, to be the most Americanized. For myself, I have never been able to nail down the meaning of "Americanization." The term might mean anything from snack bars to nylon stockings, from traffic jams to making a lot of things bigger than necessary, and to keeping one's pants up with belts rather than suspenders. It might also simply mean a synonym for successful, rich, powerful or boastful, and tawdry. Berlin was not quite like any other city in Europe. It had grown fast; it had few ancient landmarks and an appearance of improvisation. Yet, if one cared to look, there were the remnants of an older civilization.

Up until the middle of the last century, Paris, London, and Vienna had dwarfed Berlin, the capital of the poorest of the so-called Great Powers. The *ambiance* was provincial. Yet the Berliners were a special race, surprisingly unlike the rest of the king's subjects, the dull-witted, obedient farm laborers who tilled the soil of the Junkers and replenished the Prussian army.

In the early eighteenth century a colony of Huguenots, driven from France by Louis XIV, had settled in Berlin. Highly skilled artisans, they brought not only their crafts but also the intellectual and aesthetic zest of French culture. About that time immigrants from the Jewish communities along the Rhine and Moselle rivers, mostly of Sephardic origin, were attracted to the protection afforded by tolerant, commerce-minded monarchs. Freethinker, freemason, and French-speaking, Frederick II detested the German language as well as body hygiene. He proposed to make of Berlin a cosmopolite city, beautiful and rich, and, in spite of the resistance of the Spartan Junkers, he made fair progress in building his Athens on the Spree. Thus, by the first third of the nineteenth century Berlin had drawn to herself the great names of German arts, philosophy, and science. Rachel von Varnhagen, for example, presided over a salon which counted among its habitués the Humboldts, the Schlegels, the Arnims, Mendelssohn, as well as a number of second-stringers whose literary and scientific exploits are now forgotten.

After the establishment of the empire, Berlin grew by leaps and bounds into Europe's third largest city. Yet the grace, wit, and charm of the older Berlin, leisurely and slightly provincial, lived on into the metropolitan age. At a safe distance from the pretentious monstrosities commemorating the new empire, socially so insecure among the Great Powers, simple though commodious houses fronted quiet, tree-lined streets. Under their roofs one could find collections of the best in contemporary art assembled by men and women who had traveled to many places, loved music, spoke many languages, read widely, kept abreast of literary trends, and cultivated tact and moderation and the amenities of life. These were the circles of Count Kessler, patron of the avant-garde theater and literature, Princess Mechtilde Lichnowsky, friend of the Fauves; Count Pourtalès, connoisseur of eighteenth-century literature and painting; Carl Sternheim, who, a considerable private fortune notwithstanding, was one of the greatest German novelists; Max Reinhardt, the producer, Lovis

Corinth, the painter; Heinrich Mann, Thomas' more robust brother; and Helene Thiemig, the actress. Some of these people belonged to the society of the royal court, others did not and would not have cared to "belong" if birth and rank had ensured them entry. Be that as it may, the common bond of these people was civility and mutual aversion to the gross philistinism—*Banausentum*—of imperial Germany which, bellowing the word *Kultur,* threatened to squeeze the life out of German culture.

But Berlin's man in the street had never knuckled under. Armed with an expressive sense of humor, he poked fun at the helmeted and monocled clique that professed to speak for the Reich and for him. It was not that the Berliners were not good Germans; they were the best, and the only ones who were not crabbed by the national inferiority complex. They were, however, a race apart from the rest of their countrymen, the least awed by their country's martial might and the least servile. After many a storm and the passing of generations, the Berliners of today seem to have preserved their sense of humor and fierce independence. For, among all Germans, only the Berliners could have stood up, for more than fifteen years, to what is in fact an impossible situation.

When, in 1931, I came to Berlin, the prewar circles of the good life, which had defended Berlin against the barbarian invasion, had shrunk. Many of its celebrated figures had moved away, died, or sunk into the anonymity of poverty. But a few held on, and a few newcomers had worthily taken some of the empty places. Thus, in the lengthening shadow of chaos and in the midst of the rising tide of vulgarity, there were still islands of civility. I had the good fortune to be admitted to some of them. Perhaps it was the awareness of impending doom that then made life so sweet; for these were the last days of Pompeii.

How could so worldly a city and so skeptic a citizenry be taken in by so uncouth an oaf as Hitler? Why did they behave so execrably toward their Jewish neighbors? I envy those moralists and experts in national psychology who have come up with complete answers to both of these questions; for, after thirty years, I am still puzzled. I still can do no more than give a few sadly disjointed answers.

I do not believe that a very large number of Berliners were, at any time, fooled by Hitler. Hitler did not like Berlin and this for a very good reason, for he was never able to root out its hard core of stubborn, though passive, resistance. Just as the rest of the German people, the Berliners put up with Hitler because there was little else they could do. The upper classes—the high officialdom and the aristocracy as well as the high military— hardly dissimulated their outright distaste for the Nazis. A large sector of the working class, especially the non-Communist element, went woodenly through the motions of obligatory Führer-worship but kept on thinking its own thoughts. To find Hitler's genuine followers one must descend to the swamp of lower middle-class frustration and the reptile pit of turncoat "Communists." Of course, every large city has its drifters, mental misfits, perverts, and criminals. In Berlin, Hitler picked his most trusted followers from that same *Lumpenproletariat* which had harbored him in Vienna and introduced him to the anti-Semitic mumbo-jumbo of Dr. Schönerer.

So great and so understandable has been the revulsion of the civilized world against the systematic extermination of millions of European Jews that it is now no easy task to review the tense, tragic relationships of Gentile and Jew in Germany. Before World War I, anti-Semitism was no more violent and widespread in Germany than in any other major European country with the exception of Italy, where anti-Semitism had become extinct centuries ago. Next to Russia, with her periodic pogroms, anti-Semitism was strongest in France. In France it was the upper class, especially the monarchist circles, which embraced most readily the racist doctrines developed by such widely read and gifted writers as Gobineau, Daudet, and Drumont.

In England it was the lower classes that looked upon the Jew as a contemptuous and most un-English alien; as a matter of fact, they still do. Yet even educated Englishmen did not trouble to dissimulate their anti-Semitic bias. Indeed, many celebrated English novelists of the past hundred years—and not only Dickens— sketched highly uncomplimentary portraits of Jews and, in a matter-of-fact way, indulged in anti-Semitic asides.

In Germany, anti-Semitism was confined to certain middle-class citadels of snobbery such as, for example, a few, and by no means all, exclusive clubs, regiments, and university fraternities. In prewar Germany, Jews, orthodox or converts to another faith, were not denied access to any apartment building, real-estate location, country club, or resort hotel as they are in the United States to this day. Emperor William II, though a man of many crotchets, genuinely revered success and ability no matter where he found it. Among his most intimate friends were Jews, some ennobled and some just plain Herr, as, for example, the Jewish shipowner—Herr Ballin. In urban communities Jewish bankers, businessmen, and professionals were highly respected. The government suppressed with Draconic severity any anti-Semitic manifestations such as vandalism perpetrated on synagogues, a phenomenon chiefly confined to certain Rhineland cities.

Not that Germany had become the Garden of Eden. The embers of anti-Semitism still smoldered beneath quaint medieval gables of many a small German town and, even more shamefully, in many a professorial breast. Even so liberal a German historian as Meinecke let slip into his memoirs an anti-Semitic bias which made nonsense of his democratic pretensions. The Germany that rewarded Heinrich Heine so ill in his lifetime and then, upon his death, celebrated him as her national poet, remained, one generation later, as exasperatingly ambiguous as she had ever been. Yet, on the eve of World War I, anti-Semitism, though not dead, seemed at least to have lost its poisonous sting. During the war Jews fought bravely by the side of their Gentile comrades. Some of the most ardent German nationalists who, before and during the war, argued and publicized Germany's claim to a "place in the sun" were Jews. It seemed as though the community in fate of the German people at war had submerged forever the hatred of religion and race.

After the outbreak of World War I and especially after the Russian Revolution, several hundred thousand East European Jews, uprooted first by the changing fortunes of war and then by civil war, fled to Germany. A large part of them settled in Berlin. They had little in common in appearance and speech with German Jewry. Most of them spoke a German patois—a blend of

German and Yiddish—which sounded harsh and displeasing to German ears. Having lost their possessions, they were animated by a fierce will to succeed and a spirit of mutual help. They quickly adjusted themselves to the ways of German commerce and, having been long familiar with the vagaries of Russian fiscal policy, to the intricacies of German inflationary finance. Many of them made large fortunes. Many of them, who for the first time enjoyed the secure ease of a free society, no longer hid their wealth as, within the Pale, they had been forced to do. They spent conspicuously. They bought those precious things, animate and inanimate, which the luxury trades had for sale. Many of them left Germany after a while; few cared to assume German nationality and take their place in community affairs. Many of them, especially some of the most successful ones, moved on to Britain, France, and the United States. But hundreds of thousands stayed in Germany. The older German Jewish community, highly sensitive to these developments from the start, contemplated unhappily the likely and unfortunate consequences of the Eastern influx. For the first time in many centuries, there existed conditions which favored the resurgence of popular anti-Semitism: the conspicuous strangeness of a large minority to German folkways; the increase of its economic power at a time when most Germans suffered severe economic privations; and the consequent strengthening of the tendency of the masses to blame the relatively vulnerable minority in their midst for their many real and imagined misfortunes. Enough explosive stuff had accumulated; it needed only a madman or a criminal to set it off. Under normal conditions a society can control its lunatic and criminal fringe; by 1930, however, conditions in Germany were far from normal.

What I have said thus far about this painful topic almost every observant person, German or foreigner, knew at that time. But that the explosion, when it occurred, would smash the face of civilized society in Germany, this no one foresaw. I have made it plain that I do not believe in the unique nastiness of the German people. World War II was Hitler's war; a large number of Germans marched off gaily under the Swastika, confident in the magic powers of their leader and Stukas. The easy victories abroad of the first year smothered the far from negligible opposition at home. Had war not broken out, giving Hitler an ever tighter hold on the populace and insulating segments of German society such as the army, bureaucracy, church, and intelligentsia from one another, and Germany from the rest of the world, the chances are that, despite the devilish and sadistic ingenuity of the gangster elite, the persecution of the Jews would not have culminated in a genocidal orgy.

Did the great mass of the German people know what was going on or did they not? Probably they did—just as we know about juvenile delinquency, discrimination in the South, corruption in municipal government, and all kinds of atrocious goings-on in our own community. We do know about these things. By the moral principles we profess, they are our business. Yet, with the exception of a few among us, we manage to convince ourselves that they are *not* our business and that we cannot do anything about them anyway. In times of national emergency, we are even less inclined than in "normal" times to look for trouble by seeking to improve private and public morality, not to speak of the moral conduct of our rulers, whose power over us has been increased by the real or alleged necessities of the emergency. It seems to me that this analogy stands up fairly well— about as well as any analogy between a stable society like the American, on the one hand, and an unstable society subjugated by an alien usurper like the German, on the other. This still leaves a great deal unexplained.

I cannot see the beam in my own eye; worse, I cannot see the mote in the eye of others. I cannot see the world as others who suffer from the same affliction as I do see it. When, by my lights, I did right I found that others, my best friends included, did not think so. When I did wrong I was not only easily forgiven but, when the tissues of half-truths and half-lies by which we live had closed over the injury, I was credited with a noble motive which I had not had.

Though I easily compromise for the sake of my convenience, I am not tolerant. Toleration of another man's peculiarities purchases society's forbearance of our own. This bargain—a bargain with one's own sense of fitness and self-interest—is not an act of

love. Toleration, that frosty virtue, is not passionate as is love or
hate. In my magnanimity and wisdom, I do not love; I tolerate. I
tolerate almost everybody, except men who smoke cigars between courses. Those whom I have loved I can count upon the
fingers of one hand. Many people have stirred my compassion;
but with hardly any of them do I care to pass the time of day.

I tolerate Swiss, Dutchmen, Argentines, and even people who
make noises and show off, as, for example, Italians water skiing
and driving sports cars. With all of these I will settle for civil,
though distant, relationships. I am drawn to Japanese, Irishmen,
and Spaniards of both sexes, Russian women and intellectuals of
all ethnic origins, especially Jewish. I have read no further in the
book of toleration.

In the future, so we are told, cultural differences will diminish
in importance, since we are headed for the new jet and television
universal civilization. I am not so sure that the great cultural
wherry-mixer will blend all races, classes, and castes into a stable
compound. To the contrary, such a universal society is likely to
develop an intolerance far more sophisticated and snobbisms far
more differentiated and exasperating than our ethnical-minded
cultures with their relatively simple and concise class distinctions
have dreamed up.

At the behest of President Hoover, Germany's foreign credi-
tors agreed to a moratorium on the conversion of funds into
foreign currency. My negotiations with sundry banks and government offices dragged on. Business took me to Frankfurt, then a
financial center second only in importance to Berlin. Frankfurt
was then, and is now, an unattractive town. The fact that Goethe
was born there does not redeem it. The nearby Rhine, bordered
by celebrated vineyards and semirestored ruins, is one of the
most overrated objectives of international tourism. The barges on
the river, flying all kinds of pennants and the crew's underwear,
are pleasant to watch.

The Frankfurt Nazis were more uninhibited than their Berlin
comrades; the ordinary folk were more scared. I did not tarry.
To breathe an air less charged with tension and doom, I went on
to Geneva, Paris, and London. Most of the time these excursions

were justified by meetings with our fellow sufferers under the moratorium.

Late in 1931 I called upon one of the great figures of the City. His son had married the daughter of a great and debt-ridden nobleman, an almond-eyed and most un-English beauty whom I had met in Munich, where, a paying guest in a noble house, she had studied German-without-tears. The eminent financier asked my advice as to whether he and the young couple should go to Garmisch to ski or, because the snow conditions in the Vorarlberg were reported to be better, to Sankt Anton. Having settled this question to his satisfaction, he asked me what I thought about German politics. I presented to him what I thought were the obvious facts of the situation, obvious to anyone who had sat long enough in a café on the Kurfürstendamm. The financier seemed impressed, far more impressed than my information seemed to warrant. He asked me to lunch the following day at his house, where I would meet a few of his friends.

In the airy drawing room of a splendid Regency building my host introduced me to about ten men, some of whose names I had read in the papers. The mahogany tabletops had a warm sheen, the Georgian silver was polished, and the sherry translucent amber. For sheer elegance no man can rival an upper-class Englishman in his prime. And my host and his friends were English, upper class, well preserved, and rich.

In the course of the meal, served with excellent hock, our host asked me to repeat briefly what, the day before, I had told him about Germany. I chose my words carefully, awed by clear blue eyes and graying mustaches. I said that, at the rate things were going, Hitler was likely to come to power before another two years were up. I spoke of the manifest distress of a large part of the population; the increasing difficulties of the republican government, hard pressed to find the funds needed for ordinary services as well as relief and public works; and the ever more violent attacks by extremist factions upon the democratic middle. I briefly summarized the contents of *Mein Kampf*. It was here that I made my mistake.

I saw, too late, that what until then had been polite attention changed to incredulity. Finally, the most celebrated member of my audience broke in and asked me whether I took seriously all this trash. Slightly rattled, I said that I did. I tried to explain that it did not matter whether he or I took *Mein Kampf* seriously as long as its author did. And its author was likely to rule Germany provided those who could, the English and French, did not take drastic steps to prevent it. To help me back to the safe shore of common sense, my host asked me what were the drastic steps I envisaged. I suggested that a conference be called to discuss the revision of certain provisions of the Versailles peace treaty which now had become meaningless anyway since they could no longer be enforced. Furthermore, the German government should be given generous economic support instead of being badgered about the repayment of foreign credits which could not be paid off without a substantial increase of German exports.

Silence settled over the room. It was broken by the celebrated grandee, who ventured the opinion that Hitler, even if he were to come to power, would soon forget about *Mein Kampf* and settle down to the business of keeping on good terms with Germany's principal trading partners. Not to embarrass the stray young man, he casually added that not only had he talked to His Majesty's ambassador in Berlin but also somebody he knew had sounded out people in Hitler's entourage. These individual Nazi chieftains were not exactly gentlemen, but seemed to hold the English, though not the French, in high esteem.

I knew I was beaten. I also knew that I did not belong in the airy Regency room. My suit had not been cut by Anderson and Shepard. I got my coffee down, thanked my host, bowed slightly—I had been told that in England one does not bow deeply, and preferably not at all—and took my leave. I soon discovered that my host and his friends, who most certainly were no fools about great affairs, were, in fact, well in advance of informed, not to speak of popular, opinion. My uneasiness grew: did I see ghosts where these intelligent men saw but reassuring realities—the might of their own country, the impotence of Germany and an insignificant mountebank who, if ever there should be any need, could be managed like any other impecunious demagogue?

Chapter Eight

I RETURNED to the United States in the fall of 1932, when the American people had elected Franklin D. Roosevelt by an overwhelming majority. In Europe, Conservatives, Liberals, Labourites, Clericals, Fascists, and Nazis with surprising unanimity acclaimed Roosevelt's accession to power. His rhetoric was lofty; his airs grand. More important still, there had to be a change. Everybody sensed that this self-assured, sardonic man would bring it.

Perhaps my most vivid memory of the first few months following upon Roosevelt's inauguration is of the ease with which things began to right themselves. Among the several factors which brought about this reversal, the most important was the sublime confidence of the man himself. The inner strength of the man radiated—in the literal meaning of the word—into the hearts of the many. Change itself—new faces and a new style of public conduct—exercised a therapeutic effect on the temper of the masses.

More likely than not, the business cycle would have righted

itself without a change in political leadership. The physical wealth of the country was as great as it had ever been. U.S. Steel and General Motors had not been blitzed. Their plants remained. Their managers, engineers, and workers had not been deported to Kamchatka. Certainly, the general public was prepared to consume more lustily than ever before, and the producers were equipped better than ever to cater to public demand. Nothing stood in the way of that happy union except paralysis of mind. Indeed, it was this desolate stillness which gave the last and most harrowing phase of the depression its haunting dreamlike quality. Men shuffled about aimlessly, stood hunched on corners, stared vacantly at billboards.

But the Great Depression had done more than upset the economic balance; it had called forth genii that economic magic could not put back into the bottle. The Roosevelt revolution marked the culmination of social change. The historic structure was breaking down.

The Marxists, in their simplistic way, envisaged the class conflict as a contest over the means of production between entrepreneurs and wage earners, capitalists and proletarians. Yet, modern society was more complex than Marx's crude model. A new elite was reaching for the levers of power; in fact, a good many of these levers were already in its hands. The new elite still lacked the formal seal of political authority, for the exigencies of total war compelled the old ruling class to assimilate by cooption, so to speak, a growing number of technicians. Thus, the technical expert, that is, the scientist, the administrator, the manager took his place in the councils of state as well as in the board rooms of the great industries engaged in the production of strategic supplies. Moreover, the advent of the technicians, rather than growing state power and the increased burden of welfare legislation, altered traditional property and social relationships. Hence, although the various egalitarian ideologies assailed the hereditary principle,—a man's right to bequeath his property or social status or both to his kin—the most serious challenge came from the new elite of expertise and merit.

In America, Berle and Means were the first to show how wide the gap had grown between ownership and management, and

James Burnham, an early defector from Marxism, popularized this theme in his *Managerial Revolution*. Although nearly a generation earlier, Gaetano Mosca, Robert Michels, and Vilfredo Pareto in Europe had discerned the emergence of a new ruling class, their speculations did not stir the curiosity of American academic circles, for their case studies, drawn from life in the crabbed nation-states of Continental Europe, did not seem to suggest relevant analogies for Americans. Nevertheless, within the past thirty years the rise of the hierarchy of certificate and diploma—the bureaucratic, technocratic, and meritocratic elites —transformed American society beyond recognition. No doubt the forces of change were present before the New Deal accorded them recognition. Without the accession to power of new men they might have waited a long time—perhaps another twenty years—for the political act of deliverance.

If on the eve of revolution Roosevelt harbored these thoughts about momentous social change, he did not tell anybody about it. To his fingertips a man of the old, receding America, he contented himself, throughout his whole reign, to give change its head. Under prevailing conditions, this, for all one knows, was supreme statesmanship. Endowed with a canny sense of power, he gauged the momentum of the moving mass without particularly bothering about its direction. No American politician before or after him knew better how to make things happen that were going to happen anyway. Unburdened by ideological commitments, he retained to the end his jovial rapport with the masses, who shared his aversion to philosophical consistency. A clever man and hence mistrustful of intellectual subtleties, he commanded the unswerving loyalty of the great mass of American intellectuals, who for the first time had gained public recognition and access to the seats of the mighty. Like Emperor Claudius, he gave his trust to freedmen and, like Claudius, withdrew it whenever he so pleased. The freedman's sole claim to power was the master's favor.

According to Hegel, all historical happenings are necessary. In retrospect, the Rooseveltian era was "necessary," for it smoothed the perilous transition from one American way of life to another American way of life, even though the one seemed to lead in the opposite direction from the other. And who else could have presided over the precipitate, if not bewildered, debut of the United States upon the stage of world power, cast in the role of leading player?

Roosevelt was many things to many men. He baffled those who thought they knew him best. Charming and witty, vindictive and humorless, expansive and secretive, this patrician demagogue has yet to find his Tacitus.

In this age, conservative regimes have not excelled in the patronage of the arts and letters; the symbolic figure of the 1920's, for example, was the tycoon, and his species does not inspire dramatists and writers in search of tragic heroes. Though the arts and letters thrived on the periphery of the business civilization, the intellectual found business and professional politics poor pickings. To be sure, success in the arts and letters brought ample remuneration, and established academics made a fair living. But the poets and the thinkers were not in the midst of things. A few of them, especially those who had not hit the jackpot of fashion, felt themselves strangers in their own land and their wares an unessential commodity.

The disaffection of the intellectual from American society antedated the Great Depression by a good many years. During the first quarter of the twentieth century the best novels of social protest that took apart bourgeois morals were written by Americans; but their message seemed lost on the American educated public, not to speak of the masses. The New Deal not only emancipated the intelligentsia but also thrust it into the service of political and social causes. Moreover, the breakthrough of the American intellectual coincided with the exodus from Central Europe of a host of intellectuals, mostly—though not exclusively—Jewish. Thus the greatest European talent, scientific, artistic, and literary, made its way to America. On the whole, it was accorded a warm welcome.

One result of this influx and of the rise of the American intellectual with his long-standing partiality toward European culture was the Europeanization of New York. New York blossomed out in experimental theaters, avant-garde galleries, and innumerable good restaurants. Not the least contributory cause of this culture efflorescence was the repeal of Prohibition. A new era of conviviality had dawned; the café house became a focal point of American sociability and the base of a Society that was to bear its name.

The mid-thirties were one of the happiest periods of my life. My distrust of the new rulers, grounded in my readings on classic history, dissolved in a sense of well-being, heightened by a renewed zest for life which rediscovers, after the successful completion of convalescence, how green is the valley, how warm is the sun.

In this era, even a moderately intelligent man could discern that history was about to be made in the most sensational fashion.

Perhaps I was looking only for a plausible reason in the "objective" situation, absolving me from close self-examination. Nevertheless, I decided to quit my job; I had become restless.

I lived in an apartment in the East Seventies. I had a few friends and many acquaintances; I entered the ranks of that most fortunate and free-roaming band of brothers, the men-about-town. All kinds of ingredients such as good looks, wit, or some skill in public entertainment are helpful in the making of the successful man-about-town; two, however, are necessary and sufficient, namely, an air of civilty and endurance. I arrived punctually at dinner, wrote measured thank-you notes to my weekend hosts, deferred to my neighbor's conversational interests and, when the occasion was a lengthy one, sustained the proper balance of restraint and *joie de vivre* until the formal termination of the proceedings.

The rules on how to make one's way in society—how to please oneself by pleasing others—are timeless. De La Rochefoucauld, Chesterfield, Wilde, and Proust arrived at the identical conclusions, including the conclusion that the game is not worth the candle. One of the rules of the game is that in order to win, one must simulate indifference. De La Rochefoucauld wrote: "In trying to establish oneself in the world, one does all one can to seem established there already."

It is gratifying to reinforce, if one can, a highly personal decision with general considerations such as historical necessity or mission; the crusader took the cross to liberate the Saviour's tomb, not to get away from his drafty keep and nagging wife.

The publicity releases notwithstanding, most business is dull business. It takes a long time and unusual luck to reach the plateau of high adventure, to slough off the routine chores and unshackle the imagination. In whatever men do there is a place for creativity. The smooth merger of several companies is as much a work of aesthetic perfection as a battle, planned, fought, and won. To the connoisseur, both are as satisfying feats of creative imagination as the harmonies of Caravaggio and Mozart. What is perfectly poised is aesthetically peerless—Nijinsky's leap; Napoleon's center thrust at Austerlitz; the sweep of Michelangelo's brush that interposes a few inches of eternity between the hand of man and the finger of God. No doubt, circumstances and aptitude—and especially the circumstance that challenges a particular aptitude—are necessary for the liberation of creative powers.

We do not know what makes the man of genius but we know that, whatever else he might be, he is an artisan, the artful contriver of effects and master of his tools. I cannot recognize sublimity except there where I find the mark of craftsmanship. Perhaps it is my frivolous disposition which diverts my interest to how, and how well, a thing is made rather than to what purpose it serves. Perhaps Western civilization has made a fetish of self-expression, preferably self-expression in whatever one does to make a living. Be that as it may, Western man, since he does not regard work as a necessary evil but as an ennobling or, at least, a worthy pursuit, seeks a unity of life, of utilitarian pursuit and spiritual fulfillment, which no previous civilization achieved except for a small minority of the people.

The so-called moonlight civilizations of this earth, that is, the civilization in retreat before Westernization or secluded on some inaccessible or remote cliff, do not view work in the light of the Western gospel of work. Hence, the many tragicomic misunderstandings between the Western and the so-called underdeveloped peoples.

To the Hindu work means involvement with matter. It may be necessary; but it is not conducive to spiritual well-being, an unclean bond between man's inner reality and the external world of illusion. To a Polynesian, work signifies that minimal effort addressed to the collection of coconuts, the weaving of pretty baskets, and the entertaining game of catching fish. If this minimal work is done, there is time to recline in the shade, to plunge into cool pools, to dance, and to attend to the many and exacting rituals of the communal cult. To both the Hindu and the Polynesian as well as to the Catholic-Irish and the Carib-island folk, the idea of saving, of capital accumulation, is a repugnant idea which interferes with far more important and pleasurable business. There remains the gnawing thought that these people are closer to the meaning of life than are we, obsessed as we are by the twin ideas of progress and productivity, of putting tomorrow ahead of today and laying up today reserves for that greedy tomorrow.

Shortly after my return to New York, I met Mrs. C., whose intellectual interests ranged as widely as her impeccable social connections. Mrs. C. served a variety of excellent teas, Indian, Formosan, and Chinese, and the thinnest cucumber sandwiches. She bade her friends drop in any afternoon. Birdlike, vivacious, well-read and widowed, she took pleasure in swift conversation. Among her lions were literary figures of the day, rich men of assured position, a few politicians of liberal learnings, and friends of her three sons. The oldest son, an engineer, held a degree from M.I.T.; another had gone into the brokerage business, rode to the hounds, and piloted his plane; the youngest, descending from Harvard, had just made his debut on Broadway, an achievement founded in equal parts upon his considerable private means, fair schooling, and good looks. The engineer and his wife, daughter of a successful architect, had joined forthwith the patrician wing of the New Deal.

Out of heated arguments grew an enduring friendship. Not that I caviled at the general idea, a fair share for all the people in the growing riches of the land and an end to the concentration of wealth and power in the hands of a few share-pushers. But I thought that these goals could be reached at a price far lower than that which would be charged to the national account by the New Deal, its politicians, and its burgeoning bureaucracy. The common man was about to change masters. More likely than not, his new ones might turn out far more exacting and infinitely more difficult to get rid of than his old ones. My friends were far too elated by the winds of change and too certain of the future to take umbrage at my objections, particularly since, far from denouncing Mr. Roosevelt as a "traitor to his class," I conceded his ideological innocence. Without poise and counterpoise, the pall of boredom settles upon the gathering of even the most lively minds. My friends accorded a fair hearing to the views of a conservative who was not so bigoted as to quote Adam Smith and Alexander Hamilton.

At Mrs. C.'s I met Raoul de Roussy de Sales, son of a French father and an American mother. Raoul's paternal ancestors had dotted the crags of the Haute-Savoie with their castles. One member of the clan, a bishop in the reign of Henry IV, had founded an Order for "strong souls with weak bodies" deterred by their delicate constitution from entering more ascetic orders. He wrote charming letters to a widowed noblewoman who supported his good works and achieved sainthood. His shrunken body lies, preserved under glass, in the nave of an appallingly ugly church at Annecy. Raoul, himself had made a precarious recovery from a long bout with tuberculosis; was weak in body, hardly ever free of pain, and strong in soul; and reported tersely on the American scene to *Paris Soir*, the French daily with the largest circulation.

Raoul dressed immaculately. His emaciated body supported a long magnificent head. The eyes were large and opaque; the slightly crooked, heavy-lipped mouth was set between deep furrows from nostril to cheek, the nose hooked, and the skin tight and pallid. His voice was deep and resonant. A much-sought-after speaker, he could hold a crowd. Casual and terse, he was that rarest of all born conversationalists who, in a small company, could make even the dullard feel that, though he never caught the bouncing ball, he was a much-needed player on the team.

For reasons unknown to me, Raoul's family had lost, after World War I, a once ample fortune. For a while Raoul made a living as a music critic in Paris. There he met the statuesque wife of a New York banker. They fell in love and were married, the New York banker standing obligingly aside. After a while they set-

tled in New York. To make ends meet—they never did—Raoul
supplemented his reporter's pay by contributing crisp essays on
arts and letters, peoples and places to the glossy magazines. Occasionally a Gallic turn of phrase stole artfully into his smooth
English prose. His output sold well, but not well enough to meet
the added expense of the birth of a son. Raoul knew that he had
not long to live; so did his wife. As the war drew near, Raoul
joined forces with the few French non-Communist journalists
who called forthrightly for military intervention against Hitler.

Upon the fall of France in 1940, Raoul, though bedridden most
of the time, accepted General de Gaulle's appointment to the
French Delegation in New York, the quasi-diplomatic representa-
tion of the Resistance. Raoul dragged himself to Washington.
Roosevelt took a liking to this witty, disenchanted, and determined man. Raoul struggled valiantly to obtain an American
commitment less ambiguous than that which Mr. Roosevelt, loath
to offend Marshall Pétain and cross Mr. Churchill's tenebrous
diplomacy, was prepared to give to the Gaullist cause. Toward
the end of this grim year Raoul died.

Friendships that are not reinforced by habit are not likely to
endure. I am not sure that, after a lapse of twenty years, Raoul
and I would still be friends. The mobility of modern civilization
puts all human relationships, including friendship, to hard wear.
Temperamentally, Raoul and I were an oddly assembled pair.
Raoul was certain that the great clock was running down and
that he would be gone by the time it stopped ticking. My appe-
tites and curiosity, on the other hand, were boundless, all the
more boundless because the fallow years had denied them satisfaction. Not that Raoul lacked courage; the lion fought, but the
lion was tired, tired unto death. Of his deep compassion none was
left for himself.

Perhaps our friendship owed most to the fact that we were
both bilingual, had been raised in Europe, and had come to
America as young men. From experience, we knew that the
world was more fragile than most of our friends suspected; by
instinct, we expected it to break up. Since our minds had been
shaped by humanist education—Raoul's was the more finished,
mine the more rudimentary product—we liked to talk about gen-

eral issues and particular people. Thus, I surmise, we came to like
each other.

Perhaps every true friendship among men is charged by pedagogical tension: the teacher and the pupil, priest and acolyte,
master and apprentice. At any rate, friends stand at the turning
points of my life, and I hold with the idea of providential collision or destiny, mercifully veiled. I was seeking I knew not exactly what. I met Raoul. In a casual way Raoul, who managed to
give his most carefully contrived effects an improvised air, maneuvered the conversation to what I knew and cared about.
Providence had seen to it that he, too, cared about the same
things. Of all things, he cared most intensely about ideas, and I
was one of the beneficiaries of his wisdom. It was as if I had
found again what I had always cared for and had lost in hot
pursuit of a variety of unsubstantial baubles. I thought I knew
where I wanted to go. I knew for a certainty that I had to start all
over again. *D'où venons nous; où sommes nous; où allons nous?*

The question "Whither America?" we agreed, could be answered easily. America would move in the same direction as Europe, and the differences in American and European history
could be reduced to a mere gap in time of about twenty years—
more or less. Thus the New Deal retraced the pattern which the
tepid, though highly effective revolt of the Fabians had imposed,
during the first two decades of the century, upon English society.
In some respects the New Deal was a revolution from the top
down. A relatively small number of militants, a good many of
whom wore no easily identifiable labels, had captured one of the
two major political parties or, at least, gained privileged access to
its leadership. Again, a somewhat similar fate had befallen the
English Liberals. For a while the Liberal party accommodated
some of the camouflaged commandos who were later to join with
the regular troops of the Labour party. And then the Labour
party ate up the Liberal party.

Modern Western societies, bemused as they are now by the
bliss of security, are reluctant to face up to the unpleasant though
well-documented fact that history is a disorderly business. For
that matter, all great historical developments have culminated in
spasms. The idea of gradualism appeals to all those of us who

want to reconcile a quiet life with general progress. In fact, all great changes are wrought either by fear of calamity or by calamity itself. Very large numbers or even the majority of men might be agreed that far-reaching social changes are necessary; yet, so great is the inertia of a state of things that prevails simply because it has prevailed for a long time that reasonable agreement does not issue in reasonable action.

The French Revolution was an unmitigated disaster from which France has not recovered to this day. The great spokesmen of representative government from Edmund Burke to Alexis de Tocqueville, who witnessed the catastrophe or were in time to examine at first hand the resultant wreckage, were agreed that the scant achievement of the French Revolution had been bought at an exorbitant price. Yet the voices of the witnesses were drowned by the chorus of philosophers and historians who, intoxicated by the idea of onward and upward progress, profess to discern, long after the event, how constructive and noble the French Revolution had been. There was hardly a thing of goodness and beauty which, when it fell into the hands of French revolutionary leaders and their factious mobs, was not maimed or torn to shreds. The succeeding republics, notwithstanding the opulence of their ruling classes, did not lift a finger to repair the damage; to this incontrovertible fact the great historic religious and lay buildings of France, the most civilized country in Europe, bear mute witness.

Even in our times the flowering of a great industrial society, namely, the German, was topped by a revolt which exploded into the face of Western civilization as a whole. I have always held, and still hold, that the Nazis were the carriers of a Western disease that, though it raged with particular virulence in Germany, was endemic to all of Western civilization. Raoul and I debated this point a great deal. Raoul, who, like most Western intellectuals, had vanquished all myths except that of the eugenic dastardliness of the German race, professed to see the Nazi rising as the millennial revolt of the Teuton against Western civility. Since, at that time, Nazi power seemed the one and only threat to Western civilization and the Communists were discreetly lying in wait, Raoul's easy identification of Germany as the dog-in-the-

Western-manger seemed plausible and fetching. Raoul, like most New Dealers, professed himself a liberal, meaning a man who favored increasing state intervention, but who fought shy of the Socialist label. How liberalism got stood on its head is as interesting a study of semantic inversion as Marx's upending of Hegelian dialectic. Such hair-raising operations require not so much a logical mind as facility with words.

In the 1930's men who could explain the inwardness of the New Deal's random achievements, and explain it to the politicians as well as to their constituents, were in great demand. Raoul heeded the call. He rejected socialism not only because, in America, the Great Depression had failed in swelling the ranks of the various Socialist parties but also because the intricacies of Marxist dogma baffled the mass of pragmatic Americans. The varieties of European fascism had little of marketable value to offer, for their racist flavor repelled too large a segment of the American multiracial community. Capitalism, so Raoul thought, had revealed itself as both morally untrustworthy and socially obsolescent. What was to be done? The answer was—the New Deal or, rather, its brief experience: democracy *and* collectivism. Raoul, who, like most intellectuals, was more impressed by accomplished facts than are men of action, sincerely believed that President Roosevelt had answered the age-old question of authority and freedom, that the lion and the lamb would lie down together. Like most European intellectuals of his generation, he had always thought that all the issues of the times narrowed down to the confrontation of capitalism and socialism. Now, miraculously, the New Deal pointed the Third Way.

Perhaps it was the memories of my Mid-European youth that slanted my views on bold social experiments, for in my most impressionable years I had had my fill of revolutions. At any rate, I disliked revolutionary politics and even more those who eulogize, from the safe shelter of the academic tower, the destruction, in the name of social justice, of old orders. It has been said that the worst peace is better than the best war, and under modern conditions this axiom is about as true as can be any generalization about politics. The best revolution, even a bloodless one, is worse than gradual change by due legal process, no matter how exasperatingly slow be its pace. Certainly, of all forms of government, democracy is the frailest and historically the most short-lived.

Then I was far from didactically minded. Surely I did not aspire to academic expertise in political theory. The issue was highly personal: When I left Europe I carried with me the fixed image of America's wide horizons uncluttered by barracks and fences, bureaucracy and ideology. The New Deal sowed the seeds of both the bureaucratic mushroom and the ideological nettle; dismayed, I observed the indecent cross-fertilization of the two. I did not feel drawn to the New Dealers whom I met. Between ostentatious wealth and ostentatious social consciousness, I unhesitatingly choose the former, for its exponents are politically less dangerous and, in general, more pleasant to live with. Although I had not done well at making money, I was repelled by the shrill denunciation of the moneyed, the "malefactors of great wealth," the battle cry of the levelers. Then I suspected—now I firmly believe—that the Great Depression in America was a mere episode in an international tragedy. It issued from World War I and its settlement rather than from the greed or stupidity of American bankers, not to speak of the economic system. Nowadays the bankers are socially conscious. They go to any lengths not to be conspicuous. They defer humbly to authority, public and intellectual. Their banks, like the rest of us, are much safer and more closely controlled than they were before the New Deal domesticated the profit motive. One part of the human condition in America, heretofore naked before the gusts of fortune, has been decently covered; another one is now exposed to the ravages of a more intimate, more corrosive affliction. Again, it might be that the world has moved, and that America merely has moved with it.

Milk turns sour without changing its appearance. Again and again democracy has been subverted by those who profess themselves fervently and, more often than not, sincerely to be democratic. Nearly always democracy has been toppled by a process of slow erosion, imperceptible to the average citizen—a modest departure here and a little streamlining there in the name of improvement and "modernization." I believe that what has kept the flavor of American democracy sweet has been the citizenry's abiding distrust of authority and the vigor and variety of associations, from family and church to corporation and trade union, flourishing in the private sector of life. The excellence of the Constitution, devised as a safeguard against the despotism of the one and the many, monarch and mob, would have stood for little had the American people allowed politics to encroach on the profusion of their private associations and on the idiosyncrasies and the very disorderliness of their everyday lives. The New Deal's early passion for planning and centralization was the first cloud to cast its shadow upon the haphazard idyl. Since then the cloud has grown bigger. War and the speed-up of urbanization have taught the masses not so much the wisdom of order—they detest it as much as they always have—but of letting somebody else keep it for them.

In predepression America, a good many people were far from secure, though most of them did not know it. There was much disorderly dealing and brawling, and the servants of the state, now omnipresent, could not always be found to supervise the traffic and apprehend the miscreants. Corruption was more brazen, though no more insidious and rewarding, than it is now. There was, above all else, a sense of freedom, exhilarating and pungent, and books explaining that freedom meant the privilege of paying taxes and being tagged with a number remained still to be written. Like many Central Europeans of the westward migration, I rejoiced in being free in the American way which forthrightly put the individual ahead of the collectivity. Not that Americans ever lacked a high communal spirit; for no other people rivaled their voluntary dedication to the public good. But Herr Hegel's teachings, namely, that true freedom consists in obeying the all-powerful state, had not yet won a hearing in influential American quarters. Indeed, most Americans, though they had never heard of Hegel, were quite familiar with his general idea, for they and their fathers had left Europe in order to get out from under the freedom-dispensing all-powerful state. Unlike Raoul, I was far less concerned with the clash between capitalism and socialism, fascism and democracy, than with the long-standing contest between Man and State.

IN MY TIME

The problem of political power is today the same as it has always been, no easier and no more difficult. For that matter, the much-vaunted complexities of modern civilization are the most abused alibi for political skulduggery. All human relationships, whether those of two people in love, the council of village elders, the management of Dupont, or the government of the country, are as infinitely complex as the course of the stars since the beginning of time. Though modern technology has brought forth a vast number of complicated devices, it has also endowed us with the means for controlling them. If modern technology has been allowed to make undue demands on our powers of abstraction and to estrange us from the everyday world and its real and eternally perplexing problems, the fault is ours and not that of gadgets which do our bidding.

We have failed to maintain the balance, on the one hand, between techniques that dehumanize the world and, on the other, no less effective techniques for putting the machinery where it belongs, that is, in the cellar, rather than letting it clutter up our gardens, living quarters, and the isles of our dreams. This failure bears upon our politics; our rulers point, some gleefully, some sadly, at the awful and irremediable "complexity" of modern civilization, calling for ever more forceful and all-encompassing political interventions—for fighting fire with fire. The only refuge from mechanized anonymity is the number on a punch card; hence, there has to be a central computer for determining who each of us was, is, and will be. *D'où venons nous; où sommes nous; où allons nous?* The question is answered.

The compression of human beings into a faceless mass, and their alienation from nature and natural beauty, and a deepening sense of insecurity are the unmistakable harbingers of Caesarism. The Rome of the Caesars was not quite as "complex" as our civilization. Yet, without the benefit of computers, it flowered into a welfare state which in many respects equaled and in some respects even exceeded the providential solicitude of contemporary models. The guided tour from the cradle to the grave includes more planned stops than that from the free-eating place and public bath to the arena, but the latter voyage was more diverting. I suspect that the neglect in contemporary higher edu-

129

cation of Latin and Roman history is not quite accidental; though a good many modern educators genuinely doubt the "practical" value of classical studies and put their money on electronics; others remove, with a will, the naughty Romans from the curriculum so that innocent minds shall not be troubled by analogies lurking in the contemporary situation. I cannot prove my suspicions, for the rationale of public education is a closed book to me. But there is just the possibility that the desuetude of the classics must be traced to the modern educationist's own psyche. The great Freudian plunger is at work, flushing the mind of disturbing allusions. Be that as it may, the historians of the Rome of the Caesars recorded the dilemma of people like ourselves; mighty and unsure, possessed of great riches and discontented, engrossed in the rhetoric of the people's tribunes, and deaf to the tread of the Praetorians. Plutarch, Tacitus, and Suetonius speak to us.

No man can subvert democracy who does not speak fluently its language. Caesar was a charming man, deeply understanding of the common man's joys and sorrows. He had gone to the best preceptors and coaches. He cultivated the friendship of the intellectuals of his day and, though he did not always take their advice, accorded them an honored place in the affairs of the state. Although not an intellectual himself and given to more mundane diversions, he had the making of a first-class reporter and published a book that met with wide acclaim and won him the esteem of many thoughtful citizens. Though somewhat volatile in his attachments, he remained steadfast in his public devotion to his wife, the beautiful and presentable daughter of one of Rome's old and influential families. The common people were put at their ease by his simple democratic manners and guffawed good-naturedly at his occasional lapses from aristocratic decorum. From birth he was used to the handling and spending of a great deal of money. He was openhanded, principally in support of his political clients, and ever ready to associate the public treasury with his private generosity. He was superbly intelligent, especially about the uses of power. In addition, from the little we know, it seems that he had a sense of humor and a knack for the quip. He certainly did not mean to kill the Republic; rather, after a long bout of overindulgence, the Republic expired in his arms.

Caesar was the last great Roman who would have liked to keep it alive if this could have been done without undue inconvenience to his plans for modernization. Perhaps, in his heart of hearts, he meant to strike a balance between freedom and power. He hesitated, which was his undoing. But his kinsman and successor, a hard and calculating youth, did not harbor such Hamletian doubts.

The Roussy de Saleses were hosts to a variety of people in and about the arts and letters. In Paris they had met the painters, sculptors, writers, and musicians of the American exodus after World War I. Many of these men and woman—some angry with American society because it had no place for them or angry with themselves because, if there was a place, they did not fit it, and others content to live cheaply and easily in a beautiful city—were sustained by the remittances of their families, agents, publishers, and patrons. The Great Depression dried up these sources of income. The exiles, twice uprooted, returned to join their families, dun their agents and publishers, or find jobs. This influx or, rather, reflux of talent primed the charge which set off the American aesthetic revolution. As could be expected, this revolution spewed forth many weird and ungainly shapes.

Though artists as a species can subsist on skimpy and irregular diet, they, too, must eat. Since they supplied services considered by the community as nonessential, artists were hard hit by the economic crisis. Being highly articulate, they were among its most vocal victims. The government and, in some cases, the local community came to their rescue. The bounty of public works programs was extended to artists. Many a structure of utilitarian purpose, intended as a make-work project and, hopefully, as a shelter for some more or less necessary public service, was, on second thought, found to be in need of beautification. Large numbers of artists, either financially distressed or socially conscious or both, were called upon to furnish the decor. The quota of genius being fairly constant and, to a remarkable degree, unaffected by economic inducements, mass recruitment of individuals purporting to be artists tends to compound mediocrity. The organized effort of the 1930's flowered into a variety of styles among which the most conspicuous was the Potomac Symbolic Monumental—female figures with thick-jointed heaving limbs, symbolizing, I presume, hope and fertility; male figures, muscle-bound, straining mightily at wheels and levers or against some invisible obstacles, symbolizing the toilers' and tillers' sweaty struggle for ever-higher average standards of living. Not a few public buildings of the PSM epoch were embellished with large frescoes in the manner of Diego Rivera, famed as the painter of Mexico's revolutionary collectivism and much admired for his social realism by the Communist party. The structures themselves, no matter their respective height and width, seem to squat rather than stand. It is as if they had been sat upon by one of the tutelary symbolic figures, perhaps by the Colossus of Bureaucracy.

Not being an expert, I am unable to assign to Potomac Symbolic Monumental its proper chronological place in the history of officially approved architecture and decorative arts. Perhaps it should be classified as a variant of the international barrack style which, through the centuries, marked such architectural excrescences widely different in shape and yet so kindred in their pretentious spirit, as the Escorial, the Pentagon, the New and New New Department of State buildings in Washington, and the massive dirty-gray ministries in Moscow.

Although the direct contribution of the New Deal to the creative arts was not fraught by memorable consequences, it provided opportunities for experimentation which accrued to the benefit of the small minority of the gifted among the mass of the boondoggling mediocrities. Official American architecture is still about as pretentiously drab as it has ever been, yet the experiments of the 1930's set in motion the architectural revival which, especially after World War II, changed the face of American cities and changed it, on the whole, a great deal for the better. I believe it was Oscar Wilde who said, "It is better to have bad taste than no taste at all." Beginning with the 1930's America was searching for a style which would reconcile utilitarianism with grace. Although this search has gone off in many wrong directions, and the American scenery has kept on sprouting many monstrosities, it has heightened the public's awareness of accumulated ugliness and spurred the American people to preserve what is beautiful and to tackle with a will the fundamental problem of civilization, namely, that of scaling its achievements to the measure of man. *Le style, c'est la civilisation.*

In the 1930's the contemporary movements in European painting and sculpture, such as nonobjective painting and surrealism, had not yet gained a wide following in the United States. The dominant school was that of the ashcan, symbol of social realism. The bulk of American painting and sculpture stuck to realism which, except for the choice of subjects, mostly unpleasant, remained firmly grounded in the academic tradition. The novelists and playwrights, too, were increasingly obsessed by the pointless sordidness of it all, the sweaty concupiscence of the underprivileged flotsam and the ruthless profligacy of the very rich. Nearly everybody was rotten; the hero was beat. The coming of the war took the steam out of the literary boiler—unfortunately before the public, surfeited by its malodorous emanations, could make up its mind that it had been hoaxed. Be that as it may, nearly everybody now agreed that the country stood in need of heroes that were not beat.

For Western civilization, like all great civilizations before it, is beset by many mortal dangers. Throughout history, great concentrations of wealth and power have always drawn upon themselves the hate, envy, and greed of the barbarians, the have-nots, the exploited and the downtrodden, or whatever one cares to call those who did not manage to fight their way to the top. I doubt that all the resentments accumulated during five centuries of Western expansion and even the divisions within the Western camp can bring us down. Neither nuclear war nor the population explosion need break Western dominance as long as we use our wits, keep our powder dry, and apply our technological superiority to ensuring our own as well as our neighbors' survival. Our foes abroad can be kept at bay and the resources of the earth can provide its population with a living for at least another seventy years—and this is as far as even the wisest among us can now see into the future. The real danger to the West is, as it was to its parent cultures, namely, Greece and Rome, the rot from within.

The most obvious manifestation of the illness that afflicts all

Western peoples is ugliness, so obvious indeed as to suggest that ugliness is the disease itself. Previous civilizations lacked the means for altering purposively the natural environment. Deforestation and the farming methods of the Roman landed gentry contributed to the desiccation of the Mediterranean littoral. Yet learned opinions differ on how large a role these malpractices played in the impoverishment and downfall of Hellenic civilization; certainly, the consequences of the Ancients' tampering with nature were fully apparent only after several centuries had passed.

In an incredibly brief time Western civilization has succeeded in stripping vast tracts of the earth of vegetation and converting thousands upon thousands of hills and dales into level wildernesses of brick and cement shielded from the sun and moon by layers of old-fashioned chimney smoke or modern automotive smog. What made the factory towns of the nineteenth century so appalling was not the alleged misery of the average wage earner, who received a higher pay and performed no harder chores than the farm laborer, but their abysmal, soul-destroying ugliness.

Despite expensive and laudable efforts, public and private, undertaken in my lifetime to salve the lacerated face of nature and cleanse the begrimed walls of cities, ugliness, beaten back at one breach, still creeps unhindered across undefended ramparts. Furthermore, during the past fifty years its chosen instruments have been not so much the factory chimney, the tenement, and cheap mass-produced wares as the expensive motorcar. The motorcar has blighted large, once-verdant stretches of open land in this country and Western Europe, transformed farmhouses into garages and taprooms, village greens into parking lots, ancient monuments into traffic hazards, and rolling fields girded by hedge and woodland into the parceled wasteland of Suburbia. It bespeaks the unconquerable spirit of man that many among us are fighting back, seeking to escape to all kinds of remote places untouched as yet by industrial civilization or into interior decoration or simply into books about beautiful places and things. In many a community brave men and women seek to dam the tide, reorder the city, make gardens grow and noble halls rise where once tenements stood, and banish the motorcar, the destroyer, into subterranean garages where, at least for a while, it cannot clutter up streets and squares. Yet, I wonder, has ugliness not eaten so deep into the vitals of our civilization as to doom all hope of recovery by design?

A hundred years ago the descent into ugliness was inadvertent; nobody who saw, heard, smelled, and understood thought that the ravages of industrialization somehow fulfilled a deeper emotional, not to say aesthetic need. Today sensitive and gifted artists and writers clutch ugliness as if it were the flower of the dark, sweetly redolent with the scent of decay. Not that an ugly face cannot shine with beauty and that agony, death, and putrefaction have not inspired the noblest works of Western creative imagination. But in the modern cult of ugliness the ugly is the object of the creative act precisely because it is ugly. The artist savors ugliness and contrives to transmit its full flavor to his product— to spit into the face of nature and then slap the faithful rendering of the stain onto the face of the public. In our civilization, this is a novel phenomenon. That beneath the surface layer of our civilization, ostensibly preoccupied with the finer things of life as well as with security, cooperation, and toleration, a passion for ugliness and disfigurement should have gripped a large number of people, this fact signals the presence of a danger far greater than depopulation by war or suffocation by overpopulation.

The Western peoples are rapidly consuming their patrimony of natural and man-made beauty. In Europe the descent into ugliness has quickened since World War II. In the most ravaged countries the damage wrought by aerial bombing might have provided the opportunity for at least widening streets, planting lawns and trees, and replacing many an architectural monstrosity with well-designed and livable structures. Instead, the real-estate speculator and tax assessor won out. The great towns of Europe that were worst hit—London, Bristol, Düsseldorf, Frankfurt, Hamburg, Milan, and Antwerp—are now more jam-packed than they were before the war. Much that was beautiful or quaint in them has been done to the death; much plain and humble ugliness has been replaced by piles of steel and cement that flaunt arrogantly their expensive hideousness. Without the help of the blockbuster, some of the great cities of Europe have divested themselves, at a fast clip, of the precious heirlooms of the past, none more effectively than London, which has gone about the business of self-destruction in the famous, casual, national way.

I once loved cities. Most young people do. Of all cities, I loved New York most. It is the city of cities and most resilient to change, for change is its spirit. The oases of its historic past are so small and so few as not to intrude on the living present. In no other city do fame and success matter more and seem more easily within reach, and nowhere are they more fleeting; nowhere seem random meetings more fated, more charged with zest, and within the minute, more inconsequential; nowhere is it as easy to withdraw into anonymity; and nowhere is it the lot of more people to be swallowed up by anonymity forever. I won neither fame nor success, and the threads of fated communion parted, having lost their evanescent sheen. The Goncourts had a sure eye for the passing and the accidental. One rainy afternoon they sat in a café on the Place de l'Opéra and watched the hurrying passers-by. An elderly bearded man and a tall elderly woman collided, tangling their umbrellas. They cursed each other without looking and walked off in opposite directions. Alfred de Musset and George Sand, twenty years after Venice, had met and parted again.

No one who loves or hates passionately knows that he does. Those who profess to know that they are writhing in the grip of passion have surrendered only part of themselves and kept the rest back. The poet keeps his head and wrings a verse from the commitment. To sublimate passion into a work of art requires a well-regulated heart. "Wenn der Mensch in seiner Qual verstummt, gab mir ein Gott zu sagen was ich leide." (While other men fall silent in their pain, a God gives me the power to sing of my sufferings.) This escape route is not open to the average man, who simply keeps a grip on himself because passion is so unsettling. Passion that consumes the whole man has no songs, and once it is spent, only ashes, slag, and, perhaps, a few shapeless bits of molten gold are left over, enough not to let one forget and not enough to bring back to life one heartbeat of truth.

New York is a place for all seasons. In the summer, slovenly

IN MY TIME

and relaxed, she settles down in her underwear and cares even less than during the rest of the year what anyone sees or does. Despite heatwaves and the smells rising from subway, drain, combustion, refuse and disheveled humanity, I was glad to stay and let others seek cooler climes. My friends, bachelors like myself or married men temporarily deserted by their vacationing dependents, exchanged that unhurried hospitality which minds neither the clock nor the seating capacity of the dwelling. We met at our favorite outdoor restaurant. The "garden," accessible through the steaming kitchen, held a few tables pushed onto a graveled plot, twenty by twenty, sheltered by an awning and one of those remarkable trees with scrawny trunks and nervous small leaves that grow persistently in the back yards of New York.

On weekends I drove to the shaded houses on Long Island, set in well-tended lawns, flanked by paddock and tennis court, hothouse and swimming pool, and then still adequately staffed. However, most of the farmland that, in the 1930's, still evoked the illusion of rustic simplicity has now been parceled out by contractors; not a few of the great houses have been turned into institutions or sold, at a fraction of their shockingly large original cost, to the innumerable delegations, individual diplomats, and functionaries associated with the United Nations. Most of the rich have gone elsewhere in search of solitude and service. Many of the magnificent old trees that once shaded roads and lawns have been cut down. Housing developments and industries have put the acreage to most efficient economic use. Progress has triumphed over privilege.

I am sure that the psychiatrist has an answer, which I do not wish to hear, to my failure to calculate correctly the usury of time. I alternate between spurts of intense activity and protracted lassitude, relieved only by my zest for pleasantly wasting time. Love, friendship, tenderness, the happy games consume a great deal of otherwise valuable time. The dour and pompous Gibbon, whose numbing prose turns live Caesars into their own marble effigies, tells us that Hadrian was vain and curious. Hadrian was the most efficient among the Roman emperors; he could not keep his mind on his business, which was ruling the world. He built his

137

villa; he dribbled away valuable imperial time on the most inconsequential matters. He wrote verse. When he came to die he did
not rail against fate that took him from his constructive labors; he
grieved because he had to quit the "happy games of his unsteady
soul." . . . *Nec, ut soles, dabit iocos.*

Chapter Nine

I HAD turned thirty and, so I thought, had nothing to show for it. I thought, too, that I was about to wrest from this sobering realization a new sense of purpose. Yet such is the momentum of ordinary life that one keeps on pursuing a set course long after one has ceased to believe in ever reaching its destination.

Not a few of my friends with whom I had started out in "the Street" had achieved success, leaving me far behind in the quest for position and money. Now, it is much easier to bear one's own failure than the success of one's friends. Like a riderless horse, my competitive urge stayed in the race long after it had parted with my better judgment. Yet money-making, like mountaineering, does not forgive halfhearted effort. I swallowed my pride and closed the shutters on some magnificent vistas. I took the money I had left and time out to think.

I wanted to write about politics. Ever since I had reached my teens politics had impinged forcefully and unpleasantly upon my life. When I came to America I thought that I had made good my escape from politics. In America, the state had not yet intruded upon private life except for Prohibition. Incomes were taxed ever so lightly, young men were not being marched into the barracks, and foreign policy deferred to private commerce. Now, after a respite of ten years, politics had caught up with me. First, the state had moved in upon private business. Now it seemed highly probable that world politics would break into the American sanctuary. I had been only too glad to forget the great European apocalyptic writers whom I had read so avidly before I left Europe. Now their somber visions turned out to have been sober estimates of unfolding trends. They, the prophets rather than the practical men to whom the democracies had entrusted their public affairs, were proved right by the actualities of the situation. I knew that I was not a learned man. But what I had learned by eclectic forays into the philosophy of history and my wanderings in postdepression Europe seemed to me more to the point than what most of the West's politicians and their friends in the press and the colleges were saying. Perhaps mine was an unseemly pride. But a liberal dose of intellectual arrogance is indispensable for launching upon the career of political pundit.

The best way to become a writer is to write. Since my previous literary output had been composed in German and since, more recently, my written efforts had been devoted to terse business correspondence and interpersonal trivia, I had much ground to cover. Perhaps my start was favored by the fact that I had nothing to unlearn, perhaps also by the secure knowledge of my limits. My shortcoming was so obvious that even I could not ignore it: I had been born and educated in another language, and hence, try as I might, I could never aspire to that pure communion with the genius of the English language into which only her true children can enter. Not a few men and women of foreign birth who, comparatively late in life, took to writing English prose, academic or plain, are noted for their concise, though pedestrian phrasing. I tried to emulate their example.

Again, I took leave of my friends, the successful ones on the Street, the thoughtful ones behind their typewriters, and the charming ones at the candlelit table, and sailed for Europe. A classic education supplies a fair warrant for loitering under the

Mediterranean sky.

On a summer morning I left Paris, speeding over washed pavements and along shuttered façades toward the Gate of Italy, that invisible arc of promise flanked by bistros and grocery stores. Before wakening, Paris exhales her most pungent airs—spices, carbolic acid, and millions of rumpled beds. Beyond the fortified mounds, the road between the poplars curved upward to the wide plain. The city's debris—the factory sheds and the desolate red-brick villas—dropped away, and the highway cut across the broad plowland of the Ile de France. Every leaf and stalk, the day and all the days ahead were mine. Beyond Lyons, a stuffy city inhabited by tight-fisted gluttons, the valley broadens, and the names of the towns—Montélimar, Orange, and Avignon —echo the Albigensian melody.

Somewhere beyond Avignon, the moody North gives way to the Mediterranean. Within a matter of miles the landscape changes scale: enclaves of cultivation, groves of trees, vineyards, fields of wheat sheltered by lines of closely planted trees, and, beyond, the sun-baked harshness of rocky hills. Uncompromising and conventional architects, the Romans insisted upon distributing their colonnaded temples and villas all over Northern Europe within the confines of the limes. Empire builders are notoriously indifferent to their own and everybody else's convenience. Here, in the Gallo-Roman province between the Alps and the estuary of the Rhone, Roman arch and column belong to the land, no longer at odds with the vicissitudes of northern living.

At Fréjus the road branches eastward, climbs the scrubby Estérel Mountains and snakes down steeply to the shallow Bay of Cannes. For the first time in my adult years I stood on the shore of the Mediterranean Sea. Thirty years ago the French Riviera was nearly as crowded and as tawdry a place as it is now. Yet the villas along the hills still did not jostle one another, and a few miles off the beaten path fishing villages kept up bravely the pretense of being fishing villages rather than a picturesque façade for a variety of tourist industries. Here and there solitude held out behind high walls and upon rocky promontories. I stayed for a few days at Cap d'Antibes and swam off its fabled rock, whence the mass culture of the expensive tan and maximum exposure spread to all the world's beaches. I moved on, and at Ventimiglia crossed into the latest parody of the Rome of the Caesars.

During Hitler's rule I never set foot on German soil. I thought I could imagine correctly, without going to the distasteful length of personal observation, what Nazi Germany would be like. As it turned out, I had imagined correctly, at least as far as the potential of the Nazis for choking civilized life was concerned. Like many people throughout the Western democracies, I made allowances for Italian fascism which I never thought of making for the barbarous German version of the same political philosophy. I believe that the explanation for this inconsistency can be found in two considerations: first, the Italian Fascists were a great deal less fearsome than their more methodical and warlike colleagues; and, secondly, the Fascists did not take themselves quite seriously. No one else did either. To this day Italy has benefited from her record as a martial fraud and from her reputation for diplomatic inconsistency which expresses her engaging bent for pleasing everybody, especially the strong.

If nazism was the *Ring* staged by a demented drill sergeant, then Italian fascism was an *opéra bouffe* enacted by a talkative gangster. In Italy even the most radical political movements have been modulated by that cynicism which for centuries was the Italian's principal defense against a procession of foreign conquerors and more recently against the power of the state.

The Fascists came to power a few years after the end of World War I. At that time their doctrine was about as fragmentary and as mushy as that of the Nazis. They could not have stayed in power had they not followed practical policies that, on the whole, accorded with the social and ecomomic realities of Italy. They sought to alleviate the lot of the peasants and farm laborers, especially in the South. They drained marshes and settled the reclaimed land. They promoted emigration to the Italian colonies in Africa, where Italian settlers found soils and climates no worse than those of their homeland and enjoyed the psychological satisfaction of playing the role of master race. At home the Fascist government provided industrial workers with those "fringes" which, since then, have become an integral part of the real wage: vacations with pay; pensions; "centers" of sociability and sports;

vocational education, and, through membership in the party, badges of social respectability. In brief, the Fascists borrowed from all the collectivist philosophies of the time, Marxist and Christian socialism, Le Play's communalism, guild socialism and cameralism, and free-wheeled these oddments into the official doctrine of the Corporate State.

The party bigwigs grew fat and rich; so did the entrepreneurs who kept in with the party. The average Italian was better off than he had been before World War I. The opposition went into exile; the dissidents who stayed behind and did not toe the line were beaten up and jailed and some were rubbed out in that gangster fashion which, despite the Duce's intellectual pretensions, was the true style of the regime. Many found refuge in ecclesiastical establishments or simply managed to lose themselves in inconspicuous jobs. Others—probably most—made their peace with the regime.

I did not meet any officials, but among my chance acquaintances not a few proclaimed themselves members of the Fascist party. If it is possible to state one's political allegiance both boastfully and apologetically, they managed this delicate feat with traditional bravura. Unlike the *Hitler-treue* German, the average Fascist-in-the-street, posturing before the foreigner, could not help betraying a measure of embarrassment, and more often than not sought relief in slyly poking fun at the system—and even at himself.

In Germany, the Nazis were on top; Germany was theirs, and no one was permitted to forget it. In Italy, cafés along the big city corsos were thronged with uniforms, and parading black shirts erupted ceaselessly into squares overhung by balconies and hence suitable for speechmaking. Black shirt and boot seemed more fashionable for city rather than for country wear. It was possible to travel through many a village without coming across an individual garbed in this strange and impractical uniform.

To this day I have not discovered the reason for the choice of black and, for that matter, the choice of brown as the distinguishing colorations of the two respective lower-middle-class mass movements. Black boots, which so intensely preoccupied the hallucinations of Baron Sacher-Masoch, pose a much simpler

problem in psychological analysis: appurtenances of the horseman, they signify male mastery. Moreover, they can be brought
down with a thump upon the pavement. No doubt, the masses of
the militants who had never ridden a horse, and hoped that they
would never have to, found wish fulfillment in their regulation
boots and outlet for their dedication in polishing them lovingly.
Of the two leaders, one was reported to have sat his horse like a
sack of meal; the other is known to have been intensely distrustful of any and all horses. Perhaps the boots revealed more
candidly than the rest of the symbolic folderol, the absurdity of
these two kindred political movements. Though some of the leading figures were well shod, the boots of the average militant were
made of cheap leather and pathetically ill fitting. They were
useless except for stomping about on pavements; they were both
purposeless and arrogant. After a while the novelty of boots, black
shirts, and hortatory slogans scribbled on walls wore off.

The Italian is the least xenophobic of all Europeans; he rejoices
in the beauty of his land and has happily shared it with strangers
who come to marvel and to pay solid tribute to the guardians of
shrines and the keepers of shops, inns, and hostelries. I had come
to see the accumulation of the ages. As far as I could note, my
hosts were delighted that I shared with them the contemplation
and expense of their historic patrimony, and they respected my
divergent political opinions.

Italy, because she is so intensively alive among the dead monuments and melds a happy knack for modernity to her antiquarian
past, conveys more clearly than any other land the meaning of
history, the transitoriness of civilization, and the durability of
man. Great deeds are done, and after a while they do not matter.
Great transactions are concluded, and what the participants have
striven for has come to pass—with unforeseen and unwanted
consequences.

For history to be made it is not necessary that men know that
they are making it. As a matter of fact, the greatest and most
purposeful makers of history had not the slightest notion what
they were really doing. No man would have done great things if
he could have figured out beforehand the countervailing forces
which he set in motion. The fresh waters of the faith are caught

in the sluggish channels of organized religion; the conquerors are absorbed by the conquered race; the victors adopt the mores of the defeated; the quest for universal rule stirs the resurgence of nationalist fervor; and the development least noticed by contemporary society is pregnant with epochal change. The Caesars of the first century seem to have been wholly unaware of the sectarian stirrings in Palestine, not to speak of their sociopolitical significance. Count Stürgkh, the Austro-Hungarian Premier, speaking in Parliament in 1910, sarcastically asked: "Who is going to start a revolution in Russia? Perhaps Herr Trotsky in the Café Kranz?" The marble columns of Hadrian's Villa reinforce the palaces built by Renaissance popes for their nephews and nieces. One age quarries the leavings of its predecessors for the odd bits wherewith to adorn its own edifice.

The living carry off the effigies of the fallen gods, and the sacrilegious embrace begets a new purity of form and faith. When Spengler spoke of Faustian man he must have had in mind the man who plans and strives in sublime disregard of the historical evidence: a live dog is worth more than a dead Caesar; today's magnificence is tomorrow's rubbish, and the future belongs to the scavenger.

Thus, one age breaks faith with the other. What meaning bridges the distance from the dusty hillock by Lake Tiberias to the resplendent pile of marble by the Tiber? What bond of communion joins Giotto's saintly images and Bernini's enraptured St. Teresa? And how eager would have been the Founding Fathers, especially Thomas Jefferson, to complete their labors had they been able to foresee the rise of the gigantic administrative citadels on the Potomac? Our eclectic civilization vaunts its ability to discern meaningful affinities where a simpler age would have seen only flagrant contradictions. The dead cannot speak. They cannot cry abomination and withhold their sanction from frauds perpetrated in their name.

Upon the fall of Mussolini the vast majority of Italians discovered with that quick spontaneity which is their most endearing national characteristic that they had never been Fascist at heart, and embraced their conquerors and victorious democracy. The Italians are a practical people with a conversational passion for ideology. Life must go on, and in Italy it has gone on for a long time.

All political movements have had to heed the increasing secularization of human society. Since they have been confronted by the same problem—the core problem—it is not surprising that, notwithstanding their differing programmatic professions, they have come up with solutions that resemble one another far more closely than do their ideological labels. In Italy the past twenty years have been attended by seemingly portentous political changes—the Fascists, together with their shirts, boots, and imperialist posturings, have departed, and a quasi-clerical party has administered, under the watchful eyes of the Western allies, a fair likeness of parliamentary democracy. But the national economy is now about as "mixed" as it was under the Fascists; the state controls, plans, and manages as large, if not a larger sector of the economy as it did under Mussolini; and the Catholic Church, far from trying to contest new trends frontally, has sought to adapt its old dogmas to the new popular magic—the cult of science, the veneration of gadgets, and the beatitudes of an easy life upon earth.

Not the least astute insight of Hitler and Mussolini into mass psychology was their understanding of a deep popular craving—ever-larger numbers of men will eagerly exchange their civic rights for bureaucratic rank. As men fear that they are losing or have, in fact, lost their identity to the machine, the factory, and the megalopolis, they seek to re-establish it by the badge and privilege of rank. It is the "grade" that counts—and counts more even than financial remuneration, not to speak of the function, that is, the utility, of the work that goes with the grade. Napoleon, confronted with the problem of converting a mob of uncouth *arrivistes* into Imperial High Society, pioneered in the creation of a rank-and-badge society. Hitler and Mussolini tried to imitate Napoleon's hierarchical designs in more ways than one. Although the visible results of their labors were in execrably bad taste, they seemed to have satisfied the longings of millions of their now duly graded, robed, and decorated countrymen.

Of course, no self-respecting democratic society would let itself be beguiled by the tinsel of totalitarian snobbery. The styles of our status society in general, and of governmental hierarchy in particular, are removed by worlds of probity and sophistication from the ridiculous and crude designs of late and living tyrants. Yet, since the war Americans have become ever more deeply interested in such status symbols as offices which meticulously express the occupant's organizational status; protocol and precedence at public functions; and even decorations distributed by the Chief Magistrate, tastefully designed and solemnly bestowed. A growing number of specialists and, by avocation, many thousands of functionaries in the Executive Departments are bending their inventiveness to the elaboration of even-firmer differentiations in the signs and symbols that appertain to rank. Their example fires the imagination of like-minded officials in private industry. The anonymous cipher of the IBM machine is compensated for by the sweet certainty of an acknowledged place in the universal pecking order. One might not know oneself who one is and for what one labors; but one's rank tells others exactly where one stands in the scheme of things.

Gratefully, I left Italy. Much book learning had come to life. I had seen and I had touched. Furthermore, I need no longer guess at the nature of fascism. Now I knew from firsthand observation that the Fascists, too, belonged to the same species of louts which flourished in Germany. Although the Italian Fascists were not more imperialist than had been the French and the British in their respective prime, their revolting mannerisms—a grandiloquent arrogance and an exhibitionist brutality toward whomsoever they thought weaker than themselves—played havoc with the workings of traditional diplomacy. Thus, Mussolini—perhaps against his own judgment, which, in international affairs, was not always bad—heightened the sense of international insecurity haunting the democratic peoples, notably the Anglo-Saxons.

The great mass of the Italians, Fascist or bootless, did not want war—least of all a war on the side of the awesome Germans. They knew that their soldiers were poorly armed, trained, and led. Yet, the momentum of Mussolini's indecent gesticulations on the stage of world politics carried Italy into the unwanted alliance, and then the unwanted war. No one seems to have been more surprised than he when light comedy turned into gory tragedy.

On my way to the damp North I halted at Geneva. A friend of my Munich days had settled in a villa by the lake; throughout the preceding one hundred fifty years or so, his house had sheltered exiles from all over the world, neurasthenic English poets, deposed Balkan princes, absconding Latin-American dictators, escapees from a spate of abortive revolutions, and a few adulterous couples. Before the war my friend had been a rich man, but the postwar inflation consumed most of his fortune. A modestly gifted sculptor, he had employed his leisure by collecting works of art, and throughout the years he had acquired a few canvases attributed to masters of the Italian Renaissance and a score of paintings by contemporary French and German artists, some of whom had gained wide recognition. Indeed, he weathered the Götterdämmerung of the German rentier by selling part of his collection to foreign buyers against hard currencies, invested the proceeds judiciously in Switzerland, closed his house in Munich, and quietly removed himself, his handsome wife, daughters, and sundry choice possessions to the house by the lake.

Even then the Swiss cantons and, especially, the Republic of Geneva set high standards for the admission of foreigners to permanent residence. Though generous in according asylum to political exiles, ever ready to welcome solvent tourists, and punctiliously correct in accommodating the officialdom of a host of Swiss-based international organizations, the Swiss accord the privilege of residence, not to speak of citizenship, only to the chosen few among a virtually unlimited number of applicants. Surprising as this may seem to Americans, there are many people in the world who would like to settle in Switzerland rather than in the United States. Unfortunately for them, Switzerland is a very small country as well as the most exclusive community on earth.

No one, not even the Swiss themselves, agrees on what exactly are the arcane rules which govern the foreigner's admission to integral Helvetian status. Each canton makes its own. Among the criteria the most important, so it seems, are impeccable morals (as defined by the cantonal authorities) and ample funds. Among the alternatives are a Swiss grandmother or a special skill which will benefit Swiss industry. My friend qualified: his moral character passed Calvinist review; a Geneva bank guarded his tidy savings; and his great-grandmother *was* a Génèvoise.

The business which had brought me to Geneva proceeded at a leisurely pace. My host and his neighbor, Madame O., had been friends for many years. Madame O. had appointed my host executor of her last will. Separated from her husband, a German diplomat, Madame O. had lived unassumingly and comfortably in a tree-shaded villa by the lake. Earlier that year Madame O. had died, leaving a sizable estate and a son and a daughter. Madame O.'s father, a Dutch diplomat, had been posted to Washington. There he met and married the daughter of an illustrious financier. Thus, upon the demise of her parents, Madame O., an only child, fell heir to a large fortune. Unfortunately, the Great Depression had ravaged Madame O.'s portfolio. A good part of the holdings consisted of the bonded obligations issued, during the 1920's, by Latin-American governments and marketed by United States investment bankers. Interest rates were high. Shortly after the collapse of the international securities market, the Latin-American governments defaulted. My host and his fellow executors were confronted with a difficult choice: to find buyers for these battered and depressed securities forthwith or gamble on a rise in their market value and, if all went well, the resumption of interest payments. My host had sought my advice and offered me a generous fee for my services. I availed myself of the opportunity to stay, all expenses paid, in a renowned hotel by the Lake of Geneva.

The settlement of the estate proceeded at a slow pace. The probating of wills and the settling of estates are, to the heirs, a harrowing and depleting business; to bankers, lawyers, and trustees they are abundant sources of fees and commissions. We met with the celebrated Geneva lawyers who had drawn the deceased's last will. Their pondered immobility promised to extend the proceedings for an unspecified number of years. We met with the bankers of Geneva, the most punctilious and frosty ones to the east of Edinburgh. Between desultory and inconclusive meetings my duties were light. I had plenty of time for excursions into the hinterland and for observing life in Geneva. (Incidentally, a few years later the heirs entered into the unrestricted enjoyment of the fortune which, though diminished by the charges of law and administration, ensured them modest comfort. The Latin-American securities, retained upon my advice, rose in price. The respective governments resumed interest payments, for they sought to appease the old investors and to borrow new money.)

With time on my hands, I devoted myself to the study of man in Geneva, ranging from the Calvinist conscience and numbered, nameless, bank accounts to the mutation of French cuisine and language in French-speaking Switzerland, to the modesty of Geneva upper-class couture and the flamboyant polychrome sails of the racing sloops on the lake, and on to the debates in the League of Nations, then Geneva's principal attraction and source of income of its hotel and allied industries.

The League of Nations was being shaken by a series of untoward developments. The Italians, whose rape of Ethiopia had brought upon them the censure of the civilized world—international indignation, at that time, found its most forceful expression in addresses by English, French, and Soviet spokesmen—walked out, and the Germans, ferociously tearing the Versailles Treaty to shreds, soon followed.

The Geneva Disarmament Conference had come to naught. Notwithstanding the fact that the Germans and Italians were arming themselves feverishly and the Western democracies were increasingly lagging behind in the arms race, Litvinov called for general and complete disarmament. At the same time the Communist press denounced the idea of disarmament as a bourgeois preconception, and German instructors and technicians assisted in the rapid build-up of the Red Army.

In this less sophisticated age, members signified their discomfiture at or contempt of the procedures of the Parliament of Man by simply slamming the door, rather than refusing, as is the present custom, to pay their dues. One of the reasons for this summary defiance might have been the fact that the United States was not a League member and hence could not be counted upon to make up for the League's budgetary deficits. Unlike the United Nations, the League comprised only a few "emerging nations" except for the secession states carved from the Hapsburg Monarchy and the Ottoman Empire. Instead, Germany, Italy, and Japan designated themselves "have-not" nations; they were joined by the Soviets as dissident members of the international proletariat, oppressed by the Western imperialists.

These self-styled have-nots, equipped with massive and costly weaponry, and each subjecting, or proposing to subject, other peoples to their rule, attempted to incite the races of the Middle East, Asia, and Africa to rebellion against the Western colonial powers. In this endeavor, as could have been foreseen, the Soviets, unhampered by a nation-centric ideology and amply endowed with Asian affinities, and the Japanese, out of the reach of Western military power and themselves Asians, were most successful. Perhaps the simplest clue to Soviet and Japanese conduct throughout the thirties can be found in the fact that both had much to gain by a European civil war. They both did, although at one time or another they seemed to have misplaced their bets. Nevertheless, no one who during the past thirty years wagered on the collapse of the Western Empire could fail to collect. In their self-effacing way, the Japanese, bloody and deferentially bowed, too, are now reaping handsome profits from their exertions on behalf of the great cause of colonial liberation—and the end is not yet in sight.

Most of the issues that troubled the League still baffle its successor. The Western democracies, now as then, persist in viewing the "arms race" as the threat to world peace and in sweeping the political issues making for war under the rug of "peaceful coexistence"; and the Communist cry for general and total disarmament drowns out the clashing of gears in the Communist apparatus for protracted conflict. Today, as then, the lethal devices which modern technology produces as a matter of routine are inert things and hence cannot "cause," by themselves, the death of a fly or any living being. But today, even more than then, the scientific and technological intellect is *the* weapon.

Disarmament would have to begin by an international agreement to subject, in all countries, a quota of scientists and technologists to surgical prophylaxis, preferably lobotomy. If there is any lesson to be learned from the Washington treaty on the limitation of naval armament and from the Geneva negotiations in the interwar period, it is that disarmament agreements not only do not prevent evasion, they prompt it. What is science if it is not the search for solutions to seemingly insoluble problems? To tell the inventive mind that it is debarred by any law except the law of science from exploring one approach to the development of a technique is to challenge it to seek for another or to substitute an altogether novel technique for the "outlawed" one. In the field of weapons technology, the novel technique, which no one except the innovator knows anything about and which, therefore, cannot be outlawed, proves usually more effective and more lethal than the forbidden weapon. No one knows this better than the Communists, assiduous students of war and the causes of war. It is not the destructiveness or abundance of armament that tips the balance of peace and war, but the will to use them. The battle of France was lost long before it was fought, in studies and book stores, upon the stage and the screen—and in the dream world of Geneva. The Communists praised or subsidized or originated the anti-war literature which flooded the democratic countries. Their call for general and complete disarmament was tuned to a cyclic low of Western mood; the democratic peoples craved, above all things, surcease from the inexorable struggle for power which, as long as the world is half slave and half free, must remain their lot. Today, two decades after World War II, the Western mood descends again to the point of longing, a longing as futile as the anxieties of the menopause. Again, there is a "literature of fear" that caters to the quietism of the Western intelligentsia. The "Merchants of Death and Cannons" of the 1920's reappear in the even more frighteningly anonymous guise of the "Military-Industrial Complex," the murderous reptile with a thousand heads that coils around the blessed tree of life. Again the totalitarian aggressor avers his devotion to peace. Since in a straight arms race the West can always outdo him, he seeks to stall the West's military effort and to break up the Western alliance.

Nothing ever happened in Geneva. Hundreds of journalists reported more or less faithfully the goings-on in the League, rich in forensic display and devoid of tangible consequences. Some of the leading actors made good copy and knew it. The oratory of the League rolled on a higher level than that of its more polyglot successor—or, perhaps, it only seemed so to an audience not yet surfeited by televised addresses, live or canned. Yet, not even the seasoned parliamentary rhetoric of the French and British statesmen (who, if they had wanted to, might have given the League what it so conspicuously lacked, namely, muscle) could hide the futility of the proceedings. The League had been created by the victors in a world war. It reflected their image of international order, namely, the kind of world in which well-to-do democracies could live at ease. League or no League, the victors had the power, provided they stuck together, to impose their gentle vision upon mankind. They did not stick together, and it was left to the League to provide an alibi for the abdication of the West's collective responsibility. *Plus ça change, plus c'est la même chose.*

Places where nothing happens are usually more diverting than places where something does happen. There is plenty of time to talk about past events, the might-have-beens and the future. As a body, political journalists are far more intelligent and prescient than the politicians from whom they cull their copy or the scholars who commune with the deeper meaning of historical events. For one, they are more keenly aware than any other profession of the ambiguity of words. Blind hero worship is not one of their failings; they mistrust "greatness," for the intimacy of the interview and the skirmish of the press conference reveal most prominent men as being about as silly, vain, and platitudinous as the rest of us.

My host introduced me to some American and French journalists of his acquaintance. We sat in the sidewalk cafés with a view of the lake, which can be, on the shortest notice, so smilingly blue and so suicidally gray, and talked about the coming war. No one doubted that the current series of international felonies would culminate in massive shooting. The disagreement was on who would start it, where and when, and who would have joined whom at the moment of truth.

Some of us met again after the war. Even then, Clarence Streit, then a correspondent of the *New York Times,* held his audience by the ardor and the very simplicity of his argument. A prophet long before his time, a poor speaker, intransigent and awkward, he preached the gospel of Western unity. He insisted upon being right while the mighty and the famous were wrong, and for this unpardonable breach of political etiquette he has not been forgiven to this day. He has been allowed to propound his views, some of which the politicians had to embrace against their unfailingly short-run convictions, in respectable though impecunious obscurity. A similar fate befell Coudenhove-Kalergi, perennial pilgrim to Geneva and seer of European unity. To this day Coudenhove's Grand Design stands as the only valid alternative to the suicidal rivalry of European nationalisms. The pan-European union, which he created singlehanded, provided, at Europe's darkest moment, the last refuge of the unitary idea. After World War II, Coudenhove founded the European Parliamentary Union, the chrysalis of the Council of Europe, the European Common Market, and all the working organizations of European unity.

I do not know whether Clarence Streit and Richard Coudenhove-Kalergi ever met. If they did, I wish I could have seen them side by side, exponents of two ideas of international order which could be complementary as well as incompatible with each other. Streit, born in Missouri and raised in Montana, tall, angular and slow of speech, could not be mistaken for anything but an American. Coudenhove-Kalergi's paternal ancestors hailed from the remote corners of the Hapsburg Empire, the lowlands and the Eastern Marches. On the maternal side Coudenhove descended from a long line of Japanese nobles. In the matter of appearance, the maternal side had won out: small, impassive, and ceremonious, he seemed all the more Samurai for the incongruity of his immaculate European dress. This exotic effect was heightened by the Valkyrian proportions of his expansive countess. To this learned and cosmopolite man, Europe owes an inestimable debt. It is now fashionable to argue that Europe's quest for unity has been triggered by economic and military necessity. Thus the credit for historic achievement is given to those anonymous forces which are so dear to modern historiography, and not to individual men. In history—real history—there stands at every turning point one man with one idea.

I never excelled in any sport, for mine is not the athletic mold. My interest has run to sampling as many sports as were within my reach and means rather than seeking perfection in any one. At school I was taught to ride and fence. A bout at foils or sabers packs more strenuous action than any other matched game; a daily work-out at foils will, long past middle age, keep muscles firm, the spine straight, and the eyes alert.

Horsemanship requires constant application. It is not so much a sport as a way of life. In our civilization, in which the horse has lost its economic and military function, a great deal of time and some money are needed to ride enjoyably and safely, not to speak of engaging in such noble sports as fox hunting and polo. Though I have ridden many horses in diverse places, I know the beast's responsiveness to human care and love to be a myth. Horses are self-centered animals, unpredictable, impersonal, and susceptible to innumerable ailments. Not a few horses of my acquaintance, especially expensive thoroughbreds, are hardened hypochondriacs. Thus, whatever pleasure I derived from riding was vouchsafed me not by competitive gallop or my tenuous mastery pitted against reluctant power but, in contrast, by hacking across country at a slow pace, a lazy canter across a field of new-mown hay, the halt on the crest of the hill above the pasture in the valley, and fording the shaded brook, not to mention the rhythmic thud of hoofs on the turf, the tranquil creak of girth and saddle, and the pungent scent of leather.

But if I had to choose one among the sports in which I engaged and had to forsake all the others, I would settle for small-boat sailing. Most sailors are fatalists, for the will of wind and wave will be done. Skill lies not in bucking force but in leaning to it and, if need be, patiently riding it out. There is a touch of Zen in every true sailor, for he resists by nonresisting and reaches his destination by tacking past it. Again and again, there is nothing to do but to do nothing and wait for nature to change its mood.

Possibly the first scientist was a sailor and not, as we were taught, a priest-king who, from observation of sun and moon, deduced the regularities of highs and lows for the waters of the Nile. More likely, seafarers, in their unending preoccupation with position and direction, noted the path of the heavenly bodies,

the curvature of the earth, and the specific gravity of water long
before land-bound magicians in Egypt studied these and related
phenomena. In prehistory, more pure science must have gone
into the making of hull and sail than into any other thing than
wrought by the hand of man. This is probably one of the reasons
for the conservatism of sailors. To be first in possession of techniques always carries a heavy liability: figuratively speaking, the
sailor has rested on his oars. It is amazing that it took the sailor-
shipwright thousands of years to develop the centerboard, the
central rudder, and the jib. Only within the past one hundred fifty
years has he learned how to rig his sails for tacking close to the
wind. Yet, such is the constancy of the basic craft that a Phone-
cian master mariner could, upon a few hours' indoctrination, sail
without unprecedented mishap the most modern racing sloop
from the site of Tyre to the Pillars of Hercules. True conservatives, most sailors—and, at certain times, all of them—believe in
God. They have to.

Nearly every day my Génèvois host boarded his sailboat,
washed down the deck, polished brass, and attended to the many
chores of nautical housekeeping which are almost as pleasurable as
hauling close in a stiff breeze. Sometimes we participated in a
race; sometimes we cruised leisurely from one shore of the lake
to the other, dropped anchor in the lee of one of the tiny head-
lands that, here and there, jut into the lake, swam in the cool
water and lunched on cold chicken, cheese, fruit, and a bottle of
light wine from the nearby hills. My host skippered his craft
skillfully and imperturbably. From long experience he knew
every foible of the weather, the deceptively still water, the sud-
den gust of wind dropping almost vertically from the mountain,
the heavy squall funneled by the narrow valley descending to the
lake.

One afternoon a light breeze barely strained the canvas. My
host's two daughters sunned themselves on the foredeck, half-
hidden by the gently billowing balloon. The murmur of their
voices was barely audible in the cockpit where my host and I
talked desultorily about sailing, art, and islands. We fell silent,
and by an acoustic accident, perhaps sound amplified by arching

canvas, the words on the foredeck came through to us, melodious and clear. My host's daughters had been raised in the European upper-class tradition of expensive modesty and polite reticence. Slim and lithe, they moved gracefully and competently on ski slope and tennis court, deck and dance floor. Yet their allure was tempered by that touch of shyness which, in that remote past, was still prized by men more highly than all other maidenly graces. The two sisters talked about their suitors. The astute appraisal of quality and worth would have honored, by its knowing factualness, two old horse copers, confiding to each other the finer points of the trade. My host looked at me from one corner of his sardonic eye. He flipped the rudder and hauled close to the wind.

Most men go through life without knowing what women say to one another about men. One might guess that the other half of the moon looks very much like that which is visible from the earth. Then, again, it may not, and the best that science can do to still doubt is to develop a space-traveling observatory, which, having maneuvered behind the moon, casts back the image of the averted side. For a more intimate glimpse of the lunar landscape, man must launch himself upon a voyage of personal discovery from which he might not return at all or return so altered by the experience as to be unable to communicate his insights to his fellow men.

There are three universes of communication, namely, what women say to one another about men, what men say to one another about women, and what men and women tell one another. Between these three worlds the exchange of information is scanty or, some believe, impossible. Perhaps it is in the best interest of the race that they be inaccessible to one another or accessible only at extreme peril. In fact, this seems to have been the opinion of early cultures. The Greeks have held it, for in the legends of Ariadne upon Naxos and of Artemis and Actaeon, the moral is quite plain, though the trespass upon discretion is not the same in each. In our age, excessive curiosity, stimulated by the myths of science, might well undo the race, benumbed as it is by the careless camaraderie of the sexes.

Heavy clouds rolled in from the west and got stuck between

the Jura and the Mont Blanc massif. The lake looked as glum as any sunless mountain lake. Curtains of rain dropped from the soggy awnings of the terrace cafés. The boredom of parliamentary routine lay heavy upon the League Palace. The political stars, having filled their engagement, had departed. After a brief interlude of animation, the proceedings returned, not only in fact but also in appearance, to the customary state of futility. The professional diplomats who, for a while, had effaced themselves behind their political bosses reoccupied the front seats of the delegation posts. They looked as if they wished they were elsewhere, at home or in a snug embassy in one of the more affluent capitals. The lay audience had shrunk, and not a few accredited journalists had left for their vacations in some sunny place to the south of Geneva. Fall had come early. I thanked my hosts and their helpful daughters and headed back for Paris.

Chapter Ten

ALTHOUGH I had meant to write a book—my first book—about French politics, I found it irksome to settle down to work. In part my troubles stemmed from several months' indolence. The little work I do I do from habit and because I scruple to break myself of this or any other habit, even a bad one. Now I dodged the call of discipline—the awful, sedentary, and solitary discipline of the free-lance writer.

If I had a son to rear I would advise him to get the business of discipline over with early in life and then, in the prime of youth, waste time. Unfortunately, disciplined behavior is automatic behavior: first one is made to do—or, if one is clever, one makes oneself do—certain things which one does not like to do, at certain appointed times or in response to certain situations mostly disagreeable. After a while one does these things in an unthinking and unfeeling way, that is, one has become conditioned to do them; this is bad enough, but worse is to come. For if one breaks disciplines one feels badly either because of an inexplicable sense of guilt or because, having been thrown off one's routine, one's digestion kicks up and one sleeps fitfully. This is the revenge of civilization, and this is why uncivilized people behaving in an undisciplined way enjoy such rugged good health until they are brought to savor the benefits of civilization.

There is in all work, even the most creative, a large element of tedious drudgery, and it is in the efficient handling of these repetitive chores that discipline, preferably iron, pays off. This has always been so. Modern society, however, adds to this exacting and timeless condition of the race a web of do's and don'ts spun by organizational rote. Sometime or other, all of us feel that we are caught in its coils, and that we are awfully small insects to boot. I have no remedy for this depressing sensation other than sometime in one's life deserting the troops and, without any thought of tomorrow, wasting what is supposedly the most precious commodity of our civilization, namely, time. I realize that desertion from cooperative improvement is a serious crime, but only he who has committed it and returned to the ranks unrepentant of the exhilarating experience should be entrusted with the management of human affairs. Perhaps in my youth it was easier to desert than it is now. Then the geography of escape was more spacious, and even in the West the mores of unapologetic leisure still governed the conduct of important and powerful social groups as well as the customs of entire national cultures. In many parts of the world it was still sweet to do nothing or what, by the mores of the scientific-technological age, amounts to the same thing.

I might have shouldered the yoke of the solitary writer more docilely if I could have convinced myself of the importance, if not to the world than at least to France herself, of French politics. But this autosuggestive feat became increasingly difficult; I could not make myself believe that the leading French politicians, the many appeasers as well as the few resisters, still controlled the movement of the ship of state or thought themselves capable of altering course, no matter what dangerous hazards loomed ahead.

In the late thirties the various French factions had so stalemated each other that one reshuffled government after the other could do little but drift from one halfhearted improvisation to the other. In patent conflict with classic French doctrine, the French military had gone to ground in the Maginot Line; defying the logic of strategic geography, French foreign policy did not put teeth into the East European alliance or embrace the Soviets as allies—if only to test their true intentions; domestically, smouldering civil conflicts distracted the attention of the populace from the one issue that mattered, namely, national survival. Strikes, the flight of capital, and tax evasion halted economic and technological progress. Only two major highways had been improved and these led to gambling spas. The physical plant of French industry reeked of obsolescence, and the equipment of the French Army remained, but for the expansion of an air force without a definable mission, what it had been in World War I, though less well maintained.

Most Frenchmen were aware of these deplorable and unmistakable conditions. A few, like undaunted Paul Reynaud, denounced in magnificent prose the universal rot, called for an end to the tergiversations in foreign policy, and exhorted France to get ready for war. Their speeches were reported by the press, their books—French politicians can write faster about current issues than any other politicians—were displayed on most bookstands. On my rounds I did not meet a single politician, except officeholders, who did not concede, as a matter of course, that all was not well with France and that nothing could be done about it, and not a single adult Frenchman who, with the tranquil anticipation of victory, looked forward to fighting the Germans. Of course, the sentiments expressed in ministerial statements, the published communications of the Quai d'Orsay, and the speeches delivered at those Anglo-French and Anglo-American get-togethers which annually commemorated the spirit of the Somme or Belleau Wood or Yorktown, did not reflect the pervasive sense of fatality.

Under these circumstances it was not surprising that intelligent men and women should seek to wrest from the usury of time the last ounce of accomplishment and pleasure before collective calamity would overwhelm their private lives. This endeavor enlisted my deepest sympathies. My life has been a long struggle between political engagements and a deepening sense of futility.

Since I have always been a bystander, I could not seek oblivion in those absorbing and inconsequential activities which insulate officialdom against the pressure of events.

The natural inclination of a bureaucracy is to do nothing—or, rather, to do too much in a meaningless way in order to give the impression of motion. In foreign affairs this tendency increases as the gravity of the international situation mounts. Nowadays political leadership is becoming increasingly enmeshed in that very bureaucracy which supposedly does its bidding. Hence, government tends to screen the triviality of its decisions by the immensity of the commotion. The less political leadership is prepared to face up to a crucial issue the more lengthy and frequent grow departmental and interdepartmental committee meetings and international conferences. Thus, the governmental machinery —a machinery truly *sui generis*—operates the more strenuously and noisily the less output it produces. For the insider, the drone of the committee meeting, the susurrus of fluttering memoranda, and the innocuousness of agreed decisions exert a calming, healing, and fulfilling power.

This boon has been denied me, partially because of circumstances beyond my control and partially because of my congenital aversion to cooperative discipline. Furthermore, my excessive bent on the study of past ages and morbid predilection for historical analogies has estranged me from some of those influential figures into whose orbit I accidentally drifted. Could I have refrained from kindling the waning memories of what had gone before, my powerful friends might have let me tend one of those innumerable levers of the "machinery" which, though they can be raised or lowered without producing light or motion, command emolument, precedence, and psychic satisfaction.

Like nearly every disadvantageous condition, being outside the stream of "decision making"—the expression is not mine but that of newspeak—has its just rewards. Since I had nothing else to do, I fastened my attention on the end product rather than the complex process by which it had been ground out. Emboldened by what I saw, I questioned the wisdom of the management, for by their fruits shall ye know them. I turned critic; I took my seat among the observers on the balcony of history. Furthermore, since I was not wanted on the stage—not even for a walk-on part—I could absent myself from the performance whenever I felt irresistibly drawn by the need for fresh air or a glass of beer in the corner pub. Unbeholden to the management, I was free to commend and censure it; I was free even to forget about the sorry show and to pretend that it was of no concern to me.

In the 1930's the pretense of unconcern was about as healthy a posture as any reasonable person, possessed of average insight into the international situation and unable to do anything about it, could assume. As Pliny, witnessing the eruption upon Pompeii of Vesuvius noted, there are occasions when emotional identification with the catastrophe, actual or impending, not only warps the observer's judgment but also distresses him to no good purpose.

Not since that magnificent decade before World War I did the intellectual and artistic life of Paris flourish more abundantly than in the few years left to another ill-fated generation. Giraudoux mounted his iambic allegories which, on the edge of the abyss, celebrated unquenchable lust for life. His irony cleansed the human dilemma of its gritty absurdities. A compassionate man, he disdained the cruel twist with which Anouilh, the cleverest and unhealthiest among French playwrights, torments his unwary heroes and his unsuspecting audience.

Antoine de Saint-Exupéry, returning from his solitary flights across the Andes, the Sahara, and the South Atlantic, wrote of whirling galaxies, the infinity of space, the beacons at the edge of continents, and the prison from which neither winged speed nor the guidance of the constellations can free the soul. One should expect that the large fraternity of licensed pilots would have produced at least a handful of cosmic poets, singing the sunrise over Greenland, the green ocean of the Amazon, and the jet plunge through wafting clouds into the star-studded sky of night, or at least the glory and the peril of their own profession. In fact, the upper reaches remained singularly barren of literary and artistic creativity. The sole noteworthy exception has been Saint-Exupéry.

Saint-Exupéry looked like a country squire home from a long

tramp with his beagles. In relieving contrast to his literary peers, he talked neither much nor well, but always to the point. The sole mark of the Muse was a somewhat disconcerting absent-mindedness. No one I knew—except women who professed to be in love with him, and not all of these—seemed particularly eager to accompany him in flight.

Well on in middle age, he took service, toward the end of World War II, in the Free French air force. Planes now flew faster. Some of his young comrades sized him up as an erratic pilot and sought to dissuade him from undertaking the recon-naissance mission from which he did not return. It is likely that, sunk in reverie or bent over the writer's notebook, he hurtled to disaster. I believe that his personal life was unhappy and that he came to cherish the melancholic solitude from which he drew his poetic inspiration. His artistry lies in the purity of style and harmony. He was a brave man. He contrived a fitting ending. Most poets crave the death of Icarus only to be meanly carried off by hardening of the arteries or cirrhosis of the liver.

André Malraux, the most brilliant among French novelists, struggled in the coils of his checkered and controversial past. Even then—and many a metamorphosis was to follow—it was difficult to disengage the man from the legend. All the more difficult since Malraux seemed always on stage, a posturing figure from whose mask rolled a set monologue. Not so surprisingly, shadows of doubt rested upon many datum points: had he or had he not transgressed upon the academic limits dividing archaeol-ogy from profitable trade in valuable objects obtained in the course of scholarly exploration? Had he or had he not played an important role in the Communist movement? Was the exotic flavor which clung to his work and person derived from personal experience or, imaginatively, from a variety of unnoted sec-ondary sources?

A superb actor, Malraux has played many roles and changed them with an uncanny sense for the changing moods of the times: a lean scholar-adventurer, he shakes off the dust of post-war Europe, bourgeois and gross, and courses the forbidden trails of Asia in search of ancient civilization and treasure; in communism's intellectual heyday, he embraces the cause, and then plumbs the depth of Stalinist ambiguity, the "darkness at noon"; he finds his way into the Resistance, and, a tougher and more efficient Byron, he leads his crack troop in the battles of Liberation; he exchanges the sword for the pen and, secluded in his study, muses deeply over transcendent faith and the images wrought to its glory; the renowned philosopher steps from his study into the arena of practical politics, shoulders the burden of office and—apotheosis— sits in the highest council of state. The aged Prince de Ligne, having been asked how he would prefer to live his life if he could live it all over again, replied "Up until the age of thirty, a beautiful woman; till fifty, a successful general; after fifty, a cardinal." The Duke would have conceded that there is no point in putting this question to a Malraux. Malraux's most brilliant fiction pales before the flamboyance of his life. In all the tomes he has published Malraux has not let slip a word that tells about himself. Since Malraux's rise to the aesthetic pontificate and, then, the Cabinet, I can think only of one fitting coda to the life of this guarded and driven man: Malraux's autobiography composed upon a rocky crag on Patmos. At last, Malraux speaks.

Old men forget, especially those episodes of their youth which were unhappy and unedifying. Perhaps the Paris of twenty-five years ago was far less alight with the joy of living and the flame of creativeness than I now think. Perhaps in the Paris of today as many extraordinary and extravagant men and women write great plays and novels, paint explosive pictures, and carry on celebrated love affairs, mostly stormy, as met, twenty-five years ago, at the Brasserie Lipp, applauded Comte de Beaumont's last ballet, paid court to that influential patron Madame de F., and then went on to do their work and all those things that assuage the pains of creation. And yet I doubt it. I doubt it not so much because the current output strikes me as mediocre—in which judgment I might be wrong, since I might no longer be attuned to the spirit and the fashions of the age—as because political and social trends have sapped the vigor of French culture.

Today, to be sure, France is again a rich country and about to become a modern one. Yet France, rich and progressive, has lost some of that distinctness which for centuries stamped her cultural creations. The culture of France, like that of China before the coming of the Yahoos, was a closed culture, not so much hostile as simply indifferent to foreign influence. This did not mean that French men of letters, artists, scholars, and patrons were unaware of what was going on abroad. Just like their fellows in other lands, they explored and sampled foreign cultures. Nevertheless, far more choosy than other peoples, they brought home only what could be worked effortlessly into the national pattern and disdained bothering about the rest. To this extent the exclusiveness of the French intellectual and that of the Mandarin are true kin.

The Great Wall has been breached. The French middle-brow now reads several times as many books and goes to several times as many plays by foreign authors as did his father, who had worked his way through *War and Peace* (the Russians, incomprehensible, remote, savage, openhanded, and childishly eager to assimilate to French civilization, held a special place among foreigners), misquoted Goethe, and detested Shakespeare. Now Frenchmen write novels which could have been written by Americans, Germans, and Irishmen; French *haute couture* anxiously scans Fifth Avenue and the Via Veneto; French architects seek to keep step with their American, Dutch, and Italian colleagues, far more dexterous in the use of novel materials; and no longer is all of French cuisine and viticulture superior, as a matter of course, to the culinary arts practiced by other peoples.

French culture has survived many ideological schisms. Ever since the Revolution of 1789, France has been a country of political extremes. Thus, the Communist-Fascist polarization of the 1930's kept within the tradition. Now the ideological tensions have lessened.

France, like the rest of the Western world, has become surfeited with ideology. The universal tide of pragmatism creeps across the French landscape furrowed for two hundred years by dissenting philosophies about society and man. France, too, is beginning to succumb to fashionable anti-intellectualism, all the more fashionable because its avant-guard includes respected intellectuals. In modern industrial and planified France, the place of political society is being taken by the society of status. Unbeknown to themselves, Frenchmen now let their thoughts drift from the classical political divisions to the far more complex differentiations of status. Whereas in the France of the 1930's the Communist and the Fascist stood for the absolutes of social antagonism, the symbolic figures of the France of the 1960's are the scientist and the beatnik. At one terminal point lies the nuclear reactor of the French Atomic Energy Commission at Pierrelatte; at the other the cave just off the Boulevard St.-Germain. Moreover, the French economy is now fully capable of meeting the mass demand for status-giving goods.

Having completed my manuscript, I engaged a typist whom an American businessman had recommended to me as a linguist. Her tendency to reconcile English orthography with French phonetics and to improve upon my innumerable grammatical errors impressed a unique stamp upon the work which, I suspected, the most loving editorial care would be unable to erase. I sent a copy to a New York publisher who had replied to my solicitation of interest.

The work was never published. Notwithstanding its many flaws, it stood the test of time. Since I had asked no one's advice, I did not have to contend with any preconceptions except my own. Among these, the most firmly held was my opinion, derived as much from my sense of smell as from the documentary evidence, that something was hopelessly rotten in the state of France. Because French democracy was peace-loving and corrupt, it did not follow that, in war, France would prevail against the warlike and nasty Nazis.

It has been my experience that nasty people often prove to be uncommonly efficient and dirty fighters and that people who cherish peace as the supreme good and prefer an easy life to exertion often have no stomach for war. These not-so-profound insights guided me in my study of French politics on the brink of war. Though I believed that good will vanquish evil, I could not find enough good in the Third Republic to apply this axiom confidently to the impending conflict. Hence I concluded that France would crack up under the blows of her old adversary. The study was laden with statistics; the style was pedestrian; and what I had to say was the last thing a Western audience wanted to hear. The books on French politics published throughout the 1930's in America and England contained views that differed widely from mine. Indeed, many were written by Francophiles who did not wish to see or smell the decay under their noses; not a few were written by Communists and fellow travelers who labeled anyone to the right of the Popular Front as a Fascist stooge.

Many years later I rummaged among the fanciful literature which in those years passed as "Inside France." Though these books are now forgotten and their authors have gone on to other feats of political reporting, they are worth rereading; they explain much about the shocked incredulity with which the American public witnessed the fall of France, and about the slowness of America's reaction to European catastrophe.

I was eager to see in print the work which I had so laboriously wrought. Since the publisher to whom I had sent my manuscript did not seem to share in my sense of urgency, I proposed to call on him in person and arouse him to the importance of my intelligence from France. Furthermore, I expected to find a ready market for my occasional papers and, possibly, an enlightened newspaper editor who would avail himself of my services as foreign correspondent. The year was 1937. It seemed to me that anyone could see how much faster the wheels were turning. There was no time to lose. I booked passage for New York. I timed my departure so as to leave me a week in London, for King George VI was about to be crowned in Westminster Abbey.

Edward VIII, who, as Prince of Wales, had achieved unprecedented popularity, yielded to the pressures of the Establishment and relinquished the crown to his brother. The controversy over the issue—which, incidentally, revolved around Mrs. Simpson's status as a divorcee and not about her humble American antecedents—afforded Mr. Churchill the opportunity to emerge briefly from the political wilderness. He championed the King's cause. That cause lost, he retreated again into that semiobscurity which England has always reserved—in times of normalcy—to her strongest and most willful sons.

The coronation was preceded by a series of festivities, attended by the notables of the Empire, dignitaries from most other countries, and masses of ordinary peoples from all over the world. A London couple invited me to be their guest. Their house, now devoured by a high and ungainly office building, stood close to Hyde Park. Visitors from the Dominions crowded the spacious drawing room. I volunteered to assist in pushing cookies, pumping soda bottles, and cheering guests who failed to mix with the others. My host presented me to an Afrikander lady whose English reverberated with the guttural sounds of her native Dutch. She asked me whence I hailed. The general din of the party added two letters in the name of my native land. To my amazement, I found myself answering searching questions about the postnatal care of kangaroos, the trajectory of boomerangs, and the price fluctuations of sheep wool. Taking leave, the Afrikander lady told her puzzled host that she had learned much about Australia, and that South Africans and Australians should know one another better. Thus another misunderstanding had gone into cementing the solidarity of the Dominions, which—as we now know—did not survive the ravages of improved communications.

In the folklore of most European peoples, a flaming sunset heralds great calamity. In retrospect, the coronation assembled for the last time the peoples of the Commonwealth under the canopy of English power, political, economic, and military. During the subsequent era of appeasement and World War II, the centrifugal forces which, ever since World War I, had strained against the cohesiveness of the Commonwealth broke to the surface. In the Munich showdown several Dominions followed the motherland either reluctantly or not at all. At war, American power, rather than British power, shielded the members of the Commonwealth overseas and, in the last resort, secured the defense of the British Isles. At the time of the coronation, keen minds at home and abroad discerned the portents of dissolution.

Ever since the beginning of the century, Britain's industry and commerce had been losing ground, and, more likely than not, the decline of British power was one of the principal causes of World War I. Yet Britain's prestige, refreshed by victory in World War I, endured. Prestige is the gloss of past achievement; long after real power has begun to fade away, its reflected image still dazzles the beholder. For two hundred years Spain lived on little else than the inertia of history, and the ghost of Spanish power was laid to its final rest only in Manila Bay.

In 1937 the image of British power still glowed in many alluring colors. London was still the world's true capital; even the soot on the walls of her shrines, St. Paul's, the Abbey, the Houses of Parliament, the clubs on Pall Mall, and St. James's, Whitehall, and the royal palaces, seemed the patina of timeless worth and might rather than ordinary grime. White ties and tiaras gleamed through the windows of tall Rolls-Royces and Daimlers. Upon the briefest scrutiny, police constables unerringly determined who should be, and who need not be, addressed "sir." At the occasion of state, the great of the realm and their attendants wore nonchalantly their resplendent robes, uniforms, and liveries, at ease in their hieratic roles as befitted the guardians of an old yet vigorous tradition.

The men were by far handsomer than their women. Though it is true that beautiful Englishwomen of the upper classes managed to seem more beautiful than their sisters elsewhere, they were few and far between. By contrast, an average type of virile good looks could be found well represented in any club and regimental mess or at any county meet. Men dressed well, women did not. In a society as much addicted to horses as the English, the male physique is apt to model itself upon the spare grace of the horseman, whereas women, be they devotees of the sport or mere onlookers, tend to acquire the features of the steed. These generalizations did not apply to the upper-upper classes. The oddly shaped members of the seasoned peerage and their kin, deviating from the standard looks of *the* English gentleman, provided a good living to generations of caricaturists.

Throughout the realm the most unducal men in looks were the dukes. As Nancy Mitford observed, a duke may, and usually does, keep the most varied company; he draws the line against any other duke. Hence, the one and only time dukes can be reviewed en masse is when an important ceremonial occasion such as a coronation compels their joint attendance. Though I was separated from the portals of the Abbey by a considerable distance, I was able, thanks to a pair of powerful binoculars, to scan the countenances of dukes and earls. I am satisfied that the English upper-upper classes belong to a recessive species only remotely kin to the species "gentleman," which, since the beginning of the nineteenth century, has dominated the appearance of English society. Winston Churchill, member of a ducal house, has been noted to resemble, at times, John Bull and, at times, an angry baby. Never could he be mistaken for anything but a nobleman by birth and bearing. Yet he has never been commended for his gentlemanly appearance.

The English gentleman merits a place of honor among the makers of Western civilization. Without him it might not exist. As an ideal human type, he left much to be desired. Even at his best, he could not quite rid himself of that cant and snobbery which crabbed Victorian society. He prized action; he disdained thought or, at least, pretended to do so. He made a fetish of sports, especially those entailing heavy personal risks and, for the animal population, lethal consequences. At his worst he was a bore. His steadiness under any and all conditions, especially disaster, has become a legend like the kindred stoicism of the Spartans and Romans. His code was narrow. He lived and died by it. He was reliable, though not always predictable. Though with sure hand and cold eye he slaughtered certain kinds of animals, he cared tenderly for others. He loved flowers. Reverentially he stood ready to chastise any cad behaving indelicately toward any true lady. He knew how to lead men and when to leave them alone. He set a standard of honor high enough to command universal esteem and not so high as to place it beyond the reach of all but a small exclusive caste.

Because his code blended the aspirations of the up-and-coming middle classes with aristocratic privilege—the privilege that obliges—the English gentleman eased the great social transformation of nineteenth-century England. Modern parliamentary usage is unthinkable without him. Strictly speaking, Western democracy *is* gentlemanly representative government. Neither France nor Italy nor Germany was able to create an ideal human type which fused new and old values, a common denominator of conflicting class interests. In France and Italy, Catholicism stunted that sense of self-reliance which the Protestant conscience wrests from its lonely struggle with God; in Germany, Luther ranged himself with the princes who massacred their rebellious peasants, and, anyway, the German soul tarried too long in the vast, dark woods of the pagan myths. Hence the vicissitudes of democracy upon the Continent. Hence also the tragicomic fiasco of so many efforts to inculcate Western democracy into non-Western societies outside the writ of the gentlemanly code. Hence also the relative success of the democratic experiment throughout the former British colonies. Perhaps the key problem of the twentieth century is how to develop an ideal of man that can take the place held by the fair and hard-playing English gentleman.

People all over the world would like to possess American products; few want to live by the American code of values; and even fewer know what this code is. There was a time in the nineteenth century when all people who mattered, including some of England's sworn foes, wanted to *be* English gentlemen and, if they failed to become one, at least tried to look like one. Today, on the lowest of mass culture, a not-so-ideal American type exerts its attraction, and the bazaars of the East and the bars of Konakry and Augsburg teem with imitation-Americans, mostly adolescent. This grotesque parody concocted from things heard on the radio or seen on TV or read in magazines does not yet quite measure up to that sterling, hand-tooled model, the perfect English gentleman.

Of course, gentlemen, like anybody else, need to be fed and cared for. If the British Empire needed the gentleman, gentleman needed the British Empire. He administered it; if need be, he fought for it. Hunter, explorer, collector, and sometimes even trader, he roamed about in it. From it he made his living as a civil servant in the Colonial or the India Office, or as an officer in the Services, guarding "lifelines" and remote frontiers. From it he received what he cherished more highly than adequate pay and exciting action, namely, the honors which only the Monarch could bestow upon the chosen.

I do not believe that average men and women have ever benefited, in the long run, from empire. They may have taken pride in it, transferring to the symbol their own sense of inadequacy. Clearly, today's average Englishman does not think that, because

England has lost her empire, he had suffered a grievous loss. As a matter of fact, he suspects that he is better off for having been rid of the imperial burden.

To the gentleman the loss is real. All over England men and women, used to the exercise and prerequisites of authority, now putter about in small gardens, bereft of personal service. Young men, once destined to rule and to care for backward peoples and to command sailors and soldiers, now keep books, run garages, or live idly on shrinking incomes. It is far too early to say whether and how they will come to terms with their lot, or, if they do not, what will happen to them and to England.

In the age of automation, changing jobs is a difficult business under the best of circumstances. For England, the disemployment of the gentleman has created a grave problem. Like all real human problems, it eludes statistical measurement. Hence it does not receive the attention it deserves. Yet I suspect that it bears upon many other problems that we hear much about, such as the chronic weakness of the pound, the lurid goings-on in high places, and the disaffection from the Conservative party of its old guard. At the outbreak of World War II, Alfred Rosenberg, the Nazi ideologue, observed gleefully: "This is the end of the English gentleman." Hateful sayings are all the more hateful when they are true.

Chapter Eleven

Upon my return to the United
States, a small magazine published a few articles which I had
written on European affairs. After a while the editors, undaunted
by the mounting deficit, added me to their staff. Shortly thereafter I married.

I notice that autobiographies are being dedicated to the author's wife more consistently than other kinds of books, and that,
somewhere along in the text, a few sentences acclaim the author's
choice of a mate as the wisest and happiest decision he ever made.
Since I do not remember having made a decision and just got
married because, under the then prevailing conditions, this
seemed the natural thing to do, I cannot credit my wisdom for
the good things which marriage brought me. Furthermore, since
I married relatively late in life and had no children, I do not
believe that marriage affected my character as profoundly as it
must in the case of those who marry early, raise a family, and
stay married for a long time, though perhaps not to the same
spouse. Yet marriage changed many things in my life. I had

grown older and, as I began to feel less certain of the permanence of youth, I had become more mindful of the feelings of others. Be that as it may, it is only through marriage that I gained full admission to the human race. Now, not all will agree on how well I stand as a member, and I, too, have doubts on that very score. Without marriage, however, my qualifications for membership would never have been put to the test. I cannot see that one can understand one's own idiosyncrasies and hence those of others except by that compromise called marriage.

In February, 1938, Nazi armored units entered Vienna. Though the Nazis had won a strong following in Austria, especially in the Alpine provinces, they clinched the *Anschluss* with a massive military invasion. Had the Nazis left the take-over to their local Quislings, the Vienna workers and some of the Catholic organizations, as well as the minuscule Austrian army and security troops might have put up a fight. Leaving nothing to chance, the Nazis mounted so impressive a demonstration of the Reichswehr's firepower as to cow the small and helpless country into submission—and to forestall foreign intervention. Confronted by the accomplished fact, the Western democracies, as they are wont to do in such situations, wrung their hands, took legal advice, protested, and did nothing. Mussolini, who until then had supported an independent Austria as the last buffer between himself and his all-too-clever pupil, now swallowed his misgivings and welcomed the Führer at the Brenner. The outbreak of another world war had, so I thought, become a certainty. Since France and Britain were weaker than they had been in 1914 and could not count upon the support of Russia, the United States would have to redress the balance. With the zeal of inexperience, I invited my readers to accept the inevitability of armed intervention.

Raoul de Roussy de Sales, welcoming me to the profession and the band of warmongers, suggested that I launch my attack upon the public's peace of mind from the lecture platform. My agent, who had billed me as an American journalist of Austrian birth, persuaded a civic forum in Boston to let me talk on the Rape of Austria. Deeply as I loved Austria, I meant to address myself to a purpose wider than a requiem. I prepared my address, memorized every word of it, and talked for one hour about things to come. Although I did not say that Americans would and should go to war—no one said so publicly in the spring of 1938—I tried to marshal my evidence in such a way that my audience could draw no other conclusion. Although my revelations of the Nazi's deep designs and my feeling words about Austria's tragic fate were well received, my attempt at nudging my audience into the contemplation of wider and grimmer perspectives fell flat.

Today it is difficult to recapture the spirit of a vanished America: ninety-nine out of a hundred Americans thought of themselves as onlookers who, though sympathetic to the sufferings of mankind, could not possibly be sucked into mankind's dirty politics. It is, of course, utter nonsense to assert that the internationally minded many were restrained by the isolationist few: except for an exceedingly small but influential minority, *all* Americans were isolationist.

My lecture agent, who knew what kind of "message" middle-class audiences wanted to hear or would stand for—by this knowledge he made his living—and had "handled" everybody from Hindu swamis to former British Cabinet members, impressed upon me the wisdom of circumlocution. Since I had never spoken publicly and suffered the torments of stage fright, I accepted his advice. I wish now that I had unabashedly mongered war and given my first audience a run for its money.

Since then I have lectured to many audiences, academic and lay. Although I have not overcome the dread of those few minutes when audience and speaker are still estranged from each other by sticky preliminaries, I have learned that no American audience is implacably hostile. No matter how weird is the "message," there are always a few independent souls who will applaud it. A speaker need not fear to champion an eccentric cause as long as he observes the amenities of public discussion: do not impugn anybody's good faith! shun sarcasm! let go of the punch line before it turns flabby! talk straight at the average intelligent American instead of below his feet or above his head! and, above all things, be brief, briefer than the audience expects! These simple rules may not recommend themselves to a mind more subtle and discursive than mine. I am convinced, however, that in most cases their observance will contribute to the general welfare.

In no other country are as many people lecturing and letting themselves be lectured to as in America. Of course, in Communist countries attendance is a matter of survival, and whenever the apparatus does not organize, conspire, or purge, it talks complusively. In the Communist countries, however, the lecture business, which, like everything else, is the monopoly of the party, does not reflect the true workings of supply and demand.

Not all Western countries are lecture-minded. Although Frenchmen like to listen to political speeches for the pure enjoyment of oratory, they would rather talk themselves than listen to anybody else. Frenchmen do not have an open mind, nor do Italians, Spaniards, and Arabs. Intensely partisan, they have made up their mind and disown a public speaker who tries to change it. After World War II, however, the lecture business boomed in West Germany. American influence, especially the seminal forums of the *Amerika Häuser*, won over the educated and re-educated Germans to the practices of the Open Mind. In Germany, there are now nearly as many civic discussion centers and study groups as in America. I believe that, among the postwar innovations, this development contributes most to the health of German democracy.

To study the lecturer and his public in their natural habitat one must go to America. For many reasons I do not cavil at the vigor of the industry. Yet at times—especially when I must sit through somebody else's lecture—I suffer qualms. The text of a lecture can be read in a fraction of the time it takes to say it. In most instances the paper version can be obtained more cheaply and conveniently than admission to the lecturer's presence. More importantly, it can be reread at leisure or not read at all. The only good reason for jamming oneself into a drafty auditorium—all auditoriums are drafty—is enjoyment of the audio-visual spectacle rather than the quest for learning. If men must lecture and listen, then the Socratic method offers the straight approach to instruction. The audience should be small; the speaker should say his piece in fifteen minutes; and the set statement should open up a casual give-and-take. Nowadays too many words are spoken to too many people. The record is easily lost or garbled, and the purpose of its all—a little more light for the open mind—is blotted out by torrents of garrulity.

A lecture tour is a strenuous affair. Since I could not claim VIP status, the fees and expense allowance were modest. After a long night in an upper berth or a few hours' ride over icy roads, it was not always easy to muster spontaneous enthusiasm for those noteworthy landmarks in which my hosts took pride. As day followed upon day, one middle-sized town in the Midwestern lecture belt looked like the other. The faces of the chairmen melted into the one fixed countenance of patronizing benevolence.

Yet I gained much. I met many people, of whom not a few busied themselves with the political and cultural affairs of their respective communities. Some were widely read and traveled. With few exceptions, they stood with the Great Center of American politics. Ideologically temperate, if not frigid, they reserved their enthusiasm for the step-by-step pursuit of social progress. Notwithstanding their instinctive revulsion against Hitler, Mussolini, and Stalin, they viewed international conflict not as the clash of ideologies but as the logical consequence of European power politics. They suspected that old Europe was quarreling as she always had over territories and markets. As Americans, they wanted no part of it. More importantly, they were convinced that America, as long as she did not voluntarily join the fray could not be dragged into it. Today I am not so sure that then, I either fully understood or justly weighed the argument for detachment. Today it seems far stronger a case, particularly on the grounds of old-fashioned power politics, than popular historiography—what happened had to happen and, therefore, was good—makes it out to be. Certainly it cannot be refuted conclusively until another thirty or forty years have gone by.

From the lecture hall I stepped into the classroom. A few weeks after the Munich crisis a civic group in the city with which much of my life and work was to be associated for the next twenty-five years, invited me to address it. Since I had only one song to sing, I talked about the coming war. I sensed that my audience, chiefly businessmen and lawyers, did not warm up to the prospect. The meeting adjourned. The chairman, partner in one of those sprawling law firms for which Philadelphia has become a byword and a trustee of the University of Pennsylvania, asked me whether I would care to repeat my lecture to a group of teachers and students. I agreed. Soon thereafter I accepted the formal invitation of a dean, the first member of this formidable species to enter my life, and confronted, again for the first time, an academic body. The encounter led to my employment a few months later as a part-time instructor in political science and, by the slow stages of academic progression, to my present place in the hierarchy.

Of all the turns along my road, this was the most unexpected. Before I took it I had meant to travel far and wide, but never in the direction of scholarship. Then, had I known whither the turn would lead me, I would have hastened to retrace my steps. For as I saw my idealized image, its many pleasing shades did not include the pallor of scholarship.

The successful men of action whom I had known and whose example I had tried to emulate paid polite tribute to learning; they did not extend their esteem of intellectual achievement to live professors. In that remote and now improbable past, the academic stood for little in the affairs of business and of state, and for even less in the social pecking order.

The New Deal, in its springtime, had placed some of its academic auxiliaries into high government positions. Yet the populace viewed the professorial expert as an odd and somewhat comic figure. The rank and file of the old ruling elite, the businessmen, minced no words: the real world, that is, the nation's business, could do nicely without the theorizing of the professors. Since then we have come a long way. The process that began in World War II has been completed in the age of the Cold War. The academic has been fully integrated in American society. From integration he has gone on to the plateaus of political and economic power. He now meets coequally, upon the summit of society, with the banker, the corporation executive, the corporate lawyer, and the ruling politicians. His coequal status is now being acknowledged as a matter of course.

The entry of the academic expert constitutes the most revolutionary development of our times, destined to transform our haphazard society into an orderly society of merit and rank. Among the keys that open doors to advancement, the doctorate is surely one of the most important and most common. To many doors it is the one and only key. Not only has the professor gained entry into government and business, both embrace him. Professors sit on the board of directors of large corporations; and not a few of the most successful companies, exploiting novel techniques, are managed by former professors.

Who would have thought on that day twenty-five years ago when I timidly approached the campus, that purebred academics, rather than bankers, lawyers, and politicos, would hold high offices of state? As I write, both the Secretary of State and the President's Assistant for National Security Affairs are former university deans and professors; at least three U.S. ambassadors to key countries (India, Japan, and Brazil) are Ph. D.'s, professors, and noted authors. On the level of Assistant Secretary, former professors abound in various departments of the federal government. Professors sit in the Senate and House.

Academia has advanced on all fronts; professors have gained admission to those exclusive town and country clubs of the eastern seaboard which, once upon a time, excluded everyone except very rich men of Nordic origin and the sons of old families, perhaps not quite as rich as the former, yet clubbable by right of birth. With power and recognition has come affluence. Professors are making good money, and some are making a great deal of it. Top salaries compare favorably with the wages of junior executives in the big corporations. In addition, consulting jobs can be highly renumerative, and some scholarly tomes are selling nearly as well as the works of Ian Fleming. For those academics who have struck the bonanza of the Foundations, life can be sweeter still: relieved of the ordinary chores, such as teaching and departmental administration, they can pour their creative energies into long-range and very long-range projects of research which require extensive travel to interesting places and which, if they ever are completed, suggest even more searching and costlier projects. Affluent, important, and self-important, the academic elite has risen to the high places of power and prestige. Plato's designated rulers must still share with lesser men the government of the

Republic. But never have their prospects been brighter.

When I entered the profession I thought that I would sit by the still waters, a scholarly recluse remote from the mainstream of life. I welcomed the prospect. I had reached middle age. I had tried my hand at many things, and moved from place to place. Now I would settle down to the austere routine of teaching and study. We closed our apartment in New York and moved to the country.

The old farmhouse in which we made our home, and from which twenty miles of winding country roads led to the city's limits, had been for a long time in the possession of my wife's family. For many years it had stood empty. Now wax brought back the sheen to oaken floors and walnut doors, shutters gleamed in fresh green paint. We planted trees and shrubs, repaired walls, mended fences, and reclaimed the cultivable land that had lain fallow ever since, shortly after World War I, cattle and farm tools had been sold.

Up until the Civil War, the counties of Chester and Lancaster were hailed as the granary of Pennsylvania, if not the entire eastern seaboard. Their rich wheatlands and sleek cattle, vast barns and solid farmsteads, built of hewn fieldstone, evoked an image of rural well-being which, to this day, has not been entirely dimmed by the vapors of factory chimney and combustion engine. The opening up of the farmlands in the Mississippi basin, the introduction of power-driven farm machinery and the westward migration of labor worsened the competitive position of the Pennsylvania dirt farmer. Although innate stubbornness and public subsidy have kept him alive, the trends of the times have shoved him into lengthening ranks of superfluous men. In the vicinity of the big city the rise of land values permitted those farmers who had been shrewd and frugal enough to hang on to retreat in good order—into small business or rentierdom.

Suburbia has now advanced to our line fence. The last farmer has sold the homestead which the industry of seven generations had filled with a surprising variety of objects—Georgian sideboards; Victorian sofas, sinuous and brocaded; a majestic crystal chandelier; heavy carved bedsteads, sleighs, carts, and carriages; hundred years' lithographs; Franklin stoves; thirty years' electronic gadgets; sets of Lowestoft and plastic kitchen ware. At auction, the Americana fetched the highest prices; the sleighs grace whimsically suburban lawns. The last farmer, unburdened by the past, now resides near a beach in Florida. The best plowland has been made over into a golf course; the rest of the ancestral acres are being "developed."

When, two years before World War II, we settled on our farm, the shadow of progress had not yet fallen upon the rustic idyl. Contented, I went about my tasks. I had not taught before; I had not gone to school for fifteen years. Most of what I knew about international politics and diplomacy I had picked up from live politicians and diplomats of my acquaintance; from cursory reading, especially the biographies of illustrious statesmen; and from having been inadvertently at some spot where somebody was making history or pretending to do so. Thus armed, I stepped into the classroom.

What the American student lacks in deference to professional authority, he makes up by directness. The informality of the American classroom has been a cause of wonderment to many a visitor accustomed to the aloof ways of the European university. (In Continental Europe the professor is not only an academic but also a government functionary. More often than not, he is a pettifogging bureaucrat.) American education has many faults, most of which are rooted in the hedonism of an affluent society. Yet, in America the decent and lively relationship between teacher and student comes closer to the Greek ideal than in any other country. For education begins with teacher and student respecting each other as partners in a common undertaking. Although education is not a "democratic" process, the right kind of education educates free men. The roots of totalitarianism are as manifold as they are crooked. Undoubtedly, one of them is tyranny in the classroom. Up until World War II the German educational system was superior to the American in all respects except one: among the various types of toadies to authority, the German professor was the most abysmal.

I grew fond of my students and, I believe, some grew fond of me in that casual, good-humored way which is the way of the American young. I was much too absorbed in what I talked about to bother about teaching methods; in fact, to this day I have neglected to bone up on educationist theory. I suspect that teaching cannot be learned anyway. I grew fond of my colleagues who bore patiently with my ignorance of academic etiquette. I was being tried; I meant to prove myself, serve my apprenticeship, and come to rest in the bosom of the Academic Establishment. Then the war broke out.

In August, 1939, my wife and I had sailed for Europe, headed —so we thought—for Yugoslavia, Greece, and Turkey. I wanted to investigate Axis penetration in the Balkans on the spot and bring home a series of articles in which, so I hoped, political acumen would blend nicely with touches of local color. Then, before the coming of collectivization and concrete, the Balkans were still a very colorful and romantically sinister place. The kings and queens, foreign spies, and Macedonian assassins still did their best to live up to Elinor Glyn and Eric Ambler's standards. I looked forward to a voyage of exploration which would gain me access to the elite of journalism: the corps of foreign correspondents.

The news of the German-Soviet Nonaggression Pact reached us in the middle of the Atlantic. Both the Germans and the Soviets were concentrating troops along the frontiers of Poland. The crops had been brought in. The weather was fine. Europe was ready for war. We changed our plans and headed for Paris. I wanted to persuade my mother to return with us to America. We took rooms in the Hotel Georges V, just off the Avenue des Champs-Elysées. I went about settling my mother's affairs, and obtained her American entry permit from a harried but accessible consul.

In France the month of August has always been dedicated to national vacation. Thus, in Paris, every second store was shuttered; in many an apartment building only the concierge or his stand-in kept his lonely vigil by the ever-simmering cooking pot. After a few days most of the tourists had departed. In our hotel only a few guests remained. Not a few waiters and porters had received their orders of mobilization. So had the maître d'hôtel who in impeccable tails shepherded the cart with the hors

d'oeuvres across the empty dining room and suggested that we
opt for smoked salmon rather than foie gras. So had the wine
steward who poured, with a slight tremor, a summery, light Bur-
gundy into our glasses.

According to General Douhet, Italian airman and military
theorist, the next war would start with a massive air strike against
the principal cities. After their annihilation in frightfulness, little
would remain to be done for superior air power but to preside
over the mopping up of the opposing forces, deprived of their
supplies and, presumably, of their dear ones at home lying buried
under the urban debris. This theory appeared highly credible to
many city people, though to only a few professional military
trained to the waging of a long war. In fact, Hitler and Mussolini
incorporated the idea of total annihilation from the sky into their
strategy of terror, precursor to the strategy with which Americans have become familiar under the name of nuclear blackmail.
Our wine steward told us that he did not cavil—*il faut en finir*—
at joining his regiment somewhere in Alsace, but that his Parisian
wife, upon whom fell the care of an invalid mother and several
infants, viewed his retreat into the shelter of the Maginot Line as
the lesser part of valor. Those Parisians who could, especially the
rich, prolonged their vacations.

Fall had come early, and the leaves had begun to turn. The sun
was still warm and, since few people and even fewer cars were
about, one could stroll about Paris as if in a park when the crowd
had left and the gates were being shut for the night. It could have
been restful and pleasant had it not been for the suspense that
hung over the city like an enormous bat. The Germans and the
Soviets marched into Poland. War was declared. I listened to Mr.
Chamberlain's flat voice on the radio. We lunched upon a deserted terrace; we looked at the sky.

Eventually we made our way to the Atlantic port. Our car was
laden with our steamer trunks and my mother's possessions. We
passed other vehicles heavily freighted with luggage and anxiety,
the first trickle of the great exodus. The American liner on which
we had booked our passage had been commandeered to assist in
the evacuation from Europe of American tourists and other
"stranded" citizens. Aboard, we were informed that, due to the

emergency, we had been assigned to less spacious quarters than those booked and paid for. I shared a cabin, tastefully appointed for two occupants, with five adult males of diverse ages and hygienic standards. Our cabin could have accommodated another six, and all of us would have survived the voyage with less discomfort than one suffers in the course of a subway ride in the rush hour. I think we could have come to love our cozy quarters had the vessel not been billed as a spacious luxury liner. We had paid the fare, and the management pretended that we received full value for the money. But saloon and swimming pool had been converted into dormitories, and within a surprisingly short time stewards grew surly, officers curt, and lavatories filthy. Moreover, at night the blackout kept us invisible to hostile submarines and inaccessible to fresh air. Supplies ran short, especially towels, bed sheets, soap, and liquor.

My bunkmate taught logic in one of the best colleges for women and nursed a bad case of eczema under his armpit. We ran out of Russell and Husserl on the second day of the voyage. I soon found a corner in the gymnasium and bedded down on a wrestling mat. My neighbor, whose honeymoon had been cut short by events, kept nocturnal boatdeck trysts with his wife, who was assigned to an all-female cabin. Upon his return he fell instantly asleep.

Despite a crescendo of rumors about periscopes sighted afar and sabotage aboard, we reached New York. I now look back upon this unkempt voyage with gratitude, for it introduced me to the lore of living in an emergency. One day I could share vicariously a platform in the London tube with Henry Moore's family group while the Blitz pounded overhead. Moreover, I can now imagine vividly the many crowded escapes across dangerous waters to the promised land. I rediscovered the cathartic power of prolonged discomfort and even of boredom. I touched, perhaps ever so lightly, the mystery of withdrawal, of reposeful solitude in the midst of a crowd. I realized that the comforts of our civilization are truly fabulous; they rain upon us like sterilized manna. The open and hidden persuaders ask us to take them for granted; they shackle us far more tightly than we think to powers which we do not control and which, deep down in our hearts, we fear. For surfeit of comforts, a luxury liner transforming itself haphazardly into a floating refugee camp provides a mild but salutary emetic.

I returned to the university and, with half a mind, did my chores. Upon the fall of France it became plain that we, too, must go to war or, at least, that our government conducted our affairs as if we would. Did Mr. Roosevelt "want" us to go to war? This question, like all questions of a man's inmost motivations, is unanswerable. Did he pursue policies that were well-nigh certain to involve us in the fighting on the side of Britain? Of course, he did. At that time, for reasons which were rooted in my understanding of Eurasian strategy and which I still deem valid under present circumstances, I agreed with these policies. (These reasons may not have been those which informed the President's decisions, and from the subsequent course of events, I now surmise that they were not.)

In 1940 only one issue mattered, and no statesman worth his salt would ever try to deal with two, one actual and the other hypothetical. It is, however, a fact so incontrovertible as to perplex even the most adroit mythmakers that most Americans did not support the President's foreign policy; Congress passed the draft law by a majority of one. Had the Presidency not brought to bear its enormous powers of patronage and coercion, the law would have been defeated crushingly. Certainly, had any of the measures taken in the gray area between neutrality and belligerence, such as Lend-Lease, destroyers for bases, and antisubmarine patrol, been submitted to a national plebiscite, they would have met with overwhelming disapproval. As it was, his frequent recourse to executive agreements, placing before Congress accomplished facts, bespeaks the President's awareness of the nation's frigid temper.

Though most Americans detested Hitler, they did not extend this sentiment to all of his countrymen. Millions of Americans of German descent, while of two minds on the Nazis' culpability, did not relish the idea of another war against the land of their origin. Thus the intensity of the anti-Nazi current—especially anti-Nazi sentiment wedded to anti-German bias—fell off perceptibly as it flowed from the eastern seaboard to Midwest and

Southwest. Given the distribution then prevailing of economic and racial groups, this differential corresponded to the realities of popular interests, attitudes, and commitments.

We know the chronology of events that led the United States to war. Of their inwardness our knowledge is incomplete and will remain so for a long time, probably forever. Only the defeated, upon his unconditional surrender, can be forced to come across with the complete records. Be that as it may, America's approach to war raises more questions than have thus far been answered—and even put. Does a democracy like ours *make* its foreign policy? If foreign policy is offered for public inspection only after the dice have been cast, can the democratic process be made retroactive? If not, there is a break in the circuit. Can that gap between institutions and men be closed? Or should it better remain forever open? Some of my friends tell me that the answer is "leadership"—others, that it is "education." The people need a strong leader, preferably inspired; moreover, better education will enable them to understand the Problem and to support or, if need be, check the leader's policies for solving it. Unfortunately, in my metier, the stock in trade is words. Their ambiguity is harassing enough in ordinary affairs; in politics, ambiguity is the norm. In the nature of things, the professional politician is always a few jumps ahead of the public's political education. But there is no nonpartisan board of regents for supervising political education; a strong leader, inspired by whatever it is that makes men want to lead, does his own educating of the public. And this is about where we first came in. The average man has something else to do, and hence cannot give full time to the study of political science. Who keeps tabs on the gatekeeper's daughter when the gatekeeper keeps the gate?

The last war was the last war which even the bulk of the Western intelligentsia wanted to fight—for the right and the good against the unjust and the evil. Today the intellectual who does not bow to survival ethics must be willing to forgo the warming assurance of companionship. If he is so boorish as to assert that the oppressed is not as guilty as the oppressor and the aggressor not as innocent before international law as the aggressed, and to insist upon the notable difference between one's friends and one's foes, then he must manfully bear up under the charge of indifference to the survival of humanity. By one of those reversals, for the making of which only Western Progressive Thought has the precious formula, to want to fight *now* for the good against evil, or even to differentiate sharply between good and evil, is to betray the trust of the intellectual—*trahison des clercs.*

Then I was buoyed by the near-unanimous agreement of the West's leading intellectuals, except for the Communist hard core, on the goodness of fighting Hitler and Mussolini. I, too, wanted to do my bit and looked for suitable employment, preferably active and out of doors.

I had written a book on political geography. A good part of *Geopolitics* was given over to the analysis of the German school of *Geopolitik* and the teachings of its founder, General Haushofer. Strong evidence pointed to close affinity between Nazi strategy and the general's brand of geopolitics. By one of those accidents which make book publishing as exciting as Russian roulette, my book became a minor best seller. Two other books on the same topic, no worse than mine, appeared at about the same time. But mine caught on. It also brought me to the attention of one of the country's leading geographers, Dr. Isaiah Bowman, president of a renowned university.

During World War I, Dr. Bowman had advised President Wilson on how to redraw the frontiers of Europe. President Roosevelt now called upon him to serve as his consultant on the geographical problems of another war and its future settlement. Among these happened to be one of grave personal concern to the President: where to find homes for the hundred thousands of people uprooted by persecution and war? Neither strictly military nor even of immediate political importance, the problem engaged the President's generous humanitarianism; moreover, it was likely to bear upon the future peace. Events confirmed the President's foresight, though not quite his judgment as between various proposed solutions. At the President's behest, the problem was raised to the status of a Project and thus entered into the long procession of Special Projects, Task Forces and Ad Hoc Committees which marched and countermarched between the

President's office, the departments, and the innumerable emergency-born agencies. Dr. Bowman asked me to join the Project as chief of the research staff and assistant to the Project director, a widely traveled and enterprising anthropologist. Thus, a few months after Pearl Harbor, I occupied a cubbyhole in one of those temporary quarters which housed the overflow of wartime government.

Chapter Twelve

WASHINGTON seemed the most unlikely place for heroic feats at war. Certainly the Project did not spur the war effort. And so I daydreamed of atolls in the Pacific, the heaving deck of a destroyer, and the sands of Tripoli. Most of my friends had joined the armed forces and had gone to war. Some had already returned from distant battles, slimmed down and beribboned; a few I would never see again.

In America the civilian population was spared most of the inconveniences of war. We ate as well as we always had; we slept in our beds, safe from the raiders of the sky. Yet we were an ill-humored lot, given to bouts of irritation at the petty discomforts visited upon us by the Emergency. Even the official morale builders who exhorted us to step up our effort, live by our coupons, and save electricity found it difficult to make us believe in the heroism of our sacrifice and the indispensability of our contribution. Moreover, the official eulogy of our fighting men made our humdrum existence look all the drabber. I surmised that I belonged to that large part of the male population who took the traditional, tribal view of war: the fighting man has the best of war.

Had it not been for the distant thunder, I would have taken wholeheartedly to the Project. Our mission was to sift the case histories of settlement, particularly settlement of the open land. Alive to the plight of millions of people uprooted by revolution and war, President Roosevelt had asked Dr. Bowman, a long-time student of rural settlement, to launch organized research in opportunities the world over for settling those who, in the official jargon, were now "displaced people." I myself had been "displaced." I had come to a foreign land to settle. Having passed through the purgatory, I felt kin to those who, after me, had to beg the bread of exile and knock at closed doors. When World War II broke out, not all of those who had been displaced by World War I had found homes. Although the strong, the young, the skilled, and especially the moneyed refugees from lands ravaged by wars and ideologies had found new homes in the more or less hospitable countries which could put manpower and capacity to good use, the aged, the sick, and the very poor were still being shunted from place to place. Wards of international charity, the latter were permitted to reside in those countries which could not find a plausible reason for throwing them out.

Now, the Soviet-German rape of Poland and the German conquest of France, Southeastern Europe, and part of Russia had dislodged many people. About one million Jews had fled Nazi-occupied Europe. The Germans had shanghaied hundreds of thousands of workers from the lands under their occupation and impressed them into German industry and agriculture. Although it was likely, once the Allies had won the war, that a large part of this uprooted humanity could be repatriated, place would have to be found for those hundreds of thousands or even millions who could not or would not return to their countries of origin. It was to this task that our project was to be addressed. Although its mandate was broad, weighty political reasons suggested that its scope be narrowed to the investigation of opportunities for rural settlement.

Virtually everywhere, trade unions and professional organizations looked askance at the eager and hungry foreigners prepared to work hard and, if need be, at low rates of pay. In some countries, as for example in Canada, political stability had for a long time depended on the maintenance of the ethnic balance. While on the face of it such multiracial societies might have been expected to welcome the infusion of alien blood, they have, in fact, pursued highly discriminatory policies of immigration. They had welcomed those who swell the larger and, therefore, dominant racial components; they closed their doors to those who, by increasing racial minorities, might strengthen actual or potential political minorities.

Since nearly everywhere people would rather live in cities than upon the land, work short hours at high wages rather than long hours at uncertain return, go to the movies rather than rise early to milk the cows or plow the field by the sweat of their brow, in many parts of the earth fertile soil lies fallow or marginal lands are not being brought under cultivation. It is here, we thought, that a sizable number of displaced persons could be put to useful work and gain admission to a national community. They would do work which no one else wanted to do. The local folks would not envy them their prosperity. Moreover, life on the open land is healthful, and in most countries the tiller of the soils is still being acclaimed, all concrete evidence to the contrary, as the "backbone of society." There is still a lot of cultivable land upon this globe which, with varying degrees of effort, could be made to bring forth fruit.

Thus, for example, Australia, and even the allegedly overpopulated West Indies, wait for the coming of the competent agronomist, industrious farm worker—and a little capital.

We discovered, too, some less cheery aspects of the problem of settlement. Like everybody else, our prospective client, the displaced person, preferred the city to the land. Most of the uprooted had been uprooted from a city apartment rather than a farmstead. Untrained in farm work and somewhat skeptical about the delights of life in the country, they wanted to go to a city—any city—rather than a village or solitary farm. Before misfortune befell them, their standard of living generally had been higher than that of their countrymen working on the land. Now, if they were to consent to go onto the open land, certain guarantees of minimum comfort had to be given them. Housing and community services would have to be provided. In certain places, such facilities could be made available only at great cost. Furthermore, the tools of skilled and profitable agriculture—the only kind of agriculture in which both host country and prospective immigrant were interested—were expensive. Heretofore, a number of experiments in agricultural settlement had failed principally for one reason: the initial investment and preparation had been inadequate. We calculated that the cost of settling Europeans upon the land in countries overseas would run as high as $25,000 per family. Depending on circumstances, this sum would provide them with housing, farm tools, roads, schools, and medical care. Of course, circumstances would vary greatly. But even in those places where the settler would not need to build up his new existence from the "ground up," he rarely would be able to avail himself of pre-existing facilities. He would have to make a considerable investment—or somebody else would have to make it for him. Agricultural settlement in, for example, Israel was to bear out our assumptions.

I do not believe that our endeavors were entirely in vain. Only a very few of the migrants of World War II vintage have been settled upon the land. Yet some were. These would have suffered greater hardships had it not been for better planning based upon the research of geographers, agronomists, anthropologists, sociologists, and experts in legislation on migration. Although the team of the Project did not include authorities in all these fields, it could, thanks to its powerful sponsor, draw on a great variety of expertise inside and outside the government.

From everywhere, research materials and advice poured into the offices of the Project, discreetly tucked away in the upper reaches of the Library of Congress. The task of sifting these materials and distilling them into documents brief enough to be read by high officials fell upon a versatile trio: Sergius Jacobson, a huge Muscovite, émigré of the October Revolution, and one of the most meticulous scholars I have ever known; Stefan Possony, an Austrian, onetime secretary of one of Schuschnigg's ministers, economist, historian, Jack-of-all-academic-trades and a man-with-ideas, mostly new; and Gottfried Salomon-de

La Tour, sociologist, driven from his professorial chair by the Frankfurt Nazis, his slim frame crowned by a fine Voltairian head—and, until his death in 1964, lifetime professor of sociology in Frankfurt, witty and fleet of speech.

The Project called for the ordinary skills of scholarship and, since it ranged over many parts of the globe, familiarity with a variety of countries and their languages. The Project, like any undertaking started by somebody with an entrée to high places, grew and prospered. Its staff multiplied. Most of my fellow workers were exodus originals. They had been on the run for a long time. The composite of their individual fortunes told the story of freedom-in-retreat. Indeed, not a few among them, having made good their escape to some other land, again had to move on—just one train or one vessel ahead of the advancing hammer and sickle, swastika, or fasces. Nearly all of my fellow workers had to tell of harrowing adventures. They could not stop themselves from living them all over again in their dreams. They were nervous men. Unsure of their latest hosts, they could not shed that furtiveness which comes from clutching expired passports and abasing oneself before grumpy immigration officials.

In times of war the legal status of the man without a country is most precarious. Is he a victim of political persecution, deserving sympathetic hospitality? a potential spy who should be locked up? or simply a vagabond who should be told to move on? Most of my fellow workers would have settled gladly for some regular academic employment; a few would have liked to don uniforms and fight totalitarian hordes in the regular forthright way. Since, upon investigation, their personal histories revealed many gaps—how long did they live where, and with whom, how long were they employed by whom, and what had been their party affiliation in Lubeck or Bucharest or Lublin or Prague in 1931?—they could not aspire to ordinary jobs reserved for people with ascertainable good character. Even had these sedentary, myopic, and dyspeptic intellectuals been able to pass their "physicals," they could not have been trusted with a rifle, not to speak of a tank or a walkie-talkie. Unsuitable for routine employment, they had drifted into the pool of special and very special talent under the surveillance of Secret Intelligence. All kinds of odd fish swam in this pool; all kinds of odd fishermen passed their lines for a catch.

America at war plunged into an orgy of secrecy; only he who held the seal of Top Secret could enter the elite of the war effort. As could have been expected, unskilled or impious hands soon attached the seal to all kinds of things which were in plain view of friend and foe alike or should have been disclosed to the advantage of all and sundry, except perhaps some secretively bungling officials. But for that matter, in all dealings between men there is an element of secrecy; and this is as it should be. Secrecy for its own sake—the infatuation with mystification—this is another matter. It reeks of badly ventilated passions.

Nearly all internationally active countries are engaged in espionage and counterespionage, and throughout the ages statesmen have tried to bribe, blackmail, defame, and murder one another. The underworld of international politics is an interesting place. Experts disagree as to whether it is the only place where history is being made or whether at least some international business is being carried on by open dealings. Americans, more openfaced than other peoples, decry secret diplomacy and deplore the double standard of *raison d'état*. They look with revulsion upon the more or less secret and vicious activities grouped under the general heading "Secret Intelligence." Yet, the enticing scent of the flowers which grow in darkness stirs strange desires, especially in puritan breasts. Not a few among the most proper Americans and Englishmen found in Secret Intelligence, especially its most tenebrous and dirtiest fields, a fulfillment which they seemed unable to derive from more conventional pursuits. Indeed, in many departments of the Intelligence business deeds are being done which society punishes severely when they are perpetrated by its private members. In the service of Intelligence these felonies shine with the luster of civic virtues. Here many a repressed emotion finds an outlet. For in Anglo-Saxon lands, Intelligence offers its devotees catharsis; its rites of secret initiation and monastic anonymity answer a deep longing for submergence and purification.

In America, Intelligence has become not only an arm of national security but also a munificently endowed community-within-the-community. Its unpublished levies are second to the overtly acknowledged expenditure on the national establishment for conflict and violence.

When I came to Washington, Secret Intelligence had not yet risen to that place of eminence which it now occupies in the government of the Republic. Today we take it as a matter of course when we read that our Intelligence agencies make the unmake foreign governments and, by a variety of techniques, ensure our National Security, leaving it to our diplomats to tend the façade of foreign policy and to our armed services to handle the cruder means of force. Then, the makers of our Secret Intelligence recruited personnel; adapted to American requirements the methods of British Intelligence, reported to be the canniest on earth; procured enormous quantities of filing cabinets; called upon professional policemen, psychologists, and rubber-stamp and tag manufacturers to develop complex systems of security; fired personnel which further investigation revealed as posing security risks; gathered, sometimes at considerable financial and human costs, highly secret information which, it was later discovered, had been disclosed in the Encyclopedia Britannica, if not the World Almanac; created committees for maintaining liaison with shocked diplomats and bewildered soldiers as yet inexperienced in the darker arts of fighting wars, winning allies, and deceiving both enemies and allies; and had, on the whole, a roaring good time playing at cops and robbers.

Many notable and unusual people enthusiastically volunteered their services. The corridors and canteens of the building in which Secret Intelligence made its tightly guarded home teemed with the sons and daughters of the best families, alumni of the best schools, and hence deemed ideally "secure." They lent the proceedings an exclusive country club air lacking in other agencies concerned with the conduct of war. Since war had greatly reduced all social activities—cooks, maids, and butlers had taken to riveting armor plate; many fashionable resorts had been closed for the duration, turned into hospitals or occupied by the enemy—the rich and well-connected drifted to Washington in search of congenial assignments, martial or bureaucratic. As things turned out, most of the privileged recruits to Intelligence and allied activities gave a good account of themselves. They carried out successfully the oddest and most perilous missions. A few gave their lives for their country.

Henry Field, chief of our indescribable Project, had gone from England's premier public school to Oxford. Son of an American mother and an English father, he had chosen, upon his parents' separation, American citizenship. Heir of a large Midwestern fortune, he had applied himself to the study of anthropology, a discipline well-suited to minds bent on meticulous classification, travel, and life outdoors. A large number of occasional papers on the cranial measurements of various Iranian and Kurdish villagers, enriched by a miscellany of minutiae on folkways, flora, fauna, and remains *in situ*, had rewarded Henry's tireless investigations. His tales of these simple and engaging ruffians enlivened those of our lunch hours and coffee breaks which he graced with his presence. His radiant enthusiasm about the Project's contribution to the better world-to-come roused our flagging spirits; we were assured that our findings engaged the attention of an august personage, and that only ignorance of the Whole Picture, hidden to us by the indispensable curtain of Secrecy, blinded us to the Project's crucial importance. Then, having raised our morale, Henry departed, leaving us with the intimation of great and highly classified undertakings afoot.

The intellectual satisfaction which I derived from the progress of the Project did not assuage my longing for the wilder shores of war. Nor were my ruffled feelings smothered by the heavy hand laid by Security upon the Project. The Project had been classified as Secret. Its staff was answerable to the supreme arm on National Intelligence, then referred to, with lowered voice, as OSS. Had it not been for place and circumstances, I might have enjoyed my work and its associations.

I had come to Washington on what I had thought to be a temporary assignment. When it dawned upon me that my masters did not intend to let their servant go in search of excitement, I surveyed my new surroundings. My dislike for the place has been abiding.

The federal capital, laid out on a majestic scale, could have been a beautiful city. Real-estate speculation, federal architecture, and civic indifference have shared in equal parts in dissolving Washington into a conglomerate of shapeless encampments, some slovenly, some pretentious, none on speaking terms with the others. Buildings in which people make their private habitat and go after their private business shrink under the arrogant stare of the vast and expensive public barracks.

The federal capital can be reached within a few hours, and weather permitting, from Mount Vernon either by rowboat or sailboat or on horseback. This circumstance weighed heavily upon the choice of the founder who, though a hardy man, did not spurn the comforts due to his advanced age. Had the choice of the site been left to one of his successors, let us say to President Monroe, the federal capital would now stand elsewhere, probably in the highlands around Middleburg, Virginia, and the vast army of federal employees, elected officials, diplomats, lobbyists, hostesses, and supporting personnel would now be encamped in relatively salubrious environs. As it is, the capital now spreads far into the hinterland noted for its reddish, sticky soil and scrubby vegetation. Nor is Washington's climate any more healthful. In fact, it is one of the worst in the world, rivaled only by Shanghai and Baghdad. In broiling heat and dankness in summer and penetrating cold and dankness in winter, the business of the nation is being done under conditions making for a high rate of absenteeism and chronic sinus infection.

All in all, Washington is a spacious place; the streets are wide and a great deal of open ground separates individual structures. It is, therefore, surprising that there are so few places for sitting, eating, and drinking out of doors. Moreover, though nominally a city, Washington lacks most of the amenities which modern culture associates with urban life. For example, the opera houses and repertory theaters, concert halls and three-starred restaurants to be found in almost any more prosperous and self-respecting European *Kleinstadt* cannot be found in Washington. Musicians and actors visit the capital for brief performances or to lend cultural tone to state dinners. But they return quickly to New York, where Washingtonians have to go in order to enjoy the living arts. Of course, there is, in close vicinity to the eccentrically located Union Station and the Capitol, the National Gallery, an exhibit of art treasures purchased mainly by three private and public-spirited collectors. But the great art works displayed under a flattened cupola and the fine monuments do not compensate for the aesthetic defacement which federal architecture and private contractors have visited upon the city.

Site, historic origin, and architectural inspiration suggest Washington's affinity with Versailles, a town reared at the command of a strong-willed ruler upon a stretch of swampy and otherwise undesirable land. In Washington, as in Versailles, the apartments of state are flanked by barrack-like structures designed as shelters for a numerous bureaucracy and military garrison. Minimum allowance is made for those areas which serve as centers of the town's communal life. Nevertheless, the meagerness of communal facilities is probably due to lack of demand for them. For only few people expect to live out their lives in Washington.

Washington has no heart. It is not a city but an encampment which accommodates a vast crowd of transients loath to sink roots into the arid soil of the tidal flats. Toward the northwest and west stretches a complex of expensive and very expensive housing developments. But of the medley of architectural styles little needs to be said except that not a single one is pure. With the possible exception of Georgetown's plain brick, private dwellings, some of which are as vast as they are monstrous, proclaim rather than seek to dissimulate the fact that they are not what they are supposed to be.

Luckily, we found a house of inoffensive exterior and ours for the duration at a low rent. Backed by a secluded lawn under high trees, our house sat defiantly on a small hill. Beneath our windows curved the deep and vacant cleft of Rock Creek Park; fortunately its slopes were too steep to be carved up into building lots. So before breakfast and upon my return from work, I hiked along the brook which gave its name to the scenic valley, and passed the cemetery and the unkempt garden of the French Embassy on my way up to Dumbarton Oaks. Rock Creek Park redeems Washington from its pretentious shabbiness. Soon I came to know by sight its habitués, the British major in battle dress, the elder statesman in sweat shirt and sneakers, and the wizened, bird-like man who trained his binoculars upon cardinals or blue jays or, perhaps, an open window in a house overlooking the valley.

I later met the British major at a cocktail party. Of all forms of hospitality, the cocktail party is the most perfunctory and non-committal. It satisfies the social requirements of gregarious people who do not feel the need for constancy in human relationships. In Washington it is the preferred form of entertainment, for neither hosts nor guests expect or hope to see one another ever again.

The major had served in a cavalry regiment which, shortly before the war, had been converted from horse to tanks. What had been left of it was evacuated from Dunkirk, but all of its tanks and a good part of their crews could not be salvaged from strategic retreat. It might have been this practical experience or, perhaps, simply the unavailability of tanks which suggested the stunned major's transfer to one of the procurement branches of the War Ministry. Upon the entry of the United States into the War, the major, passed over for promotion, was posted to the British military mission in Washington. He did not dissimulate his distaste for desk-bound duty. Meanwhile he kept himself fit and waited for the call to battle which never came. Henceforth, once a week, we met for lunch. We talked about steeplechases, hata yoga, Bond Street tailors and bootmakers, country life, Mediterranean beaches, but never about the war. We swapped choice episodes of our lives, and did not intrude upon the rest. We liked to hike along Rock Creek, preferably in silence. Had we cared to dissect our friendship, we would have found that it consisted of little but the unavowed communion in disappoint-ment; the place to which fate had led us was the last place where we wanted to be.

Though I have pondered the nature of friendship, I find that for the sake of its enjoyment I had better leave it unexplored. It was my good fortune to pass through severe stress and great peril at the side of steady selfless men; I remember them in respectful gratitude. With others I experienced the pure joy of intellectual communion and of work well done in harness. If we became friends, it was because an unguarded moment of recognition revealed to us that we were kin in heretofore unavowed inclination or aversion. Thus the friendships of my life had sprung, more often than not, from a trivial or even a frivolous occasion which did not portend enduring association, affection, and trust. Only rarely have two of my friends taken a liking to each other; in friendships, I bore with their friends.

My wife, reserved and quizzical, has the rare capacity of enduring friendship. Not a few of her friends became mine, for she commanded their unquestioning loyalties. I do not doubt that I was accepted for her sake, for I had neither notable achievements nor many graces to commend me. Among her friends she counted Dean and Alice Acheson, who, shortly after World War I, had settled in Washington. In 1933 Dean quit his thriving legal practice and entered Mr. Roosevelt's government. When the war broke out Dean had served as Assistant Secretary of the Treasury, spoken his mind emphatically about a policy disagreement, emphatically resigned, and after a brief return to the law, accepted the offer of an Assistant Secretaryship of State.

All men are at odds with themselves. In unusual men contradictions battle one another on a scale grander than that vouchsafed to ordinary men. This is the only perceptible difference between great and little men. In history and politics the attribution "great" belongs to the specie of rubber words which, since they convey many meanings or none, delight historians and politicians. All kinds of men were "great"—because they got other people into great trouble, because their own great troubles evoked the compassion of posterity, or because their flair for publicity projected an image of greatness which the record of their actual doings does not sustain.

So frayed from ill use is the mantle of greatness that I let it descend only reluctantly upon Dean Acheson's spare and upright frame. Yet, if Dean Acheson has not been one of the greatest public servants in the employment of the Republic, then the annals of the Republic will have to be rewritten from beginning to end. The great, decisive, and creative interventions after World War II of the United States in world affairs were in part devised and launched by Dean Acheson, namely, the Marshall Plan; the North Atlantic Alliance, prefaced by the Truman Doctrine; and the restoration of German statehood. He erred on many an issue and spectacularly flopped an important one. Nevertheless, he stood upon the bridge for a long time and steered the ship through turbulent and uncharted waters.

The late 1940's were years of illusion and confusion. The American people, relaxing contentedly from the military effort, did not hanker for the bitter fruits of world power. Their "education to greatness" had to wait upon events which, when they broke, left political leadership no other choice but to trust itself to the intelligence of the people. It is now clear that much valuable time was lost and that some of the critical turns should have been made sooner. Nevertheless, Acheson—a powerful clerk but not an elected official—could not be expected to ride ahead of his political betters.

It is Acheson's sublime achievement that, when his political masters thought the time ripe for a change of course, he brought to the occasion a great design as well as the craftsmanship needed for its execution. His career has been stormy. Nevertheless, this proud, clever, and caustic man has no peer in the art of goading enemies and retaining the affection of baffled friends. Indeed, he seems to take a puckish pleasure in tripping even those who come to worship before the monument of his achievement. I suspect he thinks little of monuments, including his own, and delights in defacing them. Thus, he is famed for his quips and for the freedom with which he lets them fly in the direction of the mighty, though not of the weak.

His haughtiness, if not arrogance, would have made him an easier mark for his foes were it not for his courage. For, in the thick of battle, Acheson turns upon the commotion the same aloof, cold stare with which the Duke of Wellington is said to have gazed upon the carnage of Waterloo. In fact, by looks and demeanor, he could pass, were he not the perfect image of his celebrated self, as a lordly and tweedy member of England's Establishment. Yet his formidable presence—among living men, only de Gaulle's is more impressive—shields a mercurial temperament. Secure in the affection of his friends, he drops the disdainful stance; the loyalties which he inspires would be incomprehensible were it not for the warmth and charm of the man.

On Sundays, the Henry Fields kept open house. By suppertime some forty or fifty people crowded the living room of their narrow-chested Georgetown house and, in summertime, the diminutive garden. Thanks to Henry's years in Eton and Oxford and wanderings throughout the Middle East, the company comprised a fair variety of nationalities, including some quite outlandish ones. English diplomats; Hebrew scholars; the whole gamut of Central European refugees; Zionist emissaries; Henry's colleagues in Intelligence; American soldiers and sailors back from the war on their daily stint in the Pentagon; Oxford dons; and, of course, anthropologists, with that faraway look which still lingers on digs, bones, and mounds of primitive rites—all conversed animatedly with one another, or did silent justice to Henry's bourbon and Patsy's succulent spaghetti à la bolognaise. Among the habitués, Isaiah Berlin excelled in endurance—the later the hour the more brilliant his sallies—and in versatility. As the evening lengthened and less durable conversationalists yielded the floor, Berlin, the voluble conjuror, juggled the most diverse topics with incredible speed, tied them together in the logical exposition of a profound theory which neither he nor anybody else had ever thought of before, and, before the startled audience could take issue with his improvisation, pricked the bubble with a comical anecdote. Try as he might and addicted as he was to playful nonsense, he could not hide the fact that he was a very learned scholar and, sometimes, a profound philosopher. He wrote little; but what he wrote belongs to the classical literature of political thought.

Berlin's presence in Washington gave rise to all kinds of rumors which he took mischievous delight in first coyly ignoring and then exposing as laughable fantasies. He was said to be the Prime Minister's eyes and ears in Washington, the gray eminence of His Majesty's Embassy. According to others, he was charged with highly secret Intelligence missions. And then, again, his assignment was simply to publicize the British war effort and keep the American intellectuals happy about such unpalatable matters as, for example, British colonialism and Churchill's own concepts of what the post-World War order should be. I have not the faintest idea about Isaiah Berlin's true role in wartime

Washington; but he did manage to hold the floor—all of it—of Patsy Field's living room.

While the Project kept me busy during the day, I found that, with a little management, my evenings and early mornings could be employed in the acquisition of those academic degrees which would admit me to the guild. By the end of 1944 I had completed a manuscript which I proposed to submit as my doctoral dissertation. I asked Dr. Bowman to read it, for I valued his opinion and believed him to be well-disposed toward me. Since a large part of my work was concerned with matters of foreign policy, I needed the permission of the authorities to publish my findings so that no breach of security would expose classified information to the ever-watchful enemy.

Since my work on the Project did not afford me insight into the diplomatic and military conduct of the war, I concluded that the authorities would approve forthwith the publication of my innocuous academic tract. I was mistaken. In my study I sought to predict the international power relationships which might emerge after the defeat of the Axis powers. The estimate was based upon published statistics of population, agricultural and industrial output, raw material resources, and foreign trade of major countries. From annual indices I forecast likely rates of growth. My statistical materials were of prewar vintage, for I had been unable to obtain complete data for the war years. Upon the outbreak of war, governments had turned off the flow of statistical information on even the most innocent topics or they published data which, though purported to be statistics, were means to cheer the home folks or to deceive the enemy. Even in peacetime it was difficult enough to filter fact from fiction in Soviet statistical abstracts. I surmised that whatever figures the Soviet might condescend to disclose in wartime on, for example, the growth of population would be even more misleading than those fanciful ones on their several five-year plans. Therefore, I confined my labors to disentangling a semblance of truth from Soviet statistics published before 1939 and to deducing from this detective work likely future trends. I thought myself engaged in innocent, though tedious, research.

Yet my manuscript was not returned by the authorities. Disquieted, I sought out Dr. Bowman. Dr. Bowman adjusted his pince-nez and gazed thoughtfully through the tall window of his office upon the autumnal foliage of the White House grounds. He told me that he had read the manuscript and found nothing in it that jeopardized the security of the Republic. Having so advised the competent official, he expected my manuscript to be "cleared" for publication. Dr. Bowman, who, on occasion, could be as grand and noncommittal as befitted his high academic rank, was at heart a forthright and kindly man. He told me that he liked what I had written. I thanked him for the interest that he had taken in my work. I made to leave. Dr. Bowman bade me remain seated. He said that he had come to Washington to serve his country at war. He esteemed the President but he did not hold with the ideas of the New Deal. Indeed, he doubted the wisdom of some of the President's schemes for a future world order and, in particular, did not share the views of some presidential advisers on the dependability of our Soviet ally. No doubt, objections raised in some influential quarters would not stand for long in the way of the publication of my book. But, he added casually, I would be well advised to keep out of the way of one functionary who played an important part in the making of American policy toward the Soviets. I had not heard the name before. A few weeks later I was told that I could publish my manuscript. I was not to recall Dr. Bowman's cryptic remark until, ten years later, the case of Alger Hiss engaged the attention of the American public.

Before posting this controversial manuscript to a New York publisher, I searched its pages for a clue to the offense which its pages might have given to one of the makers of our foreign policy. Only the concluding chapters touched upon American foreign policy and the political settlement which might crown the war effort of the alliance. From the findings of the preceding chapters I had drawn two principal conclusions: First, Germany remained, even in total defeat, Europe's most advanced industrial country, and the place allotted by the peace settlement to the German people would determine ineluctably the postwar power balance in Europe and, to a considerable extent, in the world. If all of Germany were to fall to the Soviet Union, then the Com-

munist empire, thus enlarged, would not only be likely to domi-
nate, in the fullness of time, all of Europe but would also control
the largest reservoir of industrial manpower, tools and raw material resources upon earth. Second, under any circumstances, a
victorious Soviet Union would pursue, more vigorously than ever
before, policies of territorial and ideological expansion. I had not
drawn a sharp distinction between traditional Russian foreign
policies and the avowed goals of the international revolutionary
movement which had made its headquarters upon Russian soil. I
thought that the controversy between Stalin and Trotsky cen-
tered not so much upon the goals of the Communist world party
as upon a personal power struggle. No doubt, the two men had
disagreed upon tactics—"the shovel" to be used. But there was no
reason to believe that a Soviet Union, victorious at war and
aggrandized by European conquests, would repress its ambitions
as a world power *and* as the protagonist of a messianic ideology
which, even at that time when the Soviet Union had lacked
superior military power, had won over many millions of followers throughout the globe and especially in the advanced industrial
countries of the West. My reading of the United Nations draft
charter did not lead me to conclude that the two great powers of
the postwar world, the United States and the Soviet Union,
would look, in matters affecting their vital interests, to the
arbitrament of the proposed world organization. On this score, I
thought that the provision for a Security Council, consisting of
permanent members armed with veto power and temporary
members not so armed, left no room for any other interpretation.

On any issue of true power political import, the writ of the
United Nations, just as that of the League of Nations, reached no
further than the unanimity of the Great Powers. Since World
War II had reduced the ranks of the Great Powers to a two-
some of the United States and the Soviet Union, any serious
disagreement between these two giants would leave all other
members about where they had come in. I could not see that the
United States and the Soviet Union were likely to view the great
issues of world politics with serene unanimity. Hence I anticipated
a new phase in the international power struggle. This was the gist
of my findings. I did not consider them very startling nor did I

seek to insinuate to Soviet leadership motives other than those avowed *ad nauseum* in the published statements of Soviet leadership. Thus I was surprised and disquieted by the fact that conclusions so pedestrian and so innocuous had given umbrage to American officials in high places.

At this time, the autumn of 1944, the negotiations on the occupation and the division of Germany and the partition of Europe were still a carefully guarded secret. Apparently Stalin's approbation of the West's good conduct was still thought worth some solid concessions. Under the circumstances—the war against Japan had been won but not yet finished—the Western leaders might have had good reason to overlook the churlish and devious behavior of their Communist allies. On the wisdom of this course I do not presume, armed with the wisdom of hindsight, to sit in judgment. Yet, even after the last shot had been fired, the leaders of the great democracies kept mum about those massive Soviet departures from good neighborly conduct about which they possessed ample and irrefutable intelligence.

The roots of today's dilemma in U.S.-U.S.S.R. relations reach back all the way to those opaque years. In my book I had tried to decipher future trends. Nevertheless, there are times when it is more prudent to delve into the past than to speculate on the future. Be that as it may, statesmen are still more sensitive about the great and good things they propose to do tomorrow than about the mistakes they made yesterday; the latter can always be explained away: somebody else is to be blamed, and nowadays, in the age of complete and ceaseless news coverage, even the most horrible howler is quickly forgotten. Thus, for the statesman the future is everything; he can shape its image to his liking. In politics, moreover, people believe only in prophecies, not in the facts under their noses; even the most arrogant politician takes less umbrage at being called a bloody bungler than a false prophet.

The Project had served its purpose; and impressive series of case studies, embellished by polychrome maps and neat charts, attested to our zeal. The Project staff had grown in undeviating conformity with Parkinson's law: the personnel increased at the same rate at which the output of our organization diminished. At last Dr. Bowman accepted my resignation. In a gracious letter the

President commended my service to the country and to humanity at large. Grateful and unburdened, I sought and found other employment. Dr. Bowman and I met only once again. The war had been won and new frontiers had been drawn. I do not know whether Dr. Bowman's advice in dividing up the new world had been sought. (He made it clear that he did not view the latest try for just and lasting boundaries as an improvement on World War I settlements.)

Dr. Bowman was to have accompanied the President to Yalta, but a grave illness kept him from attending this last and most consequential meeting of the leaders of the war coalition. A few months later Dr. Bowman died.

Dr. Bowman's intervention set me on the track which I still follow. His devotion to meticulous scholarship—good ideas are a dime a dozen and can be put to profitable use only by close attention to minute details—set me a standard to which I still aspire. For Dr. Bowman, it seems, knew me better than I knew myself. He had told me that I would make a tolerably competent professor; I wish I could submit my performance to his review, for were he still among the living he would hand down, in his celebrated tart and offhand way, the opinion which I would accept unprotestingly as my academic epitaph.

In August, 1940, our old friend, James V. Forrestal, had been appointed Undersecretary of the Navy. I had met him in the 1930's in New York. A partner in one of the leading private banks, he moved about restlessly in those powerful and fashionable circles from which the New Deal was to recruit many of its most prominent politicians and officials. The Forrestals, spirited and handsome, had received the accolade of the old, staid, as well as the new, faster society which met in board rooms, hunting fields, paddocks, and select places of entertainment.

Jim was a self-made man. Like most self-made men of his generation, he had gone to college, sought the company of intellectuals, and zestfully discussed general ideas, particularly those concerned with man and society. At college, his performance had not been exceptional, except in sports. In a boxing bout, a blow had flattened his nose. This disfigurement set Jim's features into a hard-bitten, aggressive frown. I believe that he was well

aware of the impression which his scarred countenance conveyed
to others. Indeed, some of his mannerisms, so it seemed, were
contrived to suit his accidentally fashioned appearance; in his
highly competitive business, toughness was not the least prized
qualification for success. Jim lacked neither physical courage nor
force of character. His curt manner—laconic speech, spare gesture,
and corner-of-the-mouth wit—did not awe those whom he held
in confidence and affection.

In fact, Jim was not as tough as the world thought him and
far less tough than he fancied himself to be. Indeed, he suffered
deeply the misfortunes of others. Try as he might to compose his
stoic mien, he could not help showing the deep compassion which
flowed to young men in the toils of war, the killed, the maimed,
and the distraught. The calumnies and betrayals which are the lot
of every public man, especially if he be forceful and honorable,
stung him to the quick. Thus he wrested dicision from a conscience which scrupled at even the smallest detail left unattended
and at convenient compromise. The effigy, hewn from granite,
does not do justice to the man.

To be sure, unswerving in his allegiance, Jim did his duty. But
the burden of responsibility chafed cruelly this sensitive and conscientious man. He loved poetry. He read widely; his precise
annotations bespoke a searching and discriminating mind. He
possessed the rarest of all the statesmanly gifts, the power of
associating events—of grasping the whole where others could see
only disjointed incidents—and the sixth sense of anticipation.
Perhaps, among men then in power, he was not the only one to
gauge the drift of Soviet conduct, yet he foresaw that the ramparts in his charge would be the first to feel the full weight of the
coming onslaught. If the euphoric years following immediately
upon World War II were not permitted to erode what was left
of the invincible military power which crushed the Axis Powers,
this is, first and foremost, Forrestal's achievement. Handed
an impossible task, he guarded at least the core of national
defense—and this in the face of popular indifference and one of
the most vicious and powerfully backed campaigns of vilification
ever waged against an American in public office.

During his last years Forrestal, immolated in his solitary labors,

saw little of his old friends. We met briefly a few months before
he died. He looked older and more tired, yet he seemed sound in
body and mind. From the accounts of others I tried to put together the story of his end. The only conclusion I could reach
was that some of the pieces were missing. The official curtain had
dropped on the personal tragedy.

I went to Forrestal's state funeral in Arlington Cemetery. The
solemnities were conducted in a pillared semicircle open to the
sky, reminiscent of some Roman theater of the decadent period.
The great of the land occupied boxes; in the pit beneath them sat
the rest of the mourners. A chill wind ruffled the flag draped over
the coffin. The bishop's oration warbled through the loudspeaker.
Officialdom retained its composure. After the service, chill as the
breeze, the big black limousines drew up according to protocol. I
walked back to the parking lot. I was just in time to see the
caisson coming to a halt by the freshly dug pit. On the other side
of my car a man leaned against his. Robert Patterson, one of the
dead man's oldest friends, sobbed out his grief.

Shortly after I left the Project I had told Forrestal that I was
looking for a job. Germany was collapsing. The Japanese had
been pressed back to their isles and were expected to make a
desperate last stand. Yet we sensed that the war was nearing its
end. I thought it unlikely that, even had the services been eager
to recruit a sedentary man in middle age, I would be in time to
see action. Forrestal foresaw that America could not go back to
that comfortable era in which she could leave her maritime de-
fenses to the British Navy or, in a pinch, to hasty national improvisation; a larger peacetime U.S. Navy would have to be
officered by more men than, in the past, Annapolis had supplied.
He hoped that the navy, holding out the proper incentive, could
retain the services of experienced reservists. In addition, he proposed to strengthen the navy's reserve officer training program.

Thus, Forrestal asked me to assist the Bureau of Personnel of
the Navy Department in the preparation of course outlines to be
used in the training of midshipmen. For the war had brought to
light some alarming gaps in civic and military education; though
firmly grounded in the use of hardware, the young reservists
entertained but the vaguest notions about the purposes of na-

tional policy, means and uses of national power, and the resources and objectives of their country's allies and enemies. Of
course, men had fought valiantly and died bravely without knowing about these things. Yet, so Forrestal thought, the right kind
of instruction and understanding of national policy and strategy
would help young officers to relate their routine and mostly technical tasks to their country's stakes and goals in world politics:
theirs *was* to reason why. This knowledge should have been—and
unfortunately had not been—part of college education. Forrestal
undertook to supply it at least to the naval ROTC units on
the campus. I was deeply absorbed in my job.

Most of the men with whom I worked had served in one or the
other theaters of war. Most of them were professional military
men. Since then, especially in the past few years, a great deal has
been written about military influence in American political and
economic life. On balance, the military have had a bad press; according to their critics, it is they who have first raised and now
care for and feed such monsters as the "garrison state" and the
"military-industrial complex." I concede that military men the
world over seek to strengthen their respective services by improvement and increases of weaponry and personnel. In addition, they
also hanker for those fringe benefits—higher pay, better housing,
and greater social prestige—to which all professional groups including the clergy, aspire. Most certainly, all other employees of
government do; but only rarely are they being charged with
conspiring against the public good. The explanation of the military's predicament must be sought in two national characteristics:
although Americans like and dress up in all kinds of picturesque
uniforms, they abhor military discipline; and, although the military
have been needed for fighting several exceedingly bloody wars,
they have been kept, between wars, in strict isolation from the
rest of American society.

During the late 1920's, when I worked in the financial center
and nearly everybody had made a killing in National City Bank
Common, and bootleg champagne slaked the thirst of the guests
at the hundred-thousand dollar debutante parties, the professional
military lived quietly, though in plain view of Wall Street—
unnoticed by civilian New York—in their large though sparsely

furnished mansions on Governor's Island. My oldest American friend, the retired army captain from Savannah, had given me a few letters of introduction to his old comrades in arms. One of these was a colonel stationed on Governor's Island. His wife, a fine horsewoman and linguist, had been born on an army post. She had followed her father, a military attaché, first to Paris and then to St. Petersburg. The couple's two exceedingly beautiful daughters spoke French well; they played a fair game of tennis; they were well read and skilled at petit point.

Every so often I was invited to dances in one or the other of these spacious houses which were assigned as quarters to the officers of the garrison. Although the fare was meager and the drinks surreptitious, a great deal of ingenuity and labor went into the decor; indeed, the taste ran to fancy dress parties. The costumes, some quite exotic and elaborate, were designed and fashioned on the island; the music, the entertainment, and the *ambiance* of an island with a view of the illuminated skyscrapers of Wall Street and the Statue of Liberty, were local produce. Hardly ever did the number of civilians—the unaffiliated guests from the mainland—exceed a dozen. Some of this small band were foreigners like myself.

Isolation cut both ways. If Manhattan barely acknowledged Governor's Island, Governor's Island stood aloof from Manhattan.

Official business took my host to the city and places beyond. On rare occasions, his wife and daughters crossed the water, took in a museum and, on even more memorable occasions, a matinée. They looked at shop windows. In close order they walked down the Avenue: they descended to the subway, and, unburdened by parcels, stepped on the ferry which linked the outer world with Governor's Island. They were not the familiars of the great and sumptuous houses which, in those years, were still the centers of social gravity. In fact, by then prevailing standards, they were very poor. Indeed, any average bond salesman or junior bank executive drew an income far larger than a colonel's pay; no self-respecting apprentice on Wall Street would have dreamed of settling for a colonel's expectations. Yet life within the oasis—the post—was not without compensation: commodious houses with high ceilings—higher than those of the millionaires' manors on Fifth Avenue—orderlies, several mounts including polo ponies, and other diverse perrequisites of rank and service. Furthermore, within the oasis the tradition of gentlemanly decorum in the style of courtly society had not yet been challenged by the code of conduct of the new, the more relaxed and more pragmatic era. Indeed, in some ways Governor's Island was a land unto itself—American, yet forgotten by America, bearing a faint resemblance to an outpost on the remote imperial frontier, and retaining the flavor of a heroic though austere past.

As one is apt to do in a big city or when one is young, I lost sight of my friends on Governor's Island. If I remember rightly, the colonel retired long before the young lieutenants were to train large masses of bankers, brokers, shop clerks, and garage mechanics in the arts of war, lead them into battle, and win eagles and stars. A few years ago I met one of the daughters at a Washington dinner. She had broken a venerable tradition. She had married a naval officer.

In the past twenty-five years the American military have been called upon to "implement"—a word dear to policy makers—a number of policies which they did not make. They had to leave the oasis, sometimes against their will. Once confined to out-of-the-way stations, they have now become familiar with the nation's politics and business. Indeed, it is too much to expect from even the most self-effacing servants of the state that they refrain from thinking about public policies, for now it is more difficult than ever to say where military expertise ends and policy begins, and on what issues of national security civilian controllers should abide by or reject the soldier's professional advice.

Though I have been a civilian for most of my life, I have met, throughout the years, many military men. Among these I have found the American officer to be, if not the most glamorous, then the most competent and unassuming member of the profession. Those who now avow either mistrust of his professional judgment or fear of his designs upon power in the state should recall the oath which he has sworn to the Constitution; the service he has rendered to his fellow citizens in great and little, hot and cold wars; and, last but not least, his long isolation in the midst of the world's richest society which treated him shabbily as long as he was not needed for fighting its wars.

One day in August, 1945, I walked past the constipated statuary of Union Square toward the Cosmos Club. Just then horns started tooting, distant shouts and sirens rose to a roar— the war had ended; Japan had surrendered. I turned the corner. There three sleek Waves danced hand in hand, whirling about like a children's top on the brim of a huge sombrero.

In the evening I joined a few friends. We talked about the things we were now going to do to make up for time lost, pleasures missed. In the cool of the muggy evening we sat on a patch of green enclosed by a wattle fence. To the bystander, great events cast short shadows. To me, the surrender of the Japanese, who had thrown in the sponge months before the explosion of the most superfluous of all atom bombs, meant that I could leave Washington and need never again tarry in the promiscuous back yards of Georgetown. With a sense of relief, I put three stale years behind me. Of course, we drank to the future.

Although most of us were in our forties, not a few of us doubted that we would or could go back to the jobs we had held or even the places where we had lived before the war. As things turned out, a surprisingly large number of my friends did not go back. Some just stayed in the same, though ceaselessly reorganized government job. Some drifted into the rapidly growing proconsular bureaucracy abroad, the various occupation governments, the innumerable missions for reconstructing, punishing, and re-educating our former enemies. Soon it was to become clear that, although complete victory had been achieved, the new order at home and abroad could not be entrusted safely to the care of a bureaucracy smaller than that which had administered the war effort. Thus, many of my Washington acquaintances, confronted by the choice between the pursuit of private gain and service to the government, chose the latter.

Throughout the next decade I was to meet them in pleasant villas overlooking the Rhine and the wire-fenced cantonments of the occupation government; in Franconian chalets within easy commuting distance of the War Crimes Court at Nuremberg; in the requisitioned select hotels on the slopes of Fujiyama; and at other outposts of America's new global responsibilities. A few rose higher and higher in the official hierarchy. Indeed, much of the country's public business is still being done by those who "stayed in government" instead of returning to the unregimented joys of private life and enterprise, and the vast complex of agencies which administers the American presence abroad is largely their work.

In one way or another, this complex, together with its intricate hierarchy of jobs and abundant flow of appropriations, will be kept alive and growing as long as this group of civil servants cannot be diverted to other tasks which advance the nation's interest. Perhaps the army of these dedicated functionaries could, at any time, have been cut in half without any noticeable damage to America's welfare and "image" abroad. Nevertheless, this would have deprived many people of the opportunity of living among strange, though friendly, people and of establishing, wherever they went, enclaves of the American way of life complete with commissaries, kindergartens, and country clubs. Furthermore, these carefully selected officials introduced the lower standard of living peoples to the contemplation of the solid achievements of American civilization. For unlike the masses of American tourists traveling for a few weeks or months on their own funds and mixing indiscriminately with the local populace, they stayed on for years and maintained a proper distance from the native community. Perhaps it was because I felt unfitted for the austere discipline of service at the outposts of global responsibility or could not enter unreservedly upon the spirit of the grand scheme for the political and judicial reordering of the occupied countries that I looked for other employment. At any rate, I was forty-two; the choices had grown fewer, the test— what was it that I could do well and do for keeps?—had to be met.

Meanwhile, I harbored the unshakable belief, so necessary to the writer and so presumptuous to all around him, that I had unique insights to put on paper and that a multitude of readers waited for my revelations. Indeed, without a quota of such vanity, most books, even some great ones, would never have been written. (This might be the reason why the greatest and humblest among men are known to us through the writings only of their disciples.)

Chapter Thirteen

AFTER the victory over Japan, the United States deployed a considerable part of its naval strength in the China Sea. The Seventh Fleet established its headquarters in Tsingtao; American cruisers and destroyers rode at anchor in the roadsteads of Shanghai and Canton. As the Chinese civil war spread to the coastal regions, the U.S. Navy assumed an increasingly important role in supplying Chiang with war matériel. It ferried part of the Chinese Army across the Gulf of Pohai in order to secure Manchuria for Chiang. It became increasingly clear that the fortunes of the Nationalists would be decided by the success of this operation, for the industrial resources of Manchuria would enable Chiang to satisfy his pressing needs for war matériel and to proceed to the reconstruction of the Chinese economy, especially the railroad system. The crucial question was: how much of the industrial complex had been left intact by the Soviet forces which, after the Japanese surrender, occupied Manchuria for several months? According to Nationalist reports the Soviets had virtually wrecked the major industries of the country. How could the damage be repaired? In the winter of 1945–46 an American mission surveyed the situation. By then the Nationalist forces had advanced to the Sungari river. There they met the determined resistance of the Communists whom the Soviets, before their withdrawal, had eased into the control of Northern Manchuria.

One afternoon, at his house in Washington, Mr. Forrestal discussed the Nationalists' troubles. I expressed my interest in traveling to Manchuria. More likely than not, I would not be able to bring back any information which was not available from official sources. Yet, as a roving observer, unfettered by the chain of command, I might at least form a few general impressions which could round out intelligence more laboriously assembled by diverse, amply staffed missions and agencies. Forrestal, despite long service at the bureaucratic center, had not shed his propensity for unconventional procedures. He took up my proposal. I was to depart forthwith. If I came back with a few insights worth his consideration, this would be gravy. If my report merely covered well-trodden ground, this, too, might not be wasted effort, for my findings would serve as a spot check on available information.

Thus, in May, 1946, the Navy Department handed me a voluminous assortment of papers authorizing me to proceed to Japan, China, and Manchuria and commending me to the care of commanding officers along the way. I was to board the Naval Air Transport plane which was to take me from Washington to Oakland, California, the first lap of my westward journey. Later, while I was waiting for the plane, a familiar voice hailed me. Gero von Gaevernitz, a friend of many years, had just arrived from Europe.

After World War I, we had met in Munich. Son of a famous professor of economics and a banker's daughter, he had been reared in Freiburg, than a quaint university town on the slopes of the Black Forest. He had come to Munich to complete his studies and, whenever his course work permitted, to ski in the nearby mountains. He possessed the durable good looks common to mountain guides, skiing instructors, professional big game hunters, and all those who, since they make their living by strenuous and sometimes hazardous pursuits out of doors, must keep themselves clear-eyed, lithe, and in good wind.

In 1924 Gero arrived in New York. Equipped with a doctorate in economics and, on his mother's side, related to one of New York's leading bankers, Gero served a brief apprenticeship in a well-known Wall Street firm and then proceeded to amass a considerable fortune. I believe he could have risen to prominence had he chosen to throw in his lot with one or the other of the large financial houses. Since he shunned the routine of business and, for that matter, routine of any kind, he withdrew from the Street and devoted himself henceforth to the management of his own and his family's affairs. These affairs took him far afield: to coffee plantations in Brazil, to gold mines in Honduras, to refrigerator vessels off the shore of Peru, to the City of London, to the discreet banks of Switzerland, and to wherever judicious investment promised fair profit and fast recovery of capital.

The good things of life came easily to Gero, money, friendship, leisure, and the love of good or beautiful women. Yet his innate skepticism kept him from either losing his head or losing his heart. He believed that the days of the old order, political and economic, were numbered, that the world was headed for another war and other revolutions, and that the country of his birth which he loved would be swallowed up by folly and disaster. He did not marry. Poised and polished, he kept the world at arm's length. No man can seem enigmatic to others who is not an enigma to himself. Having so dexterously evaded the traps which life sets for ordinary men, Gero should have been happy. But, like most men to whom life has given too much for too little, Gero was not happy. Never having suffered want, he dreaded poverty. Enjoying the best of health, he dreaded illness. Practiced in the arts of seduction, he abhorred loneliness. Drawn to the Stoic philosophers, he feared death. Between travels, Gero retreated to a small villa on the Swiss side of Lago Maggiore. There he kept his well-stocked library, his skis, a few *objets d'art*, and a bountiful wardrobe.

I know little about Gero's activities during World War II up until the historic moment when he turned from corporate finance to secret intelligence. During the closing scenes of World War II he seems to have played a leading role as a lieutenant of Allen Dulles, chief of the American Intelligence operations in Switzerland. According to published accounts, Gero acted as intermediary between Dulles in Bern and the generals commanding the German Army, its back to the Alps after a long retreat along the boot of Italy. By little-traveled mountain passes, he crossed the Swiss-Italian frontier and reached the headquarters of Generals von Wietinghoff and Wolf. The generals must have found Gero's arguments persuasive, for the Germans agreed to surrender rather than make a last stand on the slopes of the Alps. Undoubtedly, many lives were saved and many a pretty village escaped destruction thanks to this extraordinary and somewhat puzzling transaction. Moreover, Mr. Dulles, who is not given to exaggeration, has praised highly Gero's contribution to the Allied victory in Italy. Gero, however, preferred to remain silent. Indeed, after the termination of hostilities, Gero, charged with urgent and confidential missions, traveled the length and breadth of occupied Germany. Then he slipped back to his private, well-guarded life.

During the fifteen minutes left to us before my plane took off, Gero and I talked about mutual friends lost from sight and about the best place to meet, preferably some remote valley in the highlands, where we could leisurely bring each other up to date on our respective exploits. Then we parted. Standing by the shed, Gero, tanned by the mountain sun, waved me to my plane.

I reached Oakland the next morning. A queer amphibious craft, lumbering and deafeningly noisy, took me to Pearl Harbor. Only a few months had gone by since the great base backstopped the Pacific armada. Now it seemed as abandoned as a resort out of season. Only the caretakers remained. Between empty sheds, a few transport planes idled on the aprons. A tanker and two destroyers lay at anchor in the harbor. Admiral Towers, Commander in Chief Pacific and veteran naval flier, introduced me to members of his staff familiar with Chinese affairs. These affairs, so I now learned, were far more complex and dismal than I had gathered from the information available to me in Washington.

I had never been to a Pacific island. Although I had read about foam-capped coral reefs, crescent beaches, and waving palm

fronds, nothing I had read or seen prepared me for the immensity
of scale, the towering volcanic cones, the endless procession of
clouds with their soaring peaks and broad, blackish bottoms. The
languorous air, the stillness of the lagoon behind the sheltering
reef, the easy grace of salt-sprayed beauty lull the senses. Yet
monstrous violence lurks beyond the horizon. The most crushing
notion of modern man's theodicy is that man does not matter to
nature and that hence God is neither in the cloud nor in the
raindrop. Nowhere does a man matter less than in that brooding
emptiness, the Pacific.

Late in the afternoon we landed on Kwajalein in the Marshalls.
First bombardment and then bulldozers had killed off all vegetation. The commodore in command of this concrete patch asked
me to spend the night in his bungalow by the beach. He whiled
away his leisure hours collecting shells and those baroque, spiky
fragments of coral which seem to have fathered Jacques Lip-
schitz' alarming sculpture. The commodore had rigged the largest
shells with electric bulbs which cast their designs—dots, waves,
and whorls—upon walls and ceiling. The glow of a lighted
aquarium inhabited by whiskered gnomes completed the cav-
ernous submarine effect. I slept badly. Fortunately, I can never
recall my dreams. Early next morning we took off for Guam.

There I swam off the celebrated horseshoe beach which, during the war, served the recreation of thousands on their way to
and from battle and which now, except for rusting gasoline
drums and rotting lean-tos, seemed oblivious of its shining hour
in naval history. The day after, the plane circled Iwo Jima, and
then, late in the evening, I unpacked my bags in one of those
cellarlike, flattened bedrooms which Frank Lloyd Wright designed to the stature, if not the comfort, of his Japanese clients.
In one week, I had crossed the Pacific. Soaking in my miniatur-
ized tub, I tried to sort out my impressions. Only one stood out
clearly:

A nation which in three years could move across as large an
expanse of hostile nature as the Pacific as many men and as much
hardware against as formidable a resistance could do anything
men need do to win dominion over this earth. More extraordinary
still, a people who will turn their back on so fabulous an exploit

as quickly as did the Americans might suffer many kinds of hubris, but the prideful lust for power is not among them.

Many of the Western-type buildings, designed to withstand earthquakes, had withstood the fire raids. The wooden structures had gone up in flames. After the surrender the Japanese, traditionally enured to recurring disaster, quckly improvised from the debris a new, though pathetically rickety, city. The occupation government and its dependents requisitioned the public buildings, hotels, and private buildings which had survived bombardment. Those Japanese, especially the former ruling classes, who could find shelter elsewhere and were not detained by the occupiers, had left Tokyo. Even so, Tokyo seemed packed with threadbare, perspiring, and ceaselessly active humanity. The docility and industry of the conquered favorably impressed the personnel of the occupation regime.

In the Imperial, a few gifts-in-kind commanded that rapid and efficient service which, in comparable American hotels, had become only a memory. Shoes were brightly shined, shirts gently laundered, suits neatly pressed, meals served hot, and all this instantly. The Imperial had been reserved for higher ranking Allied military and civilian officials. Some of them, like myself, were transients; others, on extended duty, had not yet been assigned permanent and more ample quarters; and others seemed to have settled for good in Mr. Wright's luxury bunker.

I struck up a few acquaintances. Occasionally we met at meals. An elderly naval officer talked knowlingly about tailor-made men's kimonos for evening wear, Japanese cuisine, and delightful small country hotels where neither Western customs nor gadgets intruded upon the serenity of Japanese decor. Mincing and didactic, he fitted perfectly the part of the precious bore, whose portrait Somerset Maugham has drawn with so much malice. A clipped English colonel made him his butt. His embarrassed countrymen gave him a wide berth. Yet I liked the garrulous little man. He had fallen head over heels in love with the old ways of Japan; indeed, he confided in me that he intended, upon his retirement, to settle in Japan. As a rule, senior U.S. naval officers did not avow so openly their affection for Japanese culture. One evening I walked along the moat of the Imperial Palace. The naval commander and a Japanese lady, middle-aged and prim in the traditional dress, were taking the air. A sedate couple, they walked in silence, halted to look down into the moat, and then faded into the dusk. A few days later the commander, his bulging bags beside him, stood in the lobby of the hotel. I asked him where he was going. He told me that, unexpectedly, he had been ordered back to the States. His eyes were red-rimmed. He gave me a shrunken little nod and stepped into the waiting car. Later I was told that his close affinity with Japanese folkways had been noted by his superiors.

The war crimes trials, then still in progress, necessitated the presence in Tokyo of a large number of American jurists qualified to accuse, defend, and judge General Tojo and his fellow captives of high rank. A New York lawyer, charged with the defense of a nutcracker-faced Japanese admiral, had been assigned to the Imperial mess. Sallow-faced, overweight, and truculently civilian, he sought my company, probably because I did not wear a uniform. Pulled out of the large, official hat, he had left his modest practice for what promised to turn into a long trial. He took a puzzled interest in his client.

Like all his colleagues, the lawyer took the legality of the proceedings for granted or, at least, pretended convincingly to do so. He meant to do what he could for the dour admiral. He did not doubt that his arguments would receive a fair hearing. Between conferences and briefs he meant to see what he could of Japan, her historic shrines as well as Hiroshima. He told me that, had not a physical defect assured his rejection by the draft board, he would have claimed his rights as a conscientious objector. Now, the Nazis having been crushed, there was no longer any reason why the world's peoples could not live under peace. The war crimes trials would contribute some valuable precedents to the body of international law. When I suggested that the Communists did not hold with bourgeois international law and had ideas of their own on international legality, he asked me, with that consistency which I have always admired in trial lawyers, what I would have done with the Nazi war criminals. I replied that I would have left them to the jurisdiction of the German criminal courts. He said that, even if the Germans could have been trusted to hang their own war criminals, verdict and execution would not have strengthened the body of international law, thus deterring another batch of Fascist aggressors. I rounded out my modest contribution to jurisprudence by observing that Nuremberg and Tokyo taught statesmen and generals only one lesson: if they were bent upon starting another war, they had to be sure of winning it, and that, when they had won the war, they could most economically keep the defeated nation in submission by delivering up its former ruling class to a war crimes tribunal staffed, of course, by their own jurists. Furthermore, the exhibit of Hiroshima did not seem to reinforce the moral authority of the court. Whose ox had been gored? The counsel from New York conceded that mine was not a legal mind. We adjourned the debate. The lawyer invited me to watch the proceedings. On a stifling June day I sat for a few hours through what seemed to me inconsequential exchanges between defendants and prosecution and the reading of documents adduced in evidence together with their laborious translation. I have never been an *aficionado* of bull rings or political trials. No matter how awkward the matador, the bull is doomed.

In the mess of the Imperial the Soviet military kept to themselves. A massive, bullet-headed Red Army colonel seemed to do most of the talking. I do not understand Russian. What he had to say must have carried weight, for his comrades silently kept on eating and listened attentively and respectfully to the harangue. The colonel, seeking relief from the heat, opened his tunic and thus exposed a mighty, hirsute chest, inadequately covered by a grayish undergarment. He perspired profusely; he wiped his brow with the back of his massive hand.

I later encountered the colonel under entirely different circumstances. One Sunday morning I visited the Imperial Museum. I had been told to look at the treasure of lacquer ware which a Tokugawa princess, the Emperor's bride, had brought from Kyoto to Tokyo as part of her dowry; not even the most luminous glaze of porcelain can match the sheen of fine lacquer. I walked from showcase to showcase, delighted with what I saw; a variety of cosmetic jars finished in soft gold held my attention. As I turned away, the hulk of the Soviet colonel barred the way.

Beaming broadly, he asked me in careful insular English whether I was interested in lacquer and had seen this particular exhibit before. He had spent some time in Tokyo before the war; indeed he spoke fluent Japanese. With the authority of the scholar and the reverence which finely wrought perfection inspires, he explained techniques and styles, the history and artistry of Japanese lacquer. I thanked the colonel for two hours of masterly and unobtrusive guidance. The spirit dwells in many and not a few improbable places. Having judged, I had been judged.

The ostensible purpose of my Tokyo visit was to gather information about Manchuria, my ultimate destination. With this goal in mind, I tracked down Japanese managers, engineers, and civil servants who had been stationed in Manchuria, the largest and richest of Japan's overseas possessions. Some had returned to the homeland before the surrender; others had made their escape after the Soviets had occupied the country. All told their tales of vandalism, murder, spoliation, and rape with that deferential smile with which Japanese have learned to bow to disaster.

Just when I was about to leave for Shanghai, my business finished, a member of General MacArthur's sizable public relations staff invited me to spend a few weeks with a military government team in the town of Maebashi, a few hours' ride north of Tokyo. We drove across level land planted mostly to vegetables and grains. The setting—the neat fields and the string of small factory towns along the highway—could have been anywhere in Western or Central Europe. Then, toward the end of our journey, we sighted a range of low hills and entered the rice-paddy country. Several plants which had supplied the Japanese air force ringed Maebashi; the military government team made its headquarters in the office building of one of these factories. I was quartered in a freshly painted room, redolent with the scent of dead fish. The conveniences were minimal. My hosts, however, were eager to show me around. Thus, in the company of one or the other member of the team, I saw military government at work in provincial Japan.

The team governed the sizable and populous prefecture of Gumma. Only a few months had elapsed since its assumption of rule, yet it embraced varied and staggering responsibilities with the enthusiasm, vigor, and self-assurance with which an incoming administration, dedicated to reform, bedazzles the expectant populace. The colonel in command, a fighting man recently detached from his infantry regiment, untiringly coursed from one end of his dominion to the other, inspecting schools and hospitals, receiving citizens' deputations, and looking after the moral regeneration of the slice of Japan's soul entrusted to his care. The Japanese had been taught the lesson that war does not pay—at least not if one starts a war and loses it. Japan was now to be made over into the image of the peace-loving victors.

In Gumma prefecture, one of the first measures taken by the military government was the confiscation of all lethal weapons, chiefly shotguns and Samurai swords. Among the latter were some rare and highly prized heirlooms handed down by one generation of proud Samurai to the other. The colonel, an avid collector, did not allow these choice pieces—blades honed to razor sharpness, engraved with honorable and sanguinary legends, and sheathed in polished sharkskin—to rust in the large factory shed which served as storehouse of a vast assortment of arms, ancient and modern, delivered up to the custody of a military government. With great care he had selected the finest sets, the long and the short sword and the throwing daggers snug in their finely wrought lacquer casings. The colonel, honoring me as a connoisseur, lovingly showed me his possessions.

Although Samurai families would rather go hungry than sell the ancestral armament, and although fine swords fetched large sums of money, the colonel assured me that the recent owners of his treasures were gratified at their having passed into his, a warrior's hands. After a few years, so I later learned from an old Tokyo hand, the workings of the law of supply and demand would right the balance between the oversupply of feudal weapons in the hands of transient foreign collectors and the longings of the Japanese for the mementos of their warlike past. By the end of the occupation, the thriving market in Samurai swords enabled many a Japanese to repossess himself, at going prices, of the very weapon which, upon his country's surrender, he had laid at the feet of the conqueror.

Accompanied by members of the team, specialists in education, sanitation, administration, and other branches of public welfare, I visited several show places of the prefecture. A rotund, beaming warden guided us through one of the larger of the local prisons. The inmates of a series of wooden cages topped by a flat roof resting upon closely spaced beams bowed beamingly before our presence. According to our Nisei interpreter, they praised their happy lot and the fatherly care of the warden.

Although a fair macadam road led to the jail, only a narrow footpath on top of a levee between rice paddies afforded access to the local hospital. Patients, so it seemed, were expected to make their way to the hospital by foot or wheelbarrow or upon stretchers borne by two hefty men. Like all Japanese interiors, the wards, waiting rooms, and offices were kept scrupulously clean, the ambulatory cases doing a good deal of the cleaning. The director and chief surgeon, who had graduated from a European university, professed himself deeply honored by my visit and then smartly led the way to the maternity ward. We were greeted by instant and abiding silence, a feat of collective self-control for which I have no explanation.

The team member in charge of education invited me to address a girls' high school. With unblinking demureness, four hundred students clad in blue blouse and dark-blue skirt listened to my observations on the equality of the sexes in American society, on civic responsibility, and on the inwardness of representative government. Since my host, a young lieutenant plucked from the faculty of a California high school, had asked me to address myself to these topics, I resisted the temptation to speak plainly of plain things.

I do not know what was then, and what is now, the status of Japanese women in public affairs. Whatever her public role, the Japanese woman seems marvelously well adjusted to her place in life as wife, as mother and as daughter. I do not know whether Japanese women are more or less prone than American women to drinking hard liquor or gobbling tranquilizers or consulting psychiatrists. I am sure that those Japanese women who seek these pathetic havens do not do so because they want to be, and fail to be, like men. The most salient characteristic of a Japanese woman is her ageless, entrancing femininity.

Perhaps the Japan I saw—the Japan after defeat which I searched for semblances of my literary preconception—was no longer the old Japan—the Japan of the airy perspectives, the serene spaciousness wrested by artful deceit from hardly any space at all. Perhaps the past eighteen years have transformed Japan into a replica of our own affluent society with its expensive appetite and neurosis. Perhaps in Japan, too, young men and women have settled down to that camaraderie in concupiscence which, in our civilization, so effectively levels all but the irreducible biological distinctions between the sexes. Yet I doubt that the Japanese have followed us all the way and that they ever will.

Throughout the past hundred years the very purpose of the Japanese national policy has been to Westernize in order to remain oriental. The national experiment in schizophrenia has been remarkably successful—the one and only successful experiment in Westernization in Asia. Thus in science and technology the Japanese behave like Westerners, sometimes more ingeniously and outrageously Western than Westerns themselves. Yet every day when they return from factory, office, and city street to their very private lives they shed their functional Western shell and slip back effortlessly into the old ways of Japan. Alone among non-Western peoples, they lead a happy life, apparently untroubled by the strain of impersonating one kind of man and then, with scant transition, dropping the mask and playing another kind of man, namely, themselves.

On the other hand, the Chinese, supposedly the most tradition-bound people on earth, have not managed this feat of protective Westernization. Notwithstanding their best effort to remain arrogantly Chinese, they have cut themselves off with self-mutilating frenzy from their traditional culture. The methodical iconoclasm of the Chinese Communists is liable to do what neither foreign conqueror nor natural catastrophe nor civil war had succeeded in doing, namely, to crush the cultural personality of China.

Only as clever a people as the Japanese could have captured the secrets of the power of an alien, superior, and hostile civilization without paying for these imports with its political and cultural independence. Great as was their innate genius for adaptation and organization, the Japanese were also very lucky; for the transformation of Japan coincided with the golden age of free trade. Furthermore, Japan could turn the prevailing international balance of power to her advantage: in relation to one another, the Western powers were too well matched to let any one among them grab all of Japan before she could modernize her military power. It is doubtful that, under present conditions, Japan could have leapt within one generation into the circle of major industrial exporters without getting herself deeply into hock to one of the contending Great Powers. Thus Japan has been spared the troubles which now afflict industrializing China, unable to procure from a free world market the technological means denied her by the Soviet Union. Moreover, neither defeat nor occupation appreciably altered the pattern of Japanese society; the shock of Westernization had been absorbed two generations earlier—long before World War II, Japan had come to terms with Western ways and by and large these terms were her own. Today Japan is no less her old self and not more "American," than, let us say, defeated Germany or defeated Italy. Compared with Japan, the rest of Asia has done badly: Red China has lost her soul, and the major Asian countries such as India and Indonesia have forgotten their past and cannot envisage their future.

I do not pretend to grasp the inwardness of Japan. All I see is a country among countries, a vast city and its bewildering maze, a solitary peak, windowless factories, the chrome and steel concrete of international design, tiny reposeful gardens, the calming emptiness of tatami-covered rooms, rush-caped peasants bending to the shoots in the muddy paddies, innumerable tiny booths stocked to the ceiling with merchandise; the gaudiest cinemas; the quiet of images with a faint smile, acknowledging worship. My Japan is a concoction of literary notions, chance observations, and those fickle sensations that are stirred by the smell of the trees in bloom, of bakery and fish shops and of charcoal fires; by the sight of the great mountain and a tiny patch of gravel; by the sound of innumerable tapping feet and the click and rustle of a fan.

At every turn I met the paradox. Baroness Murasaki's *Tale of*

Genji, written about A.D. 1000, combines the psychological finesse of Stendhal and Proust with the naïveté of a medieval tale of courtly love. Sensitivity without compassion, loyalty without love, courage without mercy—these men and women turn strangers just when they seem most kin to us in happiness or misfortune. In the most candid fashion they tell us about their "values," and yet they never cease to startle us by their choices. Baroness Murasaki's attractive people—the Best Society —pursue their pleasures in a well-bred, worldly way. Complex as are their intrigues and fierce their passions, their manners are impeccable and their taste exquisite. All is gaiety, and no one seems to suffer from the cares about the hereafter. Yet it is the premonition of the darkness which must fall upon Baroness Murasaki's delightful world that gives poignancy to every moment of the sunny day. Her charming people are all the more charming because they must die. "When water is scooped up in the hands, the moon is reflected in them."

I met a Japanese, famed at home and abroad for his connoisseurship, who generously showed me his rich collection of Japanese painting, scrolls, and screens from very ancient to contemporary. Invariably, the features which seemed to rouse his aesthetic satisfaction left me unmoved. Where he extolled perfection I noted but stylistic pedantry and literary allusions to some idea or feeling which did not seem suggested by the work of art itself. Then, again, the famous expert acknowledged with a casual nod the hazed perspective or the small figure beneath the brooding rock which I thought the acme of Japanese artistry. The state of noncommunication was complete. Yet, strangely enough, a total lack of rapport did not preclude our agreement on the relative perfection of various paintings as a whole. We looked at the same painting and found it beautiful for diverse and apparently unconnected reasons. In aesthetic feeling we were as far apart as the Sistine Chapel and the Temple of Nara. Yet we delighted in one and the same works of art. Beauty is an absolute. Its reduction to an aggregate of components for the sake of "appreciation" is more likely to cause sophisticated misunderstanding than reveal the meaning-within-the-meaning. Since then I have listened to many lectures on how to look at, and what to look for in, a Japanese or

Chinese or Hindu work of art. By now I am perhaps more knowledgeable about techniques, symbols, and "values." I have not come by one step nearer to understanding my own response. In the last resort, you see it or you don't.

Chapter Fourteen

A NAVY lieutenant met me at the Shanghai airfield; we drove off into the heat, humid and gritty. Sprawled over the alluvial flats at the mouth of the Yangtze river, Shanghai grew within a hundred years from a fishing village into one of the most graceless of cities. Indeed, not even Chicago can rival its shapelessness—there are no parks or impressive public buildings whatsoever. Warehouses, factories, the tightly packed workers' quarters, and the apartment houses and villas of the foreign quarter hem in the city's areas generously set aside for civic recreation, the deepwater port and the polo field. I was quartered in a tall hotel, American style, near the polo field. Early in the morning, I awoke to a listless breeze and the click of mallets.

Before the war Shanghai, an autonomous city, like the other Treaty Ports, had been governed by a mixed Western-Chinese town council. In fact, the British and French members controlled the city, conceding to their hand-picked Chinese colleagues a feeble minority voice. After the surrender of the Japanese forces,

Shanghai settled down to living under another, though more informal, condominium. Chiang Kai-shek's troops had occupied the city; units of the U.S. Seventh Fleet had secured the harbor. Now, a Chinese mayor assisted by Chinese military presided over the municipality; U.S. cruisers and destroyers rode at anchor in the harbor, and U.S. soldiers and sailors mingled with the crowds along the Bund. U.S. matériel, mostly leftovers from the war in the Pacific, accumulated in the dockyards along the river, whence some of it reached Chiang's armies deployed to the north of the Yangtze River. Part of it decayed where it had been dumped; part of it, especially jeeps and trucks, found its devious way into the civilian economy. Trade was brisk.

Once upon a time, according to the old China hands, Shanghai excelled in luxury and vice any of the great ports of Eastern Asia. Moreover, between the two wars the Sassoons, the great Parsi merchants, pulled most of their vast fortune out of India and invested it in Shanghai. The Cathay Hotel, the largest of their holdings, a grayish cigar-shaped pile, rose above the Bund. Its fabled splendors had been frayed by ill use and neglect; the Japanese conquerors, either because they did not care or because they did not have the means, did nothing to maintain the prerequisites of Western comfort such as radiators, water closets, and stuffed furniture, not to speak of croquet lawns, tennis courts, and French restaurants. The Western veneer had cracked. An era had ended.

In the foreign concessions the Japanese had evicted most of the Europeans and rich Chinese and had made themselves at home in the villas, apartment buildings, hotels, and clubs which, before the flood, had been the preserve of the foreign community and its native hangers-on. Then in the wake of Allied victory, the Chinese Nationalists not only drove out the Japanese but also abolished the autonomy of the city. Although some foreign residents, many of whom had spent the war years in Japanese captivity, managed to reclaim their property, most of Shanghai's wealth, derived from exclusive trading privileges and the world's cheapest industrial labor, passed into Chinese hands or, rather, into the hands of Chiang's officials and their business connections. Thus, in the bars of their clubs, the old China hands, Europeans and

Americans, compared notes and deplored with lowered voices—
Nationalist Army officers and civil functionaries having been
prudently admitted to membership—the deterioration of Western prestige, physical plant, and moral standards. In Shanghai the
Chinese genius for graft, extortion, and chicanery had burst into
full flower. The residual Western community knew itself
doomed, and most of its members seemed to agree that, although
Chiang's victory over the Communists would be the lesser of two
evils, the outlook for Western investment was not bright.

Shanghai had been the largest Western enclave in China, if not
in all of Asia. It was the largest *entrepôt* of China's trade with the
world and China's most important window on Western civilization. Indeed, Chinese who had been educated in Shanghai's English and French schools played an important role in the revolution which overthrew the Manchu dynasty and still runs its
course. Thus, together with Canton, Shanghai had been the principal entry port for Western missionaries, journalists, and Communist agitators. The last-named, beginning with Borodin, Chicago grain-dealer-turned-Bolshevik-agent and adviser of Sun Yat-
sen, recruited a large following not only among the gruesomely
underpaid workers but also among the sons and daughters of
those fabulously rich Chinese middlemen, the compradors, who
stood between the inland markets and the Western traders.

Until the split in the Kuomintang—or rather the Kuo Kuo
Mintang—Shanghai, Canton, and Han-Kow were the strongholds
of the Communist movement in China. Through his marriage
with Sun Yat-sen's sister-in-law, Chiang Kai-shek gained access to
the inner circle not only of the Chinese revolution but also of
Shanghai's *haute finance*, for among Shanghai's Chinese magnates
the Soong family was renowned for its wealth, international connections, and the beauty of its women. Chiang's marital ties thus
enmeshed his and the Kuomintang's fortunes in those of Shanghai, a city which, to the rest of China, stands as the monument of
Western dominance. Now some of the Chinese people's hatred
for all foreigners richocheted on those rich Chinese of low birth
who partnered Western exploitation, spoke foreign languages
better than their own, and sent their sons and daughters to Western schools. For the Chinese, including Mandarins-turned-Com-

munist, are inveterate snobs, hardened by a millennial tradition of literary conceit and striving for bureaucratic rank. Thus
the un-Chinese ways of the Soongs, their ties with foreign business, their recently acquired wealth, the brevity of their gene-
alogy, the Shanghai flavor of their Chinese speech, and their
Western polish offered rewarding targets to their enemies.
Greedy and arrogant, clever and ambitious, the Soongs always
knew how to make enemies.

I carried letters of introduction; one of these letters led to the
acquaintance of a Chinese merchant who had started upon the
road to riches, so the story had it, as a rickshaw coolie. (I do not
know how and when he improved upon this condition.) Before
the collapse of Western rule in Shanghai, he had served on the
city council as one of the members representing the Chinese
community. Denounced by the Japanese, he hid in a Fukien village; then just before the Japanese surrendered, he slipped back
into the city. When the Seventh Fleet steamed into Shanghai he
headed the delegation of notables chosen to welcome the American admiral; apparently, he had succeeded in riding out the
storms of war and inflation—no doubt, like so many rich Chinese,
well connected with one or the other of the city's secret societies, he had transferred, while Shanghai still enjoyed international
status, one portion of his capital to foreign banks and stashed
away the other portion, converted into gold and precious stones,
in diverse concealed places. Though well on in years, he stood
erect, a tall broad-shouldered man who, even in repose, conveyed
the impression of swift and powerful muscular reflexes.

No sooner had my letter been delivered to this enterprising
merchant than he sent word that he expected me for lunch. His
oldest son, accompanied by three tough individuals whom I surmised to be his guards, picked me up at my hotel. In a large and
expensive American car, the young man drove at breakneck
speed through narrow streets, barely missing a thousand rick-
shaws, climbing sidewalks and pitting his horn against the curses
of the scattering populace. Exulting in his skill, he talked about
the movies of yesteryear and his high hopes of being admitted as
a student to an American university which happened to be no
other than mine. A gate swung open. Several nondescript build-

ings stood within a walled yard; we halted abruptly at the largest.
I was led into an oblong room in which about thirty men had
assembled and was shown through another door into a high-
ceilinged hall, lined on each side with wooden benches. In the
center stood a large round table. My host stepped forward,
gravely bade me welcome, and inquired about the health of our
mutual friend. He asked me to be seated at the table and seated
himself on a chair opposite mine. The men I had passed in the
oblong room trooped in. About ten, including my host's son,
joined us at the table; the others took their places on the benches
along the wall. The meal lasted for several hours. Toasts in Scotch
whisky drunk from liqueur glasses scanned the unending procession of dishes. It seemed that I was expected to respond to all of
them; the stifling heat did not diminish the appetite of the company, and a crew of shirt-sleeved servants kept on refilling the
liqueur glasses. The men on the benches, like the retainers of a
medieval lord, silently watched the feast. Never having studied
Chinese etiquette, I cannot say whether the proceedings were
orthodox.

During my stay in China I attended several dinners given by
Chinese officials, including a high-living Communist general.
Most of them approximated Western customs of conviviality; I
was furnished knife, fork and spoon, for it was plain that I could
not manage otherwise. Always all kinds of people who neither
served nor ate drifted in and out of the room, interested spec-
tators of the repast. At first I thought their presence disturbing;
then I no longer bothered about them—just as I no longer noticed the sores of children, beggars and ponies, and the trucks
which, each morning, bore away the dead of starvation. For
China toughens Western sensibilities; this is probably why so
many of the old China hands, money grubbers as well as academic experts, know much about China and understand little.
Those who do understand because they love the Chinese people
and have chosen to live among them are likely to assume their
habits of thought and feeling, for the pull of China is immensely
strong; it is they who have moved beyond our reach and to the
other side of the barrier which stands between Chinese realities
and Western minds. Thus, one part, though not all, of the China

story—American policies toward Chiang and the ease of Communist conquest—might turn out to have been nothing more sinister than a nonsensical dialogue between one set of Americans who knew little and understood less and another set who understood and could not tell.

I barely managed to rise from my first China banquet. My impressions were blurred by acute discomfort. I had drunk and eaten too much. Of all the Chinese delicacies, only the crisp skin of Peking duck stirred my emotions; among the rest of the dishes I could not distinguish one from the other. Through the haze I saw smooth-faced men picking nimbly at an array of bowls, tucking up invisible sleeves and wiping their glistening faces with moist towels. Midway through the meal I locked my face into what I fondly imagined might look like an appreciative smile. The retired general at my right who, I was told, had fought the war lords, and who spoke basic English through clenched teeth, and the retired ambassador at my left who, so he said, had served in several European capitals, praised American determination to save China from communism.

After a while even I, dazed as I was, could not miss the purpose of these shrewd and hard-bitten men; they were fully aware of the extent to which the United States had dismantled its military power—for all their bland cheerfulness, they anticipated disaster. Only by outright military intervention could the United States halt the advance of the Communist forces, regrouped and re-armed in Manchuria. For the Soviets, withdrawing their forces, had allowed the Chinese Communists to occupy the northern regions of Manchuria along the Russian frontier and to take over the war matériel surrendered by Japan's Kwantung Army. However, the rail communications between China proper and Manchuria were poor; a massive counteroffensive launched from the sea, supplied by the U.S. Navy, and supported by two American divisions, could drive the Communists from Manchuria, cut their direct access to Soviet supplies, and ensure the Nationalists control of the most important industrial region of China. The retired general snapped his jaws and left the retired ambassador to care for my conversational needs. We talked about the excellence of American colleges, Chiang's program for the moral reawakening of China, and the eagerness with which young Chinese sought to perfect their education in America in order to serve China's New Order all the better.

My host's son drove me back to the hotel. His ardor had slackened, and we arrived without mishap. I fell into a heavy sleep and awakened to the sticky, unrefreshed breeze of the morning. I then sought out the correspondent of one of New York's great dailies. Wise and worn, he had lived for a long time in China; he had traveled widely throughout the land and spent part of the war years in Chungking. Now on a brief visit to Shanghai, which he loathed, he longed to return to Peking, where, had it not been for the turn of events, he had hoped to settle. Unlike most of his colleagues, he viewed the frailties of Chiang's regime with tolerance, if not with compassion. Having visited the Soviet Union, studied Communist doctrine and known Communists in the flesh, he doubted the benefits which China would derive from the substitution of Mao for Chiang. He knew the Yenan way to be the hard Communist way rather than the gentle path of "agricultural reform," the stock cliché of those foolish or mendacious men who denounced Chiang's regime as a clique of usurious landlords and sold the American public on the astringent virtues of the Communists.

He advised me to leave Shanghai as soon as possible, a mean city. In Peking I might not find the soul of China, a soul that, unnoticed, had departed from its body a long time ago; yet I would find there still a few shrines of tranquillity, a few thoughtful individuals, and a better climate. Indeed, the longer I stayed in Shanghai the narrower grew the perspectives and the lower fell my spirits.

The despondency of the Shanghai business community seeped into the morale of the American official presence. From the countinghouses, clubs, and hotel lobbies of Shanghai flowed the lurid tales of Kuomintang incompetence and corruption. Prettied up as reports from "reliable sources," they floated onto the desks of high officials and newspaper editors abroad.

The country had been at war for ten years, it had been ravaged by civil disorder all through the lifetime of a generation. In China, even in the best of times, food had been scarce and natural disasters, floods and droughts, frequent. Moreover, the Japanese, in occupation of the richest regions, had been much too preoccupied with fighting America to develop the resources of China with the exception of Manchuria—they took from the chunk of China under their domination whatever it had to give to their armies and domestic economy; they did not replace worn-out railroad equipment and factory tools. Thus, Chiang's ragged forces, when they descended from the highlands into the river valleys, took possession of a land virtually stripped of those facilities which China had acquired, at exorbitant costs, during a century of haphazard contact with Western civilization. Into their hands fell the Treaty Ports and what remained of their riches; however, the breakdown of the transportation system had cut off these cities from the life-giving hinterland, moribund dinosaurs stranded on the edge of the sea. Had he been left in peace, Chiang might have mastered these calamities: repaired the railroads, dredged ports, and mended the worn factory tools; but the Communists saw to it that he would not be left in peace.

Much has been written about postwar China and nearly all of it by people who preferred to obtain their insight from those "reliable sources," principally bars, located in the former Treaty Ports rather than grubbier places farther inland. And not all of it was pure fiction. Yet even those who took the trouble to see for themselves and put down faithfully what they saw succumbed now and then to the great Chinese illusion: China is the Land of the Middle, and the world around it, barbarous and foolish, does not matter.

Most foreigners who knew and loved China fell in with the thought habits of her people, the most ethnocentric on earth. That the troubles of China had now become a mere episode in a worldwide struggle between two political systems, this idea seemed both implausible and distasteful to the old China hands, the Shanghai traders, as well as the Sinologist diplomats and intellectuals. Although not more than a handful had made common cause with the Communists, nearly all of them hated Chiang— some because he threatened Western privilege, others because he could not or would not forthwith transform Chinese society in their paradoxical image of democracy in the raiment of Mandarin culture. Thus the most reactionary and the most progressive among the long-time foreign residents in China joined forces in lampooning and denouncing Chiang. They clamored for alternatives to Chiang's rickety regime which only his Western Allies' utmost resolution—and a material effort on the scale of the help later given for less pressing reasons to South Korea—could have kept from falling apart. That it did not collapse much sooner than it actually did is not the least of the enigmas of the China story.

Let us assume that Americans, a people so much less given to hysteria and corruption than the Chinese, had had to contend with a situation such as confronted Chiang in 1946. Let us assume that half the country, including Detroit, Chicago, Pittsburgh, and New York, had been occupied by a hostile army, that in the rest of the country a civil war on the order of the War Between the States was being fought, and that all these horrors had lasted for many years—what, then, would have been the chances of a U.S. government, rid of the foreign invader yet still beset by domestic rebellion, of establishing a tranquil, just, and prosperous order? Nevertheless, it is this miraculous feat which Chiang was expected to perform. Since he failed to live up to these expectations, his foreign critics scoured the scene for a more efficient and less corruptible team. In theory, there were several; in fact, however, there was only one, namely, Mao's.

French thinkers, notably Amaury de Riencourt, who sits by the Lake of Geneva and philosophizes, in full view of Mont Blanc, on history, have pointed out the close affinities of the Chinese and French cultures. Both are as tightly bound by tradition as were the feet and waists of their women, respectively. Both were highly and arrogantly literary; their world views were historicist: they both looked into the past for the prophecy of their future. Both forged from politeness and etiquette effective instruments of self-preservation.

In France and in China, a woman stood as the symbolic figure of military valor: Jeanne d'Arc and Moo-Lan. In neither country, though, has feminism made much headway. Both French and Chinese women are intensely feminine, eager to please the whims of their lords and to bask in their protection; yet, in each country, as can be seen upon a more searching look, they run the business. I do not know what is the equivalent of *la caisse* in Chinese; I am sure that whatever it is, it is in the charge of a woman.

For the illusion of male superiority, Chinese, like Frenchmen, surrender themselves happily to the tender care and iron control of their women. Since this national characteristic no longer presents a problem, thanks to the insights of modern psychology in culture traits of child rearing, I need not dwell upon it further.

Friends in Washington had written Madame Wei, widow of the Chinese wartime ambassador to the United States, asking her to receive me. They suggested that I would do well to obtain her views on the course of the civil war. A Kuomintang politician in her own right, Madame Wei had taken up residence in a modest villa in the French quarter. In the gimcrack drawing room where she received her many and influential friends, I was admitted to her formidable presence. Middle-aged, running to fat and impassive, she let me state the purpose of the errand which had brought me to China. Apparently, she found what I said to her liking. Plainly I was not a China expert and had not come with settled notions. Thus reassured, she unloosed her considerable charm. Now a gust of animation rippled over her large and handsome face. Deftly she assembled, by bits and pieces, my personal history.

Reared before World War I in the exquisite seclusion of a Mandarin family, Madame Wei had scaled the wall of the paternal palace and gone to school in the revolution against the Manchus. Member of a terrorist group bent upon assassinating high Manchu officials, she demurely traveled in a railway carriage from Tientsin to Peiping carrying in her valise bombs and fuses. Having helped to blow up the prefect of police, she was arrested; f..ed by the timely overthrow of the dynasty, she joined the opposition against Yuan Shih-kai, the dictator. When the plot miscarried, she went into exile and enrolled as a law student in the University of Paris; there she met young Mr. Wei, a fellow student.

Upon the accession of Sun Yat-sen the young couple returned

to China and opened a joint law practice which established their fame and fortune. It was widely rumored that Mr. Wei deferred, in trickier cases, to the legal opinion of his partner. Be that as it may, the Weis rose to positions of trust in the council of the Kuomintang. Indeed, Chiang offered to Madame Wei the embassy to the French Republic, but Madame Wei requested that her husband be appointed to that post. Thus Mr. Wei's diplomatic career began. Shortly before World War II, Chiang entrusted him with the all-important embassy to Washington; Mr. Wei, despite failing health, labored tirelessly to repair the bonds between Washington and Chungking, strained by the conflict of American and Chinese military commanders and all sorts of political differences rooted in the oddity of an alliance between two people who, even with the best will in the world, could not understand each other. Mr. Wei, assisted vigorously and skillfully by his wife, accomplished his mission. The alliance survived. Japan was crushed. And Chiang was awarded the status of one of the Big Five, set above the lesser members of the United Nations.

Madame Wei seemed interested in my errand. She wanted me to meet the officials who, along the way, would assist me in gathering information and, should I so desire, help me to pass my leisure hours as pleasantly as the local conditions permitted. At that time Chinese communications, even on urgent matters, must have been uncertain; nevertheless, on my travels I was to find that Madame Wei's providential arrangements proved effective.

Before World War I, Western missionaries and businessmen from all over China sought relief from the summer heat on the sandy beaches in the vicinity of Tsingtao. (The naval ensign who showed me the sights reverently pointed to the exact spot where Henry Luce, a missionary's son, then an infant, was said to have built mud castles on the beach.)

By this same commodious and sheltered bay of Tsingtao, the Imperial Germans built lovingly a fair replica of the turn-of-the-century upper-class suburb of any German city. They also constructed a fine naval base for the Asiatic squadron of their fleet, endowed the town with solid public facilities, and fostered some light industries. Shantung, like Ireland, has always exported its most vigorous youth to other countries. Indeed, the industrial

cities of Manchuria are as much Shantung Chinese as Boston and
New York once were Irish. And the Germans, who had selected
Shantung's best port as a consolation prize for their belated entry
into the spirited competition for choice Western bridgeheads on
Chinese soil, put to good use the virtually unlimited local supply
of labor; so large and so well laid out was the naval base, for
example, that it accommodated, first, the German Asiatic Squadron, then a part of the Imperial Japanese Navy and, the Japanese
having gone the way of all empires, the United States Seventh
Fleet. The Germans enjoyed only briefly the possession of their
Chinese enclave, however, for Tsingtao fell to the Japanese as
their share in the spoils of victory over the central Powers, a fair
reward for Japan's vicarious support of the Allies in World War
I. Oddly enough, though, the German flavor, solid and bourgeois,
lingered on.

Mr. Forrestal had signaled the commander of the Seventh Fleet
the purpose of my journey. Admiral Cooke requested me to
spend a few days at his headquarters.

Undoubtedly Admiral Cooke had been chosen for his seniority
in rank, technical competence, and proved ability of leadership;
this I took for granted—as I take for granted the beneficial workings of the selection process by which our vast federal bureaucracy, civil and military, purges and renews itself. Nevertheless,
men thus raised to high command are likely to score by mistakes
avoided rather than by decisions made; under ordinary circumstances, such reticence ensures the safe passage an individual
career may wend through the bureaucratic narrows, though not
the rise of the odd and bold men. It is, however, the latter who
seem to have won most wars; this is why, as Voltaire noted, the
English shot one of their most punctilious admirals—*pour en-
courager les autres.*

Admiral Cooke had come up through the staff. From Washington he guided the movements of the great fleets which, most of
the time on schedule, met and defeated the Japanese. A brilliant
planner, he was released from his desk for duty on the high seas
only after the war had ended; he took over from an eccentric, battle-worn admiral. There were now no Japanese left on

whom he could have tested his mettle. So instead of taking his mighty ships into combat he scanned reports of the shadowy maneuverings on the Chinese mainland where American diplomacy sought to reconcile the warring factions. Moreover, Admiral Cooke, though he lacked the panache of his legendary predecessor, possessed at least one prerequisite of the strategist: he knew how to reduce the obvious to order. Sophistication mistakes variety for complexity and disorder for design; war is disorderly, civil war being its most disorderly species. Yet the principles of strategy are simple, though difficult of application, and what has been called the China Tangle badly needed disentangling by a mind schooled in strategic thought. Admiral Cooke was not quite so simple a sailor as he pretended to be; a shrewd and skeptic judge of men, he had taken the measure of the principal actors on China's political stage.

Admiral Cooke thought that in China the game was all or nothing, that the Chinese Communists would not settle for less than all as long as they were not decisively beaten, and that Chiang, despite his shortcomings or because of them, was likely to keep faith with the United States—for he had no one else to turn to for military and economic support. However primly we might play the role of the neutral though sympathetic bystander, the civil war in China was a war between the United States and the Soviet Union, each backing its proxy. A defeat of the Nationalists would be chalked up by the Communists and all of Asia as a defeat of the United States. The loss of China to the Communists would decisively alter the international balance of power and, in the long run, confront us with a threat greater than the one we had just defeated in the Pacific. Thus, the Chinese civil war was as much our war as the war against Japan had ever been.

For the United States, it was more advantageous to fight the Communists in northern Manchuria than along the Yellow River and, if that line could not be held, along the Yangtze River; the farther away Communist power could be kept from the China and Japan Seas the better for the security of all the neighboring peoples and hence for the United States. If Chiang's forces could not prevail unaided, moreover, the United States would have to intervene. For military intervention now, costly and unpopular as it might be at home, would be cheaper than the future wars which would have to be fought in order to keep the victorious Communists at bay. If the welfare of the Chinese people under peace and freedom was really as dear to us as our officials in their public statements said it was, then we could do no better than back Chiang. More likely than not, Chiang would not bring to China the blessings of Western democracy, even though he would deal with his countrymen more gently than Mao. For a long time Chiang would have to look to us for help and counsel, while Mao would follow the example of Lenin and Stalin and, in order to create a powerful Communist state, turn China into one vast slave labor camp.

Chapter Fifteen

ACCOMPANIED Admiral Cooke
to Nanking, then the seat of Chiang Kai-shek's government. The
plane took us across the river and loess country which, so I read,
has sustained the world's oldest continuous civilization. From an
altitude of about 6,000 feet it looked, but for the wide, diked
channels of the great rivers, featureless and monotonous. Although
settlements varied in size, they were indistinguishable from one
another by any architectural variety which could be noted from
afar. I do not know what might have been the Chinese equivalent
of the European domes, town halls, palaces, and castles. If such
ostentatious landmarks from the hand of man ever existed, they
must have been destroyed by natural or man-made disasters or by
the wear of negligence and time.

According to reports from "reliable sources," Nationalist and
Communist armies, unmindful of the truce, were battling each
other in the very region which lay beneath our path. Though we
scanned the alleged scene of heavy combat, we failed to identify
anything like troops and tools of war, not to speak of any mili-

tary action.

I detest wars, especially wars to end wars and wars by proxy. The latter are the dirtiest. In China, the Nationalists fought the West's war against the Communists, just as from 1936 onward they had fought the West's war against Japan. For a variety of reasons, the Nationalists disappointed the trust which the United States had reposed so generously in their military prowess. By 1946 only the forthright military intervention of the United States could have stiffened Nationalist resistance. Since it had become perfectly clear that the United States would not assist its embattled proxy beyond furnishing him with castoff hardware and increasingly irritable advice, no one, except the spivs in Shanghai, had anything to gain by prolonging the contest.

Cruising over the good earth, I was gladdened by its peaceful midday slumber. Disregarding the reports from "reliable sources," the Nationalists and Communists, having reached the same conclusion, kept a respectful distance from each other. Through the mediation of the United States, Nationalists and Communists had concluded a truce and the civil war had entered upon that stage of circumspect maneuver which, in eighteenth-century Europe, obviated the necessity for battle and kept within reasonable bounds the expenditure of lives and arms.

The Chinese are eminently reasonable. Only an eminently reasonable people could have perpetuated a civilization so precariously poised for so many thousands of years. Though in China human life may always have been held cheap, it does not follow that the Chinese conceive of war as an invitation to mass slaughter. The menace of the Chinese hordes, hurling themselves upon their foes and overcoming superior armament by sheer weight of numbers, is a "paper tiger" of the West's own making. Unlike Westerners, weaned on the fables of chivalry, the Chinese are not romantics, least of all in military matters. The great strategists of their history are closer in spirit to von Clausewitz than to the executioners of Verdun and Stalingrad. The purpose of war is to destroy not men and their chattel but their will to resist. From Sun-tsu to Mao Tse-tung, Chinese military thought dwelled upon psychological gambits rather than drawn battles. In Korea, the Red Chinese suffered heavy casualties. Yet, they did not persist, as did the belligerents in World War I, in pitting brute strength against impregnable positions. Nimbly changing strategy and means, they maneuvered at the conference table in Panmunjom and successfully consolidated their position.

In Nanking, the United States naval attaché bid me welcome to his quarters and introduced me to the members of his staff. At the mess table two young lieutenants, one lean and sallow and the other squat and hairless, conducted an informal seminar on Chinese culture, the intricacies of Chinese script, nuances of intonation, the artistry that went into faking curios, and the Maoist transubstantiation of Leninist doctrine. Whatever was their mission, they must have accomplished it to their superiors' satisfaction for both rose, so I heard later, to high positions in that government agency which is concerned with the most intimate aspects of internatonal politics. They had submerged themselves so deeply into Chinese lore that only reluctantly did they come up for a whiff of Western air. Both had pursued Chinese studies at Yale University; upon receiving their commissions, both had been assigned to study in the language program of the navy. Both seemed uncannily detached from all but Chinese realities. In their company I wandered through Nanking. Within its walls, so I was told, stood once the magnificent edifices of an imperial residence. These, as seems to have been the fate of nearly all the antiquities of China, had vanished.

Since tutelary powers favor high places as their abode, part of the U.S. mission in Nanking occupied several roomy and livable houses upon a hill with a view of the town and the lowlands along the river. In a ravine at the bottom of the hill, a Chinese cooper offered tiny ponies for sale. Their running saddle sores and scarred flanks, the smell of horse dung and the jolly laughter of the dealer praising his wares and keeping his customers in stitches—this tableau still haunts my memory while other impressions which I then thought deeply moving or significant have begun to fade. It seems my memory always keeps turning up what I did not mean it to keep and drops what I expressly put in its care. It is most accurate when it plays back the unintended, the inconsequential, and the odd. It is this trick of recalling a fleeting gesture glimpsed from the corner of the eye, which makes Goya's notebooks so disturbing.

Before returning to his commodious command ship in Tsing-tao, Admiral Cooke introduced me to General George C. Marshall, Presidential Envoy to China, charged with the reconciliation of the warring factions. My appointment had been made for late in the afternoon at the general's residence. An alert aide ushered me into the presence of a lordly and slender man. The general poured me a Scotch and soda and settled me in an easy chair. He asked me what I had come to see and what I had seen. I stated my errand and my impressions. I doubt that I shone in the ensuing conversation. I was awed. I had read a good deal about General Marshall's brilliant career and legendary achievements. I knew myself face to face with greatness. I also sensed that the great man was tired and far from being a happy man.

The President had sent General Marshall to Nanking on an impossible mission. American truce teams consisting of one or several officers and a few enlisted men in charge of communication and transport equipment were posted in the various theaters of war from Central China all the way to Manchuria. They were to supervise the keeping of the truce. Neither party was either able or willing to control all of its soldiery. Since unattached guerrillas as well as bandits sporting the uniforms of the two armies roamed the country, sporadic fighting constantly threatened to touch off large-scale hostilities and thus to upset the truce.

General Marshall's task was not only to restrain the two parties from going for each other, hammer and tongs, but also to persuade them into concluding a durable arrangement. Since diplomacy alone could not appreciably alter the military situation, a compromise would have had to take into account the prevailing balance of military power. Although the Nationalists held most of the important cities, the Communists controlled most of the countryside. Hence, a settlement could be reached only by according the Communists a substantial share, probably one half, in the rule of all of China. In brief, the objective of American diplomacy could be nothing less and nothing more than the creation of a coalition government in which, but for a few minor factions, the Kuomintang and the Communist party would rule jointly. The immediate task was to obtain Chiang's agreement to sit down with the Communists, and then to keep both parties talking. The scheme suffered from one serious defect: Chiang would have had to forget all he had ever known about the collaboration of Communists with non-Communists and all he had learned, since the end of World War II, about coalition governments in Europe. In Eastern Europe the Communists had entered coalition governments only to wreck them as rapidly as the need for preserving the parliamentary decencies permitted. A short memory and an unfamiliarity with Communist stratagems were not among Chiang's failings. He demurred. The negotiations dragged on; the civil war continued, though in a minor key.

Under General Marshall's leadership, the American Army had expanded from a small and parsimoniously equipped force of mercenaries and a casual militia into the most formidable fighting machine on earth. General Marshall had organized the victories which his field generals consummated in Africa, Europe, and Asia. If America is beholden to any one man for the comparative smallness of the casualities she suffered in World War II, it is General Marshall.

Shortly after World War II, General Marshall retired from the service. Then his place in history seeemed secure—secure at least against that backwash of defamation which, after each great war, has assailed the military leaders of the great Western democracies. Only a high sense of duty could have taken him from his airy manor in Virginia to Nanking, sweltering in the July heat. Whatever part he would play in this, the messiest phase of the Chinese Revolution was unlikely to enhance his reputation. It is highly improbable that he fancied the role of peacemaker, for no one knew better than he that his government would not provide the means for enforcing a settlement.

Visibly harassed, General Marshall sat on his porch, shielded against the torrid afternoon sun by rattan mats suspended from a high scaffolding. He recounted an incident which the Communists seemed to have created for no other purpose than to test the mettle of the American presence and to divert attention from their doings elsewhere. A small detachment of Marines had been charged with the safe-conduct of a convoy from Tientsin to

Peking. The Communists attacked the convoy; two Marines were killed. General Marshall had requested Chou En-lai, the Communists' chief negotiator in Nanking, to furnish explanation and satisfaction. Chou En-lai explained. Incensed, Marshall replied: "Nothing you have said bears any relation to the facts of the case. There is only one fact which cannot be denied: two Marines were shot." Clearly, if the Communists were as devious as General Marshall knew them to be, they could not be expected to abide by the very settlement which General Marshall had been sent to obtain.

Later, when General Marshall, as Secretary of State, called a plague on both houses, Nationalist and Communist, and the great debate on the China disaster had begun, I was to recall my conversation on that listless afternoon. The United States had suffered one of the most painful defeats in its history. The world's most populous country had been lost to communism. In the ensuing hunt for scapegoats and witches, Chiang Kai-shek was awarded the largest share of the blame. Proxies are not easily forgiven by their sponsors for having let themselves be beaten. Since, in our folklore, virtue always prevails, it could have been only the sloth and corruption of the Nationalists which delivered China into the hands of the clean-living Communists.

The failure of the China missions brought upon General Marshall's head a great deal of unjust criticism, unjust because he had been picked to carry out policies made by others. If he was not the ideal choice for the occasion, then the mistake must be reckoned against those who invested his great reputation in a questionable undertaking. Like another great organizer of victory, Lazare Carnot of the French First Republic, he applied a mathematician's mind to the ordering of a great mass of factual details. Calm, precise, and tireless, he commanded the devotion of his staff. Of all his qualities, the greatest was probity. Like Carnot, he lacked the intuition and finesse of the politicians. Certainly he grasped but vaguely the workings of the Communist mind. Although his very name stands for the recovery of Western Europe, he seems to have been slow in discerning the tremendous change wrought by Communist conquests in the balance of world power. Although effective diplomacy need not be crooked and some of the most celebrated diplomats of history were honest men, a fair measure of cunning is indispensable in the practice of the craft. Whatever were General Marshall's natural endowments, cunning was not among them. The Chinese leaders, Nationalist and Communist, were exceedingly cunning men.

General Marshall's aide asked T. V. Soong, Chiang's brother-in-law and foreign minister, to grant me an interview. Soong received me in his cool and sparsely furnished office at the Foreign Ministry. He dismissed his hovering aides and we talked. He expressed himself somewhat less than sanguine about the ultimate results of the truce negotiations. A well-set man, running to that rubbery fat which marks the Chinese man of distinction, he affected the manners of an American bank president, brisk, affable, and noncommittal. In his opinion the Communists were using the truce to regroup their forces. In one of the few drawn battles of the civil war the Communists had been defeated on the Sungari River north of Mukden. Instead of affording them a breathing spell, an offensive should be mounted forthwith. Of course, the Nationalists could step up operations only with increased American help. I asked the minister as to whether he could give me an estimate of Soviet help to the Chinese Communists. He replied that the Soviets had handed over to the Communists the arms which they had taken from the Japanese. Furthermore, the Chinese Communists, having established themselves with Soviet connivance in Manchuria, had now direct access to Russian territory and thus to Soviet supplies. The minister refrained from criticizing the Soviet Union which, at that time, maintained diplomatic relations with the Nationalist government and had not recognized the government of Mao. I believe that the Soviets, having helped the Communists to improve their strategic position, waited on events. They were not eager for a head-on collision with the United States. They watched the rapid dissolution of America's military power. They gauged the drift of American public sentiment. Heartened by the military progress of the Communists and the indecisiveness of American policy, the Soviets openly disowned their old ally, Chiang, and hailed Mao as the rightful ruler of China.

In the summer of 1946 the Soviets still marked time. Conceivably, they might have settled for a partitioned or a neutralist China. Soong's remarks left me with the impression that he did not believe Stalin irrevocably committed to the Communists. He carefully refrained from censuring Soviet conduct. Having drunk Mr. Soong's weakish tea and then his more potent Scotch, I walked back through the torpid heat to my quarters. I am sure now that the China Tangle could have been untied by one method only, namely, that applied by Alexander to the Gordian knot. It is difficult to see why weakness should beget anything but weakness.

The two naval sinologists invited me to join them on a jeep ride through the countryside. For a few miles we followed the river and then ascended a low escarpment. Traversing a plain fringed by low hills, we passed several villages to the acclaim of numerous, scantily clad, and bouncy children. We stopped and bought a magnificent watermelon. We conversed with the elders. On the hillside above the village peasants straightened up from their work, glanced briefly at the three men in a pea-green jeep, and then turned back to their labors. These invaders, too, were only passing through. Clad in shirt and shorts, sturdy and straight, men and women worked side by side. My companions told me that Kiangsu Province was one of the most fertile regions of China, famed for the beauty of its women. As the sun was setting, we drove on.

I stopped off in Tsingtao and then went on to Peking. I have lived in several of the world's great cities. It is only when I return to them as a tourist that I realize how little I had known about them. The inhabitants hold the tourist in low esteem, for he looks about for no other purpose but looking and, so the old inhabitants allege, does not get to the bottom of things. Yet the tourist, at least if he is a reasonably industrious one, has one advantage over the old inhabitant: since he has no other business on his hands but seeing the sights, he gives his undivided attention to the obvious and does not grudge it his time.

I am told that Peking is the most secretive of the world's great cities. Nowhere else, not even in the old Arab towns, have men expended more ingenuity to wall in their private lives and keep

the stranger out. Entering a Peking compound is thus like un-
wrapping a surprise package: the main gate, set inconspicuously
into a grayish wall along a malodorous unpaved alley, opens reluctantly. Penetrating through several lesser walls and empty
courtyards, one finally reaches the delightful center, the spacious
living quarters, the pond with the lotus flowers, the secluded
library and the stillness which always must have been the height
of privilege in this crowded, noisy city. Over the centuries this
illusion of solitude must have been very costly. The world resents
being kept out, and this is probably one of the reasons why the
history of this Peking has been so murderous.

Having read *Peking Picnic*, I insisted upon traveling senti-
mentally to a dilapidated temple on the outskirts of the city. We
lunched on cold duck and Four Roses, a brand which mysteri-
ously had swept the bars of non-Communist China. Four Nationalist soldiers cradled their tommy guns and watched the
mountains to the north. Beneath them the tombs of the Ming
emperors, grassy mounds, marked the safe limits of Nationalist
control; beyond them, I was told, Communist patrols were likely
to halt the tourist.

Communist guerrillas had filtered into the outskirts of the city.
One American military mission provided the local Nationalist
forces with advisory services; another, under the guidance of Mr.
Walter Robertson, U.S. Minister Plenipotentiary in Peking, su-
pervised the keeping of the truce. The presence of a large number of Americans, military and diplomatic, ensured the flow to
Peking of staple goods which, though unobtainable from the local
economy, were nevertheless needed to keep the American official
community in good health and spirits.

With a thermos bottle of strong coffee and sandwiches, I
visited the summer palace in the midday quiet. Since at that time
not many American tourists, except military personnel on leave,
visited Peking, I had no trouble finding a guide. Or, rather, a
guide, after considerable altercation with his colleagues, claimed
me. Though fierce looking, he proved learned. When I told him
that I had come to stay for a few hours, he cut his standard spiel.
We sat down on the steps of the Pavilion in which, seated high
upon his throne, the Emperor recived the homage of the foreign

ambassadors.

I had come, so my guide told me, at the wrong time of day. In the morning, just before the sun had risen above the walls of the palace, the envoys of foreign rulers were made to wait in the forecourt. Just when the rays of the rising sun fell upon Emperor and gilded throne, the gate opened and the ambassadors were led into the imperial presence. The effect must have been startling. For hours the ambassadors had been made to cool their heels in the dark enclosure, bare of ornament and guarded by high walls and massive towers. The staging of the ceremony—the ambassadors' long approach to the pavilion, the glow of gold leaf, and the Emperor seated high upon his throne—was intended to overawe the envoys of less sophisticated though more quarrelsome lands and thus to ensure without excessive military exertions the smooth flow of tribute. Count Schlieffen, father of the celebrated plan which twice went awry, once said: *"Mehr sein als scheinen"* (Be more than you seem); only a people as insensitive as the Germans would take pride in living by so imperceptive a maxim. Chinese diplomacy, for example, seems to have been based upon the principle that a good show is worth a good deal of real power and that the savings in the military budget thus achieved should be put into gold leaf, magnificent vestments and ceramics, fireworks, and all the things of good living.

We talked about Chinese history. The guide, of whom I liked to think as having been an impoverished Mandarin, bemoaned the fact that most of the heirlooms of Chinese culture had been destroyed or carried off by the barbarians. No doubt China has been the most looted country upon earth; hence the piety of the Chinese is reserved exclusively for his own ancestors and property. Since most of China's historic relics, unlike those of more ill-favored and hence more forward-looking people, are fashioned from highly perishable materials, it is just as well that at least part of the China loot is being cared for by public and private collections abroad. Someday the objects thus preserved might return to China, possibly in the same fashion in which their present owners acquired them.

I went to see the Summer Palace, contemporary in feeling to Monte Carlo baroque. I cannot think of any place where the meeting of West and East achieved more inadvertently startling results.

Mr. Robertson invited me to join him on a flight to Kalgan, the Communist-held capital of Chahar. We circled the Ming tombs and dipped down for a good look at the processional way flanked by the famous fierce and haggard lions. Then we crossed the range which separates Hopei Province from the Outer Mongolian plains. A high pleateau, cleft by dry and barren river beds, extended northward to the far horizon. Within a few minutes we had left behind the fertile, densely settled coastal lands and had crossed into the dust-blown emptiness of Inner Asia. Though well this side of the Great Wall, this part of the empire still vaunts its untamed past, the debated frontier between the herdsmen-raiders and the settled peoples of the great river valleys.

After this excursion I joined Mr. Robertson and his sons and aides in a spirited game of water polo in the legation pool. That evening I reread Marco Polo's travelogue. Modern geographical and archaeological exploration has confirmed the veracity of this great ancient reporter whose stories made him the laughingstock of his fellow townsmen. Nearly five hundred years after Marco Polo, Giovanni Giacomo Casanova set down his account of travel and adventure, and for a long time it met with the same disbelief. Nevertheless, modern research has revealed Casanova to have been one of the most reliable witnesses of eighteenth-century society, its customs, speech, dress, diet, mores, and everyday routine. Thus the two sons of Venice, the merchant-adventurer and the pimp-informer, bequeathed to later ages masterpieces of reporting unrivaled for accuracy and readability. For both Marco Polo and Giovanni Giacomo Casanova went forth to live with people, to get the better of them in trade or at the gaming table, to win the favor of their rulers and their women, and to return from their odyssey with fame and fortune. Then, in old age, illused and disappointed, they found solace in recollection. Indeed, so vividly did they relive the past—the past being all that was left of life—that, against the urgings of shame and vanity, they kept faith with truth. I have read many books written by men and women who traveled for no other purpose than to write them,

yet none of them are free from the distortion which results from
looking too hard at a few things and therefore not being able to
take in all the others. Marco Polo and Giacomo Casanova were
much too busy living to know that they were looking.

The U.S. Marine courier plane which took me to Mukden
crossed the Jehol Mountains and then followed the railroad
tracks which join Mukden to Port Arthur and, by a branch line,
to Shanhaikwan and Peking. Edmond Clubb, the U.S. Consul
General in Mukden, showed me to my quarters; I had been assigned to a suite of rooms which one had been reserved for Pu-yi,
the boy Emperor of China, later the Japanese puppet ruler of
Manchuria. I understand that this unfortunate monarch, by then
in his fifties, was not only taken prisoner by the Communists but
made to study Marxist-Leninist doctrine. According to a French
journalist who was permitted to interview him, the ex-Emperor
expressed his gratitude to his captors and his joy at learning
dialectical materialism. His evil grandmother, who hated all foreigners, would not have been pleased.

In the Emperor's apartment most of the original furniture,
representational French, had been replaced by quartermaster
functional. The bathroom, however, remained intact; the color
scheme was predominantly black. A generous tub, large enough
to hold several persons, had been sunk into the black imitation
marble floor. The fixtures were wrought from highly polished
brass. My delight in this somber luxury was short-lived, however: no water gushed from the taps. As a matter of fact, there
was no running water, the Communist guerrillas having cut the
city's water supply and captured the electrical generating station.
I was supplied with buckets.

During my stay in Mukden I came to know Edmond Clubb
well, as well as one comes to know a man with whom one lives
under the same roof for a few weeks in the intimacy of shared
discomfort. Years later Edmond Clubb was dismissed from the
service. I do not know what were the grounds for this action.
When I knew him his stated views accorded with those of the
high American officials whom I had met on the way and with my
own views; although not uncritical of the Nationalists, he de-

clared them to be our only and, therefore, our best bet.

The Japanese had transformed Mukden into a large modern city; about five hundred industrial plants and a large number of trading concerns provided employment for a million inhabitants, the great majority of whom were Chinese immigrants or of Chinese descent. Upon the surrender of the Japanese, the Soviets occupied Mukden, proceeded methodically to strip the factories of movable equipment and looted whatever private and public property seemed worth looting. In addition, they inflicted a great deal of damage on all kinds of objects which they judged too bulky for transportation, for the purpose either of sabotaging reconstruction or of simply venting their passion for smashing things.

Now the Chinese Communists had surrounded Mukden. Food was scarce. Deprived of running water, the householders dug for the old wells which, before the coming of modern hygiene and sanitation, had satisfied the needs of preindustrial Mukden. Soon cholera and typhoid ravaged the city. The stench was appalling. Nor was this condition improved by the indiscriminate use of disinfectants. To make matters worse, the breakdown of public services such as street illumination and telephones emboldened bandits and infiltrating Communist guerrillas; occasionally their activities stung the Nationalist garrison into frenzied retaliation. When bursts of gunfire died away in one part of the city the firing started all over again in another.

UNRRA sought to alleviate the sufferings of the civilian population. Although considerable stocks of food and medical supplies had accumulated in coastal ports, their movement inland was hampered by the scarcity of rolling stock. Before their withdrawal, the Soviets removed not only the locomotives and freight cars but also much of the track; it is unclear what they meant to do with the rolling stock, for the gauge of their railroads is wider than those of other countries, the Argentine excepted. They also carried off whatever stores of coal and petrol they could lay their hands on. An advance party of UNRRA officials, quartered in our hotel, surveyed the unpromising situation.

One of the members of the multinational team was a young, slender Hindu youth. Although the nights were warm and the days stiflingly hot, he covered his spare frame with layers of sweaters topped with a thick woolen shawl. He descended from his room to share our meals, talked much and charmingly about cricket, the erotic themes in Hindu sculpture, his years in the London School of Economics, and British imperialism. Having finished his meal, he would then withdraw to his room. To the best of my knowledge, he did not leave the hotel during the weeks I stayed in it.

Large organizations, such as armies and international bodies charged with humanitarian missions, obey their own laws of motion. By the courtesy of the U.S. Navy, UNRRA acquired rolling stock and fuel from other lands, mostly Japan. Supplies began to trickle into Manchuria. The nature of some of the items destined to succor the needy was surprising. Some hundred cases of Four Roses, the brand favored by the bars of China, safely reached our hotel. Because of the dubious quality of the water rationed to the guests of the hotel, some of us put the heady stuff to all kinds of sanitary and cosmetic uses. Ever since, I have suffered from some sort of block which deters me from the untrammeled enjoyment of whisky, even the more venerable brands.

I made the acquaintance of two bearded White Russians famed for their skill at tracking wild game in the more inaccessible hill country to the north and east of Mukden. Under various Manchurian regimes, they had made a good living guiding hunting parties to their quarry, notably the ferocious Manchurian tiger, and assuring their clients an easy shot or, in case of a miss, personal safety. The two gnarled old men had met with many an adventure. Tersely, and not without humor, they told their stories of sportsmen, some famous and some infamous, some bold and some craven, who had come from all over the world to seek excitement and trophies. Now, they thought, their skills would no longer be in demand. In their old age, they would have to learn a new trade to make a living. Not only they, but all the hundreds of thousands of Russian émigrés living in Manchuria and China-inside-the-Wall faced an uncertain future.

Although Russian settlement in Manchuria antedated the Russo-Japanese War, most Russians in Manchuria and China were either refugees or the children of refugees from the Bolshevik Revolution. Their status, stateless and passportless, had always been precarious. They made their living as small shopkeepers, restaurateurs, artisans, and middlemen. In Czarist Russia they had been petty officials; not a few had served in the civil administration of Siberia. Hardly any were skilled in a profession such as medicine and engineering. Their education had not fitted them for coping with the vicissitudes of exile.

After the Japanese conquest, the lot of the Russian émigré worsened. Masters at chicanery, the Japanese took pleasure in humilating the helpless exiles of a country which they had defeated in war and professed to despise. Racial animosity found an easy butt in these, the first white people under Japanese domination. Now the Chinese Nationalists emulated the example of the Japanese. While the Japanese accorded the Russian émigré at least a semblance of legal protection, the Chinese, in their uninhibited, boisterous way, made him fear for his very life. Russians were fair game, and beatings were the order of the day. When the Soviets offered passports to these desperate people, many chose to return to the country of their fathers. Since no one else seemed to care, they could not think of any alternative. I cannot think of any other example of voluntary mass emigration into the Soviet Union.

The fortunes of the White Russian communities in Manchuria and China proper anticipated those of other white minorities in several Asian and, later, several African countries. Their humiliation and rejection furnish a stark and unpalatable lesson: the non-white peoples will not tolerate a white minority in their midst once they have rid themselves of the West's political and military dominance.

At last the preparations for my journey to Anshan, Manchuria's great steel center, were completed. It was decided that I should go by rail rather than by jeep. The equipment consisted of a diesel engine, a parlor car of 1910 vintage, and a flatcar upon which had been mounted two machine guns. Several officials of the Chinese Ministry of Economics, the crew of the diesel engine, and about twenty soldiers made up my entourage. We proceeded at a speed of about fifteen miles per hour. We stopped frequently

at culverts and switches, which our guards gingerly examined
for explosives. An abundant lunch—cold chicken, melons, peaches,
and the ever-present Scotch—had been prepared for the occupants of the parlor car.

In perfect weather we crept past lush fields, grassy hillocks. At
each stop we got off the train, our escort to ensure our safety and
we of the parlor car to stretch our legs and admire the scenery. I
shook hands with stationmasters and local military commanders.
All official Chinese occasions are enlivened by much laughter and
banter. Everybody seemed enchanted by my presence. Only the
soldiers seemed somewhat glum and apprehensive.

We arrived safe in Anshan. The welcoming ceremonies were
brief. I went to bed in the local hotel. Next morning my rounds
began. Japanese engineers were to lead me though the steel plant.
Captured and released by the Soviets and now impressed by the
Chinese as "consultants," these two unhappy men, too, professed
to rejoice at my arrival. The Chinese had asked them to fix up the
plant and to start forthwith the production of steel plate, rails,
and other strategic items. They thought that never again would
they see Japan. It was not at all certain that they ever would, for
their masters had grown impatient and hinted at severe penal-
ties if they failed to meet expectations. Both had graduated from
American engineering schools and served their apprenticeship in
the steel mills of Pittsburgh. Discreetly, they suggested to me that
the expectations placed by their Chinese employers upon the potential of their plant were unfounded. Clad in soiled shirt, shorts,
and canvas shoes—the rest of their wardrobe having followed the
withdrawing Soviets—the two top managers of Eastern Asia's
largest steel mill doubled as electricians, plant foremen, and
steeplejacks.

A large part of the work force had melted away. Some of the
workers had drifted to Mukden; others had joined the Communists. The plant seemed to have been methodically looted and
then wrecked. It had been completed during the first years of the
war. Some of the machinery had been imported from the United
States; some of the equipment as, for example, devices for bene-
ficating low-grade iron ore, had been furnished by Krupp. The
Soviets had left nothing to chance: They dispatched to Anshan a

contingent of German engineers whom they had captured during the war, to ensure the efficient dismemberment of the mills. Having carted off all movable things of value, the Soviets sought to dynamite the rest. Since the charges were either weak or inexpertly placed, the blast furnaces had escaped serious damage. Harried by the Chinese, the two Japanese managers, working the remainder of the work force three shifts a day, had restored one tenth the plant's capacity—a miraculous feat of improvisation, for only a trickle of spare parts had reached Anshan from Japan. The Chinese officials who had accompanied me from Mukden listened dourly to the Japanese engineers' estimate of the situation. Obviously, they had never been inside a steel mill. Whatever their expertise, it was not metallurgical engineering.

The Nationalist presence did not gladden the local Chinese population. Perhaps it was Manchurian *Lokalpatriotismus* or life in an advanced industrial environment which restrained the Chinese working population in Manchuria, some fifty million strong, from embracing the Nationalists as liberators from alien rule. Rather, it seemed that they looked upon Chiang's soldiers and administrators as carpetbaggers, representatives of the older, less advanced China. Indeed, Manchuria could claim its own flag with a good deal more justification than most countries which have achieved their independence since World War II. It is the one region on the East Asian mainland which possesses at least the rudiments of modern industrial civilization. It is a rich country, and a beautiful one, its features—rolling land, fields planted to soy beans and grains, and pastures—reminiscent of the Polish and, in some places, of the Hungarian plains. Within a few miles of the city, birds of all kinds thrive on plentiful feed. The Manchurian cock pheasant, resplendent and swift, resembles the ring-necked pheasant of Hungary.

Thanks to the mediation of one of my White Russian acquaintances, I found a pony for hire and set off, accompanied by its owner, for a ride across fields and gullies and up the slope of low hills. My companion wore his mustachios suitably long and sat his horse with the crouch of the Mongol rider. Since we had no language except equestrian grunts in common, we rode in blessed silence. On this, the most memorable day of my journey I felt at peace with the world. Unbeknown to me, this land, torn by savage factions, had come to obsess me. Later, reading Orwell's *Homage to Catalonia*, I relived the sense of involvement of nightmarish transfigurations: to the "good" cause sticks the grit of shabby betrayal; decent men turn into informers, and only fools and brutes stand fast. On that cool summer day the creak of leather, the eternal sky, and the grassy turf released the ducts of catharsis. I returned to Mukden; even Pu-yi's bathroom looked less funereal.

The Nationalists had failed to exploit their victory over the Communist armies north of Mukden. Their lines of supply had become tenuous, and over the Mukden grapevine traveled rumors of impending retreat. General Tu Li-ming, Nationalist commander in chief, sent me word that he could see me in Changchun, Manchuria's administrative capital under the Japanese. I reached that city in an American courier plane. My fellow passengers, two army officers and two enlisted men, were to relieve the personnel of a truce team assigned to a town just this side of the Manchurian-Mongolian border. Only a few days before, a band of Mongol horsemen had ridden into the town, killed all the male inhabitants, carried off the women, and left unmolested a stunned American colonel and his radio operator.

General Tu had just returned from the United States, where he had undergone surgery. Still convalescing, he had resumed his duties. General Tu had been trained abroad, followed Chiang to Chungking and then led the forces which accepted the Japanese surrender in China. He may have been an incompetent general; generals who cannot accomplish their mission are always said to be incompetent. But though he possibly lacked superior strategic insight, Tu possessed one inestimable military virtue: in the face of mounting odds he remained calm and kept on fighting. In front of a large war map, he explained the deployment of his forces and the provisions made for supplying them with food and munitions. We talked about the international situation. Clearly, conditions abroad, the demobilization of the Western Alliance, did not favor Nationalist China.

Tu expected the truce to come soon to an end—as soon as the Communists had succeeded in realigning their forces. He expressed his appreciation of military and diplomatic assistance which the United States had given China. He praised the morale of his troops who, far from their homes, faced an enemy superior in numbers and operating, so to speak, on the doorstep of the Soviet Union. As events were to bear out, his answers to my questions were forthright. I could not judge the quality of his generalship; I liked the man. Some of Tu's staff officers, several of whom had attended American service schools, shared our frugal meal. I took my leave.

Later Tu's army retreated in good order from Manchuria. It covered Chiang's retreat and the evacuation of the bulk of the Nationalist forces to Taiwan. The Communists captured Tu and displayed him, chained in a cage, to the populace as a token of their victory, thus honoring their fallen foe with the same magnanimity which Tamerlane showed Sultan Bayasid.

When I returned to Peking I found a message inviting me to the house of the chief of the Communist truce mission. General Yeh, a veteran of the Long March and famed as a guerrilla fighter, made his quarters in a compound near the Imperial Palace. The general, short and square, welcomed me with elaborate formality. He was flanked by a silent, sallow, youngish Chinese and an unmistakably Western person, fiftyish and unprepossessing. I took the former to be the general's political adviser and guard of his class conscience, and the latter for the interpreter. Both aides handed me their cards. That of the Caucasian-looking individual sported a Chinese name. Later I was told that, many years ago, its bearer, a New York physician, had come to China, married a Chinese woman, and entered the inner council of the Chinese Communist party.

My fellow guests were Benjamin Wells, American journalist, whose shrewd commentaries should have commanded the attention not only of the American public but also of official Washington, and an American woman, a sturdy Midwesterner. Miss Strong grabbed the conversation and ran with it. An ardent admirer of Stalin's Russia, she had reached China via Moscow and now proceeded to take me to task for my published views on the policies of the Soviet Union. General Yeh intervened. He spoke briefly. The interpreter cut into the harangue of the indignant lady and asked me, on the general's behalf, how I liked Chinese cooking. I said that I liked Peking duck. The general raised his glass and proposed a toast. The lady fell silent and bashfully contemplated her plate. No further breach of party discipline troubled the luncheon. Again, the general raised his glass and, so the interpreter reported, praised me as a keen observer of the Chinese scene.

I asked General Yeh to tell me about the Communist program for the development of China. Yeh consulted briefly the protective young Chinese at his left. Then he spoke. China was an agricultural country, he said. Her situation differed only by degrees from that of Russia before the October Revolution. In compliance with Leninist principles and practices, China would have to step up the pace of industrialization. As the experience of Russia had shown, this endeavor would impose considerable hardships on the Chinese people. Nevertheless, the United States could lighten the burden and turn a good profit by supplying China with industrial equipment and technical knowledge. For the Chinese market offered American capitalists virtually unlimited opportunity for rewarding investment.

I then asked General Yeh what would happen to American investments once China had passed into the stage of advanced industrialization. Without a second's hesitation General Yeh replied: "Then we will expropriate the exploiters." I said that this prospect, appealing as it might be to a Leninist, was likely to cool the enthusiasm of prospective American investors. "Not at all," said the general, "it is well known that American trusts operated on the basis of a twenty percent return on capital per year." "Where," I asked, "could I find shares on the New York Stock Exchange in so profitable an enterprise?" I added that I would like to invest my savings with the general's advice. The general professed to find my reply vastly amusing. Miss Strong unhappily poked at her duck.

A few days later a furtive messenger delivered a package to my hotel. It contained a piece of jade carved into the likeness of a goggle-eye fish. Three inches long and flat, it fitted my pocketbook. I showed General Yeh's gift to a knowledgeable friend. He told me that I had been the recipient of a soldierly compliment.

Fish leap upstream; by suitable exertion, a soldier advances in
rank. Yeh participated in the campaign which drove Chiang from
the mainland. Mao raised him to marshal and the governorship of
Canton.

After a brief stay in Okinawa, torn up by one of the war's
bloodiest battles and lashed by a mighty typhoon in the fall of
1945, I returned to the United States. I scanned my notes. I
summed up my findings. At considerable cost, the Communist
bid for domination could be defeated in China. The Soviets were
as deeply involved in China as was the United States. At no better
time and at no better place could the United States call upon the
Soviets to "put up or shut up." No doubt, such a policy would
involve risks, including the risk of war. The prize, were the
Soviets to turn down the challenge as they surely would, was not
only a non-Communist China but also a free hand for the West in
shaping the New Order. Certainly, anybody could see that the
Communists' subjugation of five hundred million Chinese would
alter decisively the balance of world power, thus largely canceling
out America's gains from victory over Japan. If Japan's defeat
had been worth a full-scale war, then the defense of China was
surely worth the intervention of two American divisions on the
side of Chiang and, if need be, an even larger force. I stressed the
crucial importance of Manchuria, for the loss of that province
would doom the Nationalist cause. If the Nationalists were to
receive U.S. help, they needed that help now and nowhere more
promptly than in Manchuria.

I handed in my report to Forrestal. It confirmed the opinions
of certain influential officials and did not change the mind of
other no less influential officials who held contrary opinions.
While I was saying what I had to say I realized that my news
from Tartary would not add the weight of a feather to the scales
of official policy. The lead-time of a great country's foreign policy is long. In the midst of commotion the decision had been
made, the marching orders had been given and received. The
troops—chiefs of bureaus, ambassadors, generals, and nameless
public spokesmen, identified and unidentified—were moving forward on their appointed course. Since the operation would cause

considerable inconvenience to an old and faithful ally and since that ally was likely to voice his discomfort, it was necessary to explain the situation and prepare the case for the impending disengagement: it was in China, not in Europe, that the Cold War began. The revolution which ran its course uninterruptedly since the end of World War I had entered upon a new and decisive phase. The unpleasant messes to come were unavoidable; their true cause was Chiang's longstanding, though only recently discovered, reactionary inclinations. In brief, Chiang was not being brought to fall by Communist might but by his own weakness and wickedness. With the pungent odor in my nostrils which such proceedings are wont to discharge, I left Washington and joined my wife at a summer resort on the coast of Maine.

I arrived on a Sunday and joined the crush at the club buffet. The table was laden with delicious and plentiful dishes. Tanned by sun and salt-sprayed air, young and not so young people danced gaily to the tunes of an expensive band which had helped to "bring out" generations of expensive debutantes. Surely, nearly everybody in the room remembered the Great War and, in a general way, for what it had been fought. Naturally, everybody rejoiced in all the good things which peace had brought back to those who could afford them. The fact that somewhere in a far-off corner men were still fighting and testing the hard-won New Order with bullets was not permitted to interfere with well-earned rest and enjoyment.

The transititon had been abrupt. The shapes of things to come were still hazed by the smoke of the propaganda and the diplomatic small-arms fire. Yet, had I not seen their menacing shadow creep up on the horizon? They boded ill for the West and those freedoms which Western leadership had inscribed in the Charter of the New Order. Pointing in alarm is not a gesture which can be unduly prolonged in polite society. I stopped pointing.

Chapter Sixteen

THAT, one day, the great revolution will come to an end and will give birth to a universal world order is inevitable. Upon closer inspection, no other alternative except an absurd one is left to man. Yet, while mankind stands on the threshold of a new age and the great organism is about to mutate, more is at stake than survival. It is on this question that the best and the wisest among us divide. To be sure, the craven will settle for safety at any price; the opportunist will back the winner. It is not easy for the wisest and the best to stand fast among the stampeding mob, to resist the temptation to be not only wise and good but also expedient and smart. Barring the absurd alternative, the great revolution should come to an end and issue into a universal state within about fifty years. It would be unlikely that the government of this universal state could be brought to fall by an internal revolution, for it will hold the monopoly of military power. Armed with all the devices for destruction and for population control which science and technology can supply, the universal state will maintain for a long time, if not forever, the political institutions with which it was endowed at its birth.

In whose image will these institutions be created? This is the burning, the ultimate question. It cannot be talked away by sophistries about the alleged relativism of democracy and totalitarianism. Freedom and tyranny are opposites and no amount of dialectic finesse can join them in unholy wedlock. Thus, I take my stand with those who hold that the right answer to the question is worth life and property, all that man has wrought throughout the ages, and the happiness of this generation. If men do not now stake their lives they will not win life for themselves and for the generations to come.

Increasingly, euphoric visions of the ever-abundant material life dull the luster of the great political ideals which, from Periclean Athens to twentieth-century America, inspired whatever progress man has made toward living as a free individual among free individuals. We are coming perilously close to living in a child's world. A child's world is a beautiful world, so we are told. This may be so, though mine was not. In any case, children are hard realists. We know that they can be cruel, more naïvely and realistically cruel than the most depraved adults. Indeed, the imaginings of children are reflected by the illustrated yarns, comics, and cartoons which represent the single largest segment of contemporary literature. These musings have anticipated with uncanny accuracy the progress of modern technology and, which is even more significant, the emergence of modern technological man—*homo technicologus*.

There is nothing wrong with a child's world, provided its untrammeled imagery and innocent savagery be not exported into the adult's world. The observance of this proviso is becoming more and more perfunctory, however, as can be gleaned from the stuff ground out by what are called, euphemistically, the media of mass communication, or simply from what goes on around us. For the world of technological man is a primitive world, as primitive as the modern child's world. It lacks, however, the innocence of the latter. Thus it is a pragmatic world and, because adults cannot keep on at playing children without some debilitating consequences, a cynical world. In it live, together with all kinds of ordinary people, many scientists, engineers, social scientists, and publicists. In it it is proper to speak of politics as a problem in social engineering and of the human condition as a problem in biochemistry and statistics. It finds the idea of the irreconcilable conflict between ideas a repugnant idea, for the proof of this idea can be found only by introspection, an activity deemed nowadays unsociable and unscientific.

What makes Soviet man so formidable a contender for mastery of the future universal state is such a union of pragmatic materialism with fanatical belief. Tragicomic pathos is not wanting. The Communists' capture and perversion of Western idealism may well triumph over its authentic, though decadent, heirs. If this should be so, then a future universal order will be of no other than biological interest. I would not want to live in it, nor do I wish that anyone I care for should live in it. Here I take my stand. Now, of late, the company of like-minded men has been dwindling. All along I suspected that one day we would be read out of meeting. Now it seems that well we might. One consolation remains: better than half of the lost causes of history were good causes.

I returned to the square house commanding a fair view of the valley and the woods beyond. My wandering years had come to an end. I settled down to my books and jotted down what I would teach. Having received my doctorate, I entered upon the cyclic rounds of instruction, examination, and the scheduled lengthy in-betweens, with tenure as my staff. During a hiatus, an apprentice professor like myself is well advised to pursue studies, reveal his findings in publishable form, and thus establish his claim to advancement in knowledge and rank. Perhaps because unaccustomed security lulled my ambition or because the taste of bitter tea still clung to my tongue I attended perfunctorily to my duties and, during the rest of the time, did no work at all. Be that as it may, I indulged my thirst for fresh air. I followed the local hunt.

Although I never mastered the finer points of horsemanship, I became fair enough a rider to keep the master within sight and to watch the hounds working. The companionship of the field is undemanding. A rider's monologue about his mount calls for neither comment nor agreement. After a day in the saddle, tired and happy, the complete fox hunter tacks home to a box stall and hot bath. Among my friends of the field, quite a few had served in the war. Because life was too pleasant to look back and a retrospective frown does not become the horseman, the less reticent among them volunteered the bare essentials, the number of a unit, a few dates and names of places, and let it go at that; the others said nothing. The war had been won. A few years had gone by. Even the worst blunder had mellowed into a wry anecodote. Business had started humming. The shows on Broadway were sold out for months ahead. After so strong a dose of foreign affairs, it would have been unmannerly to examine too closely what all the travail and contingent discomfort had brought forth. To my friends, the domestic scene looked all the more inviting for the things that they had seen abroad. Since, by nature, I cannot stay morose for any length of time and make up by gregariousness what I lack in inner peace, I kept my troubling visions to myself and from my cheerful companions. This is a good rule. The gods, mindful of the continuity of the race and their own prestige, saw to it that those to whom it was given to see the future should not be believed when they reveal it. It is tiresome to search for black specks in the sunny sky. I had grown tired of looking in one direction and turned to the here and now.

In the summer of 1947 I went to Europe for the first time since 1939. I stayed for a few days in Paris, its people still shabby and pinched. Not all friends and friendships had survived. At any age, a gap of eight years is hard to close; at mine, one looks sympathetically across it, waves politely, and then turns away. Middle Europeans of my generation had lived through the collapse of one order and the aftermath of another defeat. Now all Europe had been laid low and its age had closed with considerable finality. I had not come to study the European Problem, but once again to walk through the streets of Europe's old cities, inspect her old monuments, savor the variety of her old ways—before another generation concerned with parking its cars rather than strolling in the old streets, with modern living rather than past splendors, would remake Europe to the specification of efficient production and distribution.

Within the walls of a large estate on the Rhone we found a small cottage. For a few months we went to market at the local village and drank the wines of the country. We searched the graveled banks of the Rhone for polished stones and cast for fish in the river.

I had brought from Paris a small stock of books I had meant to read years ago and others which I had read and wanted to read again. Among the former were Comines's *Mémoirs;* Pirenne's *History of Europe;* the diaries of Pepys, Saint-Simon and the Chevalier de Gramont; the autobiographies of Cardinal de Retz; Chateaubriand's somber and noble *Mémoires d'Outretombe.* I reread novels which, in my youth, had stirred my imagination and touched my heart: Stendhal's *Le Rouge et le Noir* and *La Chartreuse de Parme;* Thackeray's *Henry Esmond* and Gottfried Keller's *Der Grüne Heinrich;* Forster's *Passage to India.* All my life I have searched for the land of the Greeks, *Das Land der Griechen mit der Seele suchend.* I read Bowra's *Greek Experience,* and let myself be guided by the light hand of consummate scholarship across the crowded Agora, resounding to the voices of quick, observant, and contentious men, and up the steep rocky path to the polychrome profusion of the gods.

Although much of my search was in vain, it rewarded me with at least a patch of blue between the clouds: the meaning of the quest and, beyond one man's striving, the goal of the great journey. Not that all the wisdom of the ages is to be found in books. Indeed, at times it seems to me that I have read too much, and I am quite certain that I have written too much.

The best writers have not been literati but men of action seeking to publicize or to justify their deeds or while away old age and enforced inaction. I must confess to the most grievous among my many scholarly inadequacies: but for rare exceptions, I write or read when I do not have better things to do, as, for example, exercise in the open air or converse with bright, attractive people about everything and nothing. The summer's retreat by the Rhone was one of the rare exceptions; I recaptured time lost. From the musings of men who walked upon the stage of history and the fortunes of imaginary heroes, all the more alive for having been contrived in the artist's mind, flowed those verities which, in each generation, men do their worst to deny and their best to affirm, the same voice echoing and re-echoing across time. My own vignette of history-observed was not as sharply drawn as I wished; at least, its perspective had undergone considerable improvement.

Toward the end of the holiday I received word that I had been commissioned to prepare a study on the making of a new Constitution for Germany. The donor of the small grant, the Council on Foreign Relations, long and intimately concerned with foreign affairs, requested me to proceed with dispatch. I traveled to a reed-fringed lake in Bavaria where, upon a small island, the fantasy of a demented king had reproduced the centerpiece of the Versailles Palace. There, between delightful breaks for tea or midmorning coffee, lunch and afternoon tea, the representatives of German democracy, cleared and certified by the occupation regime, pondered the draft of the Organic Law. I warmed to these good men, most of whom had chosen to suffer prison, exile, and poverty rather than compromise with the Nazis. I thought that to a considerable extent the new Germany would be what these few men on the island would make it.

Early in the Spring, we traveled to Rome. We climbed the noble stairs of the Palazzo Caetani. In its airy penthouse, the last heir to that ancient name and his Philadelphian wife made music, wrote poetry, and edited the best and most voluminous literary magazine of Europe, *Botteghe Oscure*. Friends from everywhere and from every school of the creative arts, as well as from Europe's left-of-center political factions, talked art and politics over tea served in the ceremonious English fashion. Italy, too, was still digging out, disheveled and underfed, from the rubble of war and smashed institutions. With a fine view of tarnished domes and pineclad hills, the penthouse offered refuge from Rome's cold drizzle and the staleness of Italian politics.

Our hosts had never dissimulated their detestation of Fascism. Because their name belonged to Italian history and their international connections were powerful, they escaped all but minor harassment. Their faith in Italy had never wavered. They wanted us to meet her new men and women.

It is not easy for literary men to live up to their best pages. Through the mediation of his fair Irish wife, Ignazio Silone, a ruggedly-wrought and unpretentious man, explained to me the infighting in the Socialist Party and its rear-guard action against the Communists. A famous convert to Communism, he had resigned disgustedly from the party when Stalin and Ribbentrop shook hands. The light had failed; and, dazed by Communist betrayal, he now ruminated distractedly on what had gone wrong. He put his words cautiously and emphatically. Among all the intellectuals who had embraced the purging discipline of Communism and, disenchanted, had fled the promised land, he seemed the most pathetic. It was fortunate that simplicity of heart kept him from seeing the cruel irony of his predicament.

Carlo Levi asked me to his icy studio. His powerful, compassionate novel, *Christ Stopped at Eboli,* was to bring him fame, yet he wanted most to be known as a serious painter. Steeped in religious philosophy, he searched for the pure sources of the faith. Neither his paintings nor his philosophical tracts received the public acclaim accorded his novel. The new Italy has no place for troubled mystics. The dragging anguish of which Levi wrote is the last thing that modern Italy, motorized, noisy and showing off, wishes to remember.

A friend of the Caetanis led me to a modest hotel and, after an introduction over the telephone, turned me over to a porter. I was shown to a room under the eaves. The furnishings consisted of an unmade bed, a chair on which rested an untidy valise, and a washstand with metal pitcher and basin. A balding, pudgy man, about to put on his socks, invited me to sit beside him on the bed—there being no other place to sit. Thus started my long friendship with Adriano Olivetti, one of the most successful and one of the most controversial industrialists of modern Italy. Under his brilliant, though eccentric management, the family firm, domiciled in Ivrea near Torino, expanded its operations into every corner of the globe, and its production from portable typewriters to a great variety of automated devices. His genius wedded aesthetics to engineering, efficiency to beauty. In the improvement of working conditions, he led Italian industry. His fellow industrialists followed him, most of them reluctantly. If any one man can be said to have set in motion the development of Italy's industrial culture, Olivetti was that man.

During Mussolini's rule, Adriano spent several years in Swiss exile. He returned not only to reclaim his paternal possessions but also to infuse a sense of community into industrial society. While Adriano completed his toilette, we talked of the community lost and the community regained. Our thoughts met: How to restore the civilized community? How to shelter it in free institutions? How to make it whole? How to make manifest its unitary spirit in home and meeting place, in the products of collective labor and in individual creativity? Adriano had profited hugely from Italy's recovery and export boom. He proposed to engage in exhilarating social experiments. He set out to build the model community in Ivrea. Wages and working conditions, meeting halls and playing fields, workers' housing and cultural centers set standards for Italian industry.

Adriano's encouragement of new directions in the architectural and decorative arts fostered that style of functional harmonies which, from Italy, spread to the urban-industrial centers of Europe. He founded a publishing firm and a richly illustrated periodical which introduced the Italian public to international thought on sociology and economics, especially in the field of urban development and industrial relations. He founded a political party—the Party of the Community—and represented it in the Italian parliament. He acclaimed and supported a variety of movements toward the unification of Europe and of the peoples of the North Atlantic. He reversed a trend in international finance: he put European capital into American enterprise, acquiring a leading American producer of typewriters. He commuted between Rome, Milan, Paris, and New York. He died in a sleeping car of the Milan-Rome express.

Not easily deceived, Adriano had learnt to bear with the ingenious spongers who fasten on very rich men and their causes. He kept his trust, for his compassion exceeded his passion for ideas. I count him among the few superbly clever men possessed of heart.

I returned to America and handed in my report on constitution making by a Bavarian lake. The draft constitution, though it granted the states a fair measure of autonomy, provided for firm federal controls. Thus it approached the American model rather than the French idea of a loose confederation of sovereign states —the quaint Germanies who, up until 1870, opposed their combined impotence to a powerful, highly centralized, France. My report summarized the views on the constitutional problems of the political parties: the Socialists wanted to grant great powers to the federal government, the Christian Democrats, especially the Bavarians, held out for states' rights. The draft constitution represented a fair compromise between the contending views.

Allen W. Dulles, on behalf of the Council, expressed his satisfaction with my presentation. Thus encouraged, I set myself to sedentary tasks which, although they kept me increasingly from the meet, proved satisfying and rewarding. As time went on, I anticipated pleasurably the beginning of a new term, the new faces in the classroom, some strained by attention, some slackened by boredom, and some smoothed by sleep. I savored the effects of my pedagogical rhetoric. I anticipated eagerly the publication of my works, scanned anxiously the journals for reviews. Unawares, I had begun to travel by rote. The groove held the wheel.

What has life taught me? Since the ultimate experience is still to come, my answer cannot be complete. I am not a humble man. I admit to having grown wiser. Hypocrisy is not one of my besetting vices. I do not conceal the fact that I have grown kindlier. I have not found the one great truth, perhaps because no man is wise and good enough to find it, or, as seems more likely, life does not teach one great truth—except that very truth. One cannot step twice into the same river.

I have not been the identical man to those whom I knew well enough to bid the time of day, to address with levity or pondered thought, and to like and to dislike. Nor have I been on any day the same man to myself. Anyone who grows old and has his wits about him comes to know men—of how nobly and how dastardly one and the same person is capable of conducting himself, of how people in cogitation scratch their noses, of how others avert their eyes when they speak the truth, and of how the forthright look deceives. This kind of knowledge had been of little help to me. Each time I got a little closer to a human being I had to learn all over again about the tragedy and comedy of being human. Then I forgot. Hence the wonderful and shattering surprises.

My life has not conformed to any intelligible design; I do not know of any life that does. I see coincidence and I see accident; I do not see the logical unfolding of potentialities with which birth, station, and education endowed me. If I had completed my training as a surveyor, I might have gone to Guiana, built roads, married a mulatto and . . . If I had not waited for that traffic light on 62nd Street and Park Avenue, I would not have met X who asked me to dinner and introduced me to Y, who started me in a completely new direction.

I have learned a good deal from living, yet virtually nothing from my life. Of course, my life suggests a few unprovable hypotheses; the one that I find most plausible is that, nowadays, no one could live a life such as mine has been. There is a lack of sequence, a stultifying dystrophy which is irreproducible. Certainly not at any time was I the master of my destiny—which is a pompous idea anyway. The current tripped me, caught me and floated me, right side up, in the direction I sometimes least wanted to go.

A man of my times, I looked to science for answers which, in times gone by, were supposed to be given by common sense or taken on faith or not given at all. Science has many uses, except telling us how to live with any live man or woman. That men and what they do can be reduced to numbers, this belief is an innocent scientific conceit. The attempt to do so in practice rather than in theory should evoke that spirit of resistance with which, all throughout history, the defenders of freedom have risen against sundry schemes for turning men into cattle. I, too, have toyed with numbers. As long as numbers are not being taken too seriously and not allowed to march over the tender grass of life they can furnish us the handy information about how often men do certain things and how many men do often certain other things. This knowledge cannot hurt anybody lest it encourage the belief that it unlocks such mysteries as, for example, the mystery of being human. Numbers do not lie. Yet the world of numbers is to the real world what were the shadows from which the denizens of Plato's cave derived their knowledge of the world outside. Life has taught me to revere its infinite variety. Life has taught me to sleep lightly and to beware of the age-old conspiracy against the variety of life. The horrible simplifier stands always at the gate. I was raised in the Protestant faith. Of its theological teachings I kept little. Yet is spirit of resistance—man alone against the legions of arbitrary authority—is still alive in me. *Ut ardeat!!*

Life has taught me to expect the unexpected and not to try to outwit it. By nature a schemer, I now recall not so much the many schemes which miscarried as the unanticipated and often untoward consequences of those which succeeded. In brief, I learned the common lesson that the greatest unhappiness lies in receiving everything we desire. The most terrifying story I ever read was Balzac's *Peau d'Ane*.

The strongest forces for evil in human affairs is *amour propre*. Vanity and hypocrisy, rather than greed and lust, are the besetting vices of our civilization. The masses will grant their masters almost any privilege or whim except privacy. The politically ambitious must, as never before, shun the pleasures of the flesh which the going mores deny the average man or, at least, contrive the appearance of conformity. Thus the vainest and most dangerous prophets of our age pretend to be, and often really are, good family men. Indeed, some of the most unpleasant of the breed were devoid of all compromising urges—as virtuous as Robespierre.

My interest in politics has taught me the corrosiveness of ambition in the guise of egalitarian good-fellowship. I have met saintly men, all the more saintly for the confession of their many frailties. Moral perfection, especially when it uses service to humanity as its vessel, put me on my guard. Not a few servants of humanity whom I have met seemed to reserve their compassion for their elevated cause. I would not have cared to get in the way of their promotion to a better job.

In brief, I learned those homely lessons which the rub of life prints on average intelligence. Had my faith been greater, my memory more retentive, the world around me not so distracting,

I would not have had to relearn, at considerable cost, what I had been taught to start with. The end is in the beginning. Since I do not hold one great truth and since my haphazard progress has not traced any intelligible pattern, I do not believe that the story of my life as set down in these pages can teach other men how to live their lives better. My own design which enriched the art of living will perish with me. So will the yards of spoiled canvas. So characteristic of the times has been the setting that my performance no longer bears repetition. Although no man's life is, as he thinks, unique, I take the artist's pride in placing my signature on mine.

Index